ABOUT THIS PUBLICATION

FOR SERVICE ASSISTANCE

Please call Customer Service Department At:
1.704.898.0770

North Carolina General Statues is published by The Muliti-Media Group of Greater Charlotte in Charlotte, North Carolina. Copyright 2015 by the Multi-Media Group of Greater Charlotte. This book or parts thereof may not be reproduced in any form, stored in a retrieval system, or transmitted in any form by any means—electronic, mechanical, photocopy, recording or otherwise—without prior written permission of the publisher, except as provided by United States of America copyright law.

The records required by U.S. Code 2257(a) through (c) and the pertinent regulations 28 C.F.R. Cli. 1, Part 75 with respect to this publication and all materials associated with such records are maintained by The Multi-Media Group of Greater Charlotte, Publisher and available for review by Attorney General.

www.visionbooks.org

Copyright © 2015 by MMGGC
All rights reserved!

TID: 5061475
ISBN (10) digit: 1502913380
ISBN (13) digit: 978-1502913388

123-4-56789-01239-Paperback
123-4-56789-01239-Hardback

First Edition

090520140547

Printed in the United States of America

2015 EDITION

North Carolina Criminal Law And Procedure-Pamphlet # 36

Printed In conjunction with the Administration of the Courts

North Carolina Criminal Law and Procedure
Pamphlet Reference Guide

Chapters	Pamphlet
Chapter 1 Civil Procedure	1
Chapter 1 Civil Procedure (Continue)	2
Chapter 1A Rules of Civil Procedure	2
Chapter 1B Contribution.	2
Chapter 1C Enforcement of Judgments.	2
Chapter 1D Punitive Damages.	2
Chapter 1E Eastern Band of Cherokee Indians.	2
Chapter 1F North Carolina Uniform Interstate Depositions and Discovery Act.	2
Chapter 2 - Clerk of Superior Court [Repealed and Transferred.]	3
Chapter 3 - Commissioners of Affidavits and Deeds [Repealed.]	3
Chapter 4 - Common Law	3
Chapter 5 - Contempt [Repealed.]	3
Chapter 5A - Contempt	3
Chapter 6 - Liability for Court Costs	3
Chapter 7 - Courts [Repealed and Transferred.]	3
Chapter 7A – Judicial Department	3
Chapter 7A – Continuation (Judicial Department)	4
Chapter 7A – Continuation (Judicial Department)	5
Chapter 7B - Juvenile Code	5
Chapter 8 - Evidence	6
Chapter 8A - Interpreters for Deaf Persons [Recodified.]	6
Chapter 8B - Interpreters for Deaf Persons	6
Chapter 8C - Evidence Code	6
Chapter 9 - Jurors	6
Chapter 10 - Notaries [Repealed.]	6
Chapter 10A - Notaries [Recodified.]	6
Chapter 10B - Notaries	6
Chapter 11 - Oaths	6
Chapter 12 - Statutory Construction	6
Chapter 13 - Citizenship Restored	6
Chapter 14 - Criminal Law	7
Chapter 14 –Criminal Law (Continuation)	8
Chapter 15 - Criminal Procedure	9
Chapter 15A - Criminal Procedure Act (Continuation)	10
Chapter 15A - Criminal Procedure Act (Continuation)	11
Chapter 15B - Victims Compensation	11
Chapter 15C - Address Confidentiality Program	11
Chapter 16 - Gaming Contracts and Futures	11
Chapter 17 - Habeas Corpus	11

Chapter 17A - Law-Enforcement Officers [Recodified.]	11
Chapter 17B - North Carolina Criminal Justice Education and Training System [Recodified.] Chapter 17C - North Carolina Criminal Justice Education and Training Standards Commission	11
Chapter 17D - North Carolina Justice Academy	11
Chapter 17E - North Carolina Sheriffs' Education and Training Standards Commission	11
Chapter 18 - Regulation of Intoxicating Liquors [Repealed.]	12
Chapter 18A - Regulation of Intoxicating Liquors [Repealed.]	12
Chapter 18B - Regulation of Alcoholic Beverages	12
Chapter 18C - North Carolina State Lottery	12
Chapter 19 - Offenses against Public Morals	12
Chapter 19A - Protection of Animals	12
Chapter 20 - Motor Vehicles	13
Chapter 20 - Motor Vehicles (Continuation)	14
Chapter 20 - Motor Vehicles (Continuation)	15
Chapter 20 - Motor Vehicles (Continuation)	16
Chapter 21 - Bills of Lading	17
Chapter 22 - Contracts Requiring Writing	17
Chapter 22A - Signatures	17
Chapter 22B - Contracts Against Public Policy	17
Chapter 22C - Payments to Subcontractors	17
Chapter 23 - Debtor and Creditor. r 24 - Interest	17
Chapter 24 – Interest	17
Chapter 25 – Uniform Commercial Code	18
Chapter 25 – Uniform Commercial Code (Continuation)	19
Chapter 25A – Retail Installment Sales Act	20
Chapter 25B - Credit	20
Chapter 25C - Sales of Artwork	20
Chapter 26 - Suretyship	20
Chapter 27 - Warehouse Receipts [Repealed.]	20
Chapter 28 - Administration [Repealed.]	20
Chapter 28A - Administration of Decedents' Estates	20
Chapter 28B - Estates of Absentees in Military Service	20
Chapter 28C - Estates of Missing Persons	20
Chapter 29 - Intestate Succession	21
Chapter 30 - Surviving Spouses	21
Chapter 31 - Wills	21
Chapter 31A - Acts Barring Property Rights	21
Chapter 31B - Renunciation of Property and Renunciation of Fiduciary Powers Act	21
Chapter 31C - Uniform Disposition of Community Property Rights at Death Act	21
Chapter 32 - Fiduciaries	21
Chapter 32A - Powers of Attorney	21
Chapter 33 - Guardian and Ward [Repealed and Recodified.]	21

Chapter 33A - North Carolina Uniform Transfers to Minors Act	21
Chapter 33B - North Carolina Uniform Custodial Trust Act	21
Chapter 34 - Veterans' Guardianship Act	22
Chapter 35 - Sterilization Procedures	22
Chapter 35A - Incompetency and Guardianship	22
Chapter 36 - Trusts and Trustees [Repealed.]	22
Chapter 36A - Trusts and Trustees	22
Chapter 36B - Uniform Management of Institutional Funds Act [Repealed.]	22
Chapter 36C - North Carolina Uniform Trust Code	22
Chapter 36D - North Carolina Community Third Party Trusts, Pooled Trusts	23
Chapter 36E - Uniform Prudent Management of Institutional Funds Act	23
Chapter 37 - Allocation of Principal and Income [Repealed.]	23
Chapter 37A - Uniform Principal and Income Act	23
Chapter 38 - Boundaries	23
Chapter 38A - Landowner Liability	23
Chapter 39 - Conveyances	23
Chapter 39A - Transfer Fee Covenants Prohibited	23
Chapter 40 - Eminent Domain [Repealed.]	23
Chapter 40A - Eminent Domain	23
Chapter 41 - Estates	23
Chapter 41A - State Fair Housing Act	23
Chapter 42 - Landlord and Tenant	23
Chapter 42A - Vacation Rental Act	23
Chapter 43 - Land Registration	23
Chapter 44 - Liens	24
Chapter 44A - Statutory Liens and Charges	24
Chapter 45 - Mortgages and Deeds of Trust	24
Chapter 45A - Good Funds Settlement Act	24
Chapter 46 - Partition	24
Chapter 47 - Probate and Registration	25
Chapter 47A - Unit Ownership	25
Chapter 47B - Real Property Marketable Title Act	25
Chapter 47C - North Carolina Condominium Act	25
Chapter 47D - Notice of Settlement Act [Expired.]	25
Chapter 47E - Residential Property Disclosure Act	25
Chapter 47F - North Carolina Planned Community Act	25
Chapter 47G - Option to Purchase Contracts	25
Chapter 47H - Contracts for Deed	25
Chapter 48 - Adoptions +	26
Chapter 48A - Minors	26
Chapter 49 - Bastardy	26
Chapter 49A - Rights of Children	26
Chapter 50 - Divorce and Alimony	26
Chapter 50A - Uniform Child-Custody Jurisdiction and	

Enforcement Act	26
Chapter 50B - Domestic Violence	26
Chapter 50C - Civil No-Contact Orders	26
Chapter 51 - Marriage	26
Chapter 52 - Powers and Liabilities of Married Persons	27
Chapter 52A - Uniform Reciprocal Enforcement of Support Act [Repealed.]	27
Chapter 52B - Uniform Premarital Agreement Act	27
Chapter 52C - Uniform Interstate Family Support Act	27
Chapter 53 - Banks	27
Chapter 53A - Business Development Corporations and North Carolina Capital Resource Corporations	28
Chapter 53B - Financial Privacy Act	28
Chapter 54 - Cooperative Organizations	28
Chapter 54A - Capital Stock Savings and Loan Associations [Repealed.]	28
Chapter 54B - Savings and Loan Associations	29
Chapter 54C - Savings Banks	29
Chapter 55 - North Carolina Business Corporation Act	30
Chapter 55A - North Carolina Nonprofit Corporation Act	31
Chapter 55B - Professional Corporation Act	31
Chapter 55C - Foreign Trade Zones	31
Chapter 55D - Filings, Names, and Registered Agents for Corporations, Nonprofit Corporations, and Partnerships	31
Chapter 56 - Electric, Telegraph and Power Companies [Repealed.]	31
Chapter 57 - Hospital, Medical and Dental Service Corporations [Recodified.]	31
Chapter 57A - Health Maintenance Organization Act [Recodified.]	31
Chapter 57B - Health Maintenance Organization Act [Recodified.]	31
Chapter 57C - North Carolina Limited Liability Company Act.	31
Chapter 58 - Insurance.	32
Chapter 58 - Insurance (Continuation)	33
Chapter 58 - Insurance (Continuation)	34
Chapter 58 - Insurance (Continuation)	35
Chapter 58 - Insurance (Continuation)	36
Chapter 58 - Insurance (Continuation)	37
Chapter 58 - Insurance (Continuation)	38
Chapter 58A - North Carolina Health Insurance Trust Commission [Recodified.]	38
Chapter 59 - Partnership.	39
Chapter 59B - Uniform Unincorporated Nonprofit Association Act.	39
Chapter 60 - Railroads and Other Carriers [Repealed and Transferred.]	39
Chapter 61 - Religious Societies	39
Chapter 62 - Public Utilities	39

Chapter 62 - Public Utilities (Continuation)	40
Chapter 62A - Public Safety Telephone Service And Wireless Telephone Service	40
Chapter 63 - Aeronautics	40
Chapter 63A - North Carolina Global TransPark Authority	40
Chapter 64 - Aliens	40
Chapter 65 – Cemeteries	40
Chapter 66 - Commerce and Business	41
Chapter 67 - Dogs	41
Chapter 68 - Fences and Stock Law	41
Chapter 69 - Fire Protection	41
Chapter 70 - Indian Antiquities, Archaeological Resources and Unmarked Human Skeletal Remains Protection	42
Chapter 71 - Indians [Repealed.]	42
Chapter 71A - Indians	42
Chapter 72 - Inns, Hotels and Restaurants	42
Chapter 73 - Mills	42
Chapter 74 - Mines and Quarries	42
Chapter 74A - Company Police [Repealed.]	42
Chapter 74B - Private Protective Services Act [Repealed.]	42
Chapter 74C - Private Protective Services	42
Chapter 74D - Alarm Systems	42
Chapter 74E - Company Police Act	42
Chapter 74F - Locksmith Licensing Act	42
Chapter 74G - Campus Police Act	42
Chapter 75 - Monopolies, Trusts and Consumer Protection	42
Chapter 75A - Boating and Water Safety	43
Chapter 75B - Discrimination in Business	43
Chapter 75C - Motion Picture Fair Competition Act	43
Chapter 75D - Racketeer Influenced and Corrupt Organizations	43
Chapter 75E - Unlawful Activities in Connection With Certain Corporate Transactions	43
Chapter 76 - Navigation	43
Chapter 76A - Navigation and Pilotage Commissions	43
Chapter 77 - Rivers, Creeks, and Coastal Waters	43
Chapter 78 - Securities Law [Repealed.]	43
Chapter 78A - North Carolina Securities Act	43
Chapter 78B - Tender Offer Disclosure Act [Repealed.]	43
Chapter 78C - Investment Advisers	43
Chapter 78D - Commodities Act	43
Chapter 79 - Strays [Repealed.]	43
Chapter 80 - Trademarks, Brands, etc.	44
Chapter 81 - Weights and Measures [Recodified.]	44
Chapter 81A - Weights and Measures Act of 1975.	44
Chapter 82 - Wrecks [Repealed.]	44
Chapter 83 - Architects [Recodified.]	44

Chapter 83A - Architects	44
Chapter 84 - Attorneys-at-Law	44
Chapter 84A - Foreign Legal Consultants	44
Chapter 85 - Auctions and Auctioneers [Repealed.]	44
Chapter 85A - Bail Bondsmen and Runners [Recodified.]	44
Chapter 85B - Auctions and Auctioneers	44
Chapter 85C - Bail Bondsmen and Runners [Recodified.]	44
Chapter 86 - Barbers [Recodified.]	44
Chapter 86A - Barbers	44
Chapter 87 - Contractors	44
Chapter 88 - Cosmetic Art [Repealed.]	44
Chapter 88A - Electrolysis Practice Act	44
Chapter 88B - Cosmetic Art	45
Chapter 89 - Engineering and Land Surveying [Recodified.]	45
Chapter 89A - Landscape Architects	45
Chapter 89B - Foresters	45
Chapter 89C - Engineering and Land Surveying	45
Chapter 89D - Landscape Contractors	45
Chapter 89E - Geologists Licensing Act	45
Chapter 89F - North Carolina Soil Scientist Licensing Act	45
Chapter 89G - Irrigation Contractors	45
Chapter 90 - Medicine and Allied Occupations	45
Chapter 90 - Medicine and Allied Occupations (Continuation)	46
Chapter 90 - Medicine and Allied Occupations (Continuation)	47
Chapter 90 - Medicine and Allied Occupations (Continuation)	48
Chapter 90A - Sanitarians and Water and Wastewater Treatment Facility Operators	48
Chapter 90B - Social Worker Certification and Licensure Act	48
Chapter 90C - North Carolina Recreational Therapy Licensure Act	48
Chapter 90D - Interpreters and Transliterators	48
Chapter 91 - Pawnbrokers [Repealed.]	48
Chapter 91A - Pawnbrokers Modernization Act of 1989	48
Chapter 92 - Photographers [Deleted.]	48
Chapter 93 - Certified Public Accountants	48
Chapter 93A - Real Estate License Law	49
Chapter 93B - Occupational Licensing Boards	49
Chapter 93C - Watchmakers [Repealed.]	49
Chapter 93D - North Carolina State Hearing Aid Dealers and Fitters Board.	49
Chapter 93E - North Carolina Appraisers Act	49
Chapter 94 - Apprenticeship	49
Chapter 95 - Department of Labor and Labor Regulations	49
Chapter 95 - Department of Labor and Labor Regulations (Continuation)	50
Chapter 96 - Employment Security	50
Chapter 97 - Workers' Compensation Act	50
Chapter 97 - Workers' Compensation Act (Continuation)	51

Chapter 98 - Burnt and Lost Records	51
Chapter 99 - Libel and Slander	51
Chapter 99A - Civil Remedies for Criminal Actions	51
Chapter 99B - Products Liability	51
Chapter 99C - Actions Relating to Winter Sports Safety and Accidents	51
Chapter 99D - Civil Rights	51
Chapter 99E - Special Liability Provisions	51
Chapter 100 - Monuments, Memorials and Parks	51
Chapter 101 - Names of Persons	51
Chapter 102 - Official Survey Base	51
Chapter 103 - Sundays, Holidays and Special Days	51
Chapter 104 - United States Lands	51
Chapter 104A - Degrees of Kinship	51
Chapter 104B - Hurricanes or Other Acts of Nature	51
Chapter 104C - Atomic Energy, Radioactivity and Ionizing Radiation [Repealed and Recodified.]	51
Chapter 104D - Southern States Energy Compact	51
Chapter 104E - North Carolina Radiation Protection Act	51
Chapter 104F - Southeast Interstate Low-Level Radioactive Waste Management Compact [Repealed]	51
Chapter 104G - North Carolina Low-Level Radioactive Waste Management Authority Act of 1987 [Repealed]	51
Chapter 105 - Taxation	51
Chapter 105 - Taxation (Continuation)	52
Chapter 105 - Taxation (Continuation)	53
Chapter 105 - Taxation (Continuation)	54
Chapter 105A - Setoff Debt Collection Act	55
Chapter 105B - Defaulted Student Loan Recovery Act	55
Chapter 106 - Agriculture	55
Chapter 106 - Agriculture (Continue)	56
Chapter 106 - Agriculture (Continue)	57
Chapter 107 - Agricultural Development Districts [Repealed.]	57
Chapter 108 - Social Services [Repealed and Recodified.]	57
Chapter 108A - Social Services	57
Chapter 108B - Community Action Programs	58
Chapter 108C Medicaid and Health Choice Provider Requirements.	58
Chapter 108D Medicaid Managed Care for Behavioral Health Services.	58
Chapter 109 - Bonds [Recodified.]	58
Chapter 110 - Child Welfare	58
Chapter 111 - Aid to the Blind	58
Chapter 112 - Confederate Homes and Pensions [Repealed.]	58
Chapter 113 - Conservation and Development	58
Chapter 113 - Conservation and Development (Continuation)	59

Chapter	Page
Chapter 113A - Pollution Control and Environment	59
Chapter 113A - Pollution Control and Environment (Continuation)	60
Chapter 113B - North Carolina Energy Policy Act of 1975	60
Chapter 114 - Department of Justice	60
Chapter 115 - Elementary and Secondary Education [Repealed.]	60
Chapter 115A - Community Colleges, Technical Institutes, and Industrial Education Centers [Repealed.]	60
Chapter 115B - Tuition and Fee Waivers	60
Chapter 115C - Elementary and Secondary Education	60
Chapter 115C - Elementary and Secondary Education (Continuation)	61
Chapter 115C - Elementary and Secondary Education (Continuation)	62
Chapter 115C - Elementary and Secondary Education (Continuation)	63
Chapter 115D - Community Colleges	63
Chapter 115E - Private Educational Facilities Finance Act [Recodified]	63
Chapter 116 - Higher Education	63
Chapter 116 - Higher Education (Continuation)	63
Chapter 116A - Escheats and Abandoned Property [Repealed.]	64
Chapter 116B - Escheats and Abandoned Property	64
Chapter 116C - Continuum of Education Programs	64
Chapter 116D - Higher Education Bonds	64
Chapter 117 - Electrification	64
Chapter 118 - Firemen's and Rescue Squad Workers' Relief and Pension Funds [Recodified.]	64
Chapter 118A - Firemen's Death Benefit Act [Repealed.]	64
Chapter 118B - Members of a Rescue Squad Death Benefit Act [Repealed.]	64
Chapter 119 - Gasoline and Oil Inspection and Regulation	64
Chapter 120 - General Assembly	65
Chapter 120 - General Assembly (Continuation)	66
Chapter 120 - General Assembly (Continuation)	67
Chapter 120C - Lobbying	67
Chapter 121 - Archives and History	67
Chapter 122 - Hospitals for the Mentally Disordered [Repealed.]	67
Chapter 122A - North Carolina Housing Finance Agency	67
Chapter 122B - North Carolina Agricultural Facilities Finance Act [Repealed.]	67
Chapter 122C - Mental Health, Developmental Disabilities, and Substance Abuse Act of 1985	67
Chapter 122C - Mental Health, Developmental Disabilities, and Substance Abuse Act of 1985 (Continuation)	68
Chapter 122D - North Carolina Agricultural Finance Act	68

Chapter 122E - North Carolina Housing Trust and Oil Overcharge Act	68
Chapter 123 - Impeachment	69
Chapter 123A - Industrial Development [Repealed.]	69
Chapter 124 - Internal Improvements	69
Chapter 125 - Libraries	69
Chapter 126 - State Personnel System	69
Chapter 127 - Militia [Repealed.]	69
Chapter 127A - Militia	69
Chapter 127B - Military Affairs	69
Chapter 127C - Advisory Commission on Military Affairs	69
Chapter 128 - Offices and Public Officers	69
Chapter 128 - Offices and Public Officers (Continuation)	70
Chapter 129 - Public Buildings and Grounds	70
Chapter 130 - Public Health [Repealed.]	70
Chapter 130A - Public Health	70
Chapter 130A - Public Health (Continuation)	71
Chapter 130A - Public Health (Continuation)	72
Chapter 130B - Hazardous Waste Management Commission [Repealed.]	72
Chapter 131 - Public Hospitals [Repealed.]	72
Chapter 131A - Health Care Facilities Finance Act	72
Chapter 131B - Licensing of Ambulatory Surgical Facilities [Repealed.]	72
Chapter 131C - Charitable Solicitation Licensure Act [Repealed.]	72
Chapter 131D - Inspection and Licensing of Facilities	72
Chapter 131E - Health Care Facilities and Services	72
Chapter 131E - Health Care Facilities and Services (Continuation)	73
Chapter 131F - Solicitation of Contributions	73
Chapter 132 - Public Records	73
Chapter 133 - Public Works	74
Chapter 134 - Youth Development [Recodified.]	74
Chapter 134A - Youth Services [Repealed.]	74
Chapter 135 - Retirement System for Teachers and State Employees; Social Security; Health Insurance Program for Children	74
Chapter 135 - Retirement System for Teachers and State Employees; Social Security; Health Insurance Program for Children	75
Chapter 136 - Transportation	75
Chapter 136 - Transportation (Continuation)	76
Chapter 137 - Rural Rehabilitation [Repealed.]	76
Chapter 138 - Salaries, Fees and Allowances	76
Chapter 138A - State Government Ethics Act	76
Chapter 139 - Soil and Water Conservation Districts	76

Chapter 140 - State Art Museum; Symphony and Art Societies	76
Chapter 140A - State Awards System	76
Chapter 141 - State Boundaries	76
Chapter 142 - State Debt	76
Chapter 143 - State Departments, Institutions, and Commissions	77
Chapter 143 - State Departments, Institutions, and Commissions (Continuation)	78
Chapter 143 - State Departments, Institutions, and Commissions (Continuation)	79
Chapter 143 - State Departments, Institutions, and Commissions (Continuation)	80
Chapter 143A - State Government Reorganization	80
Chapter 143B - Executive Organization Act of 1973	80
Chapter 143B - Executive Organization Act of 1973 (Continuation)	81
Chapter 143B - Executive Organization Act of 1973 (Continuation)	82
Chapter 143C - State Budget Act	83
Chapter 143D - The State Governmental Accountability and Internal Control Act	83
Chapter 144 - State Flag, Official Governmental Flags, Motto, and Colors	83
Chapter 145 - State Symbols and Other Official Adoptions.	83
Chapter 146 - State Lands	83
Chapter 147 - State Officers	83
Chapter 148 - State Prison System	84
Chapter 149 - State Song and Toast	84
Chapter 150 - Uniform Revocation of Licenses [Repealed.]	84
Chapter 150A - Administrative Procedure Act [Recodified.]	84
Chapter 150B - Administrative Procedure Act	84
Chapter 151 - Constables [Repealed.]	84
Chapter 152 - Coroners	84
Chapter 152A - County Medical Examiner [Repealed.]	84
Chapter 152A - County Medical Examiner [Repealed.] (Continuation)	85
Chapter 153 - Counties and County Commissioners [Repealed.]	85
Chapter 153A - Counties	85
Chapter 153B - Mountain Resources Planning Act	85
Chapter 153C - Uwharrie Regional Resources Act	85
Chapter 154 - County Surveyor [Repealed.]	85
Chapter 155 - County Treasurer [Repealed.]	85
Chapter 156 - Drainage	85
Chapter 156 – Drainage (Continuation)	86

Chapter 157 - Housing Authorities and Projects	86
Chapter 157A - Historic Properties Commissions [Transferred.]	86
Chapter 158 - Local Development	86
Chapter 159 - Local Government Finance	86
Chapter 159 - Local Government Finance (Continuation)	87
Chapter 159A - Pollution Abatement and Industrial Facilities Financing Act [Unconstitutional.]	87
Chapter 159B - Joint Municipal Electric Power and Energy Act	87
Chapter 159C - Industrial and Pollution Control Facilities Financing Act	87
Chapter 159D - The North Carolina Capital Facilities Financing Act	87
Chapter 159E - Registered Public Obligations Act	87
Chapter 159F - North Carolina Energy Development Authority [Repealed.]	87
Chapter 159G - Water Infrastructure	87
Chapter 159H - [Reserved.]	87
Chapter 159I - Solid Waste Management Loan Program and Local Government Special Obligation Bonds	87
Chapter 160 - Municipal Corporations [Repealed And Transferred.]	87
Chapter 160A - Cities and Towns	88
Chapter 160A - Cities and Towns (Continuation)	89
Chapter 160B - Consolidated City-County Act	89
Chapter 160C - Baseball Park Districts [Repealed.]	90
Chapter 161 - Register of Deeds	90
Chapter 162 - Sheriff	90
Chapter 162A - Water and Sewer Systems	90
Chapter 162B Continuity of Local Government in Emergency.	90
Chapter 163 Elections and Election Laws.	90
Chapter 163 Elections and Election Laws. (Continuation)	91
Chapter 164 Concerning the General Statutes of North Carolina.	92
Chapter 165 Veterans.	92
Chapter 166 Civil Preparedness Agencies [Repealed.]	92
Chapter 166A North Carolina Emergency Management Act.	92
Chapter 167 State Civil Air Patrol [Repealed.]	92
Chapter 168 Persons with Disabilities.	92
Chapter 168A Persons With Disabilities Protection Act.	92

§ 58-49-50. Filing of application.

An association sponsoring a MEWA shall file with the Commissioner an application for a license on a form prescribed by the Commissioner and signed under oath by officers of the association. The application shall include or have attached the following:

(I)   A copy of the articles of incorporation, constitution, and bylaws of the association;

(2)   A list of the names, addresses, and official capacities with the MEWA of the individuals who will be responsible for the management and conduct of the affairs of the MEWA, including all trustees, officers, and directors. Such individuals shall fully disclose the extent and nature of any contracts or arrangements between them and the MEWA, including possible conflicts of interest.

(3)   A copy of the articles of incorporation, bylaws, or trust agreement that governs the operation of the MEWA.

(4)   A copy of the policy, contract, certificate, summary plan description, or other evidence of the benefits and coverages provided to covered employees, including a table of the rates charged or proposed to be charged for each form of such contract. An actuary who is a member of the American Academy of Actuaries or the Society of Actuaries and has experience in establishing rates for a self-insured trust and health services being provided, shall certify that:

a.   The rates are neither inadequate, nor excessive, nor unfairly discriminatory.

b.   The rates are appropriate for the classes of risks for which they have been computed.

c.   An adequate description of the rating methodology has been filed with the Commissioner and such methodology follows consistent and equitable actuarial principles.

(5)   A copy of a fidelity bond, in an amount determined by rules adopted by the Commissioner, issued in the name of the MEWA and covering any individuals managing or handling the funds or assets of the MEWA. In no case may the bond be less than fifty thousand dollars ($50,000) or more than five hundred thousand dollars ($500,000).

(6)   A copy of the MEWA's excess insurance agreement.

(7) A feasibility study, made by an independent qualified actuary and an independent certified public accountant with an opinion acceptable to the Commissioner, that addresses market potential, market penetration, market competition, operating expenses, gross revenues, net income, total assets and liabilities, cash flow, and other items as the Commissioner requires. The study shall be for the greater of three years or until the MEWA has been projected to be profitable for 12 consecutive months. The study must show that the MEWA would not, at any month end of the projection period, have less than the reserves as required by G.S. 58-49-40(d).

(8) A copy of an audited financial statement of the MEWA reflecting the minimum statutory reserve as required by G.S. 58-49-40(d).

(9) Evidence satisfactory to the Commissioner showing that the MEWA will be operated in accordance with sound actuarial principles. The Commissioner shall not approve the MEWA unless it is determined that the MEWA is designed to provide sufficient revenues to pay current and future liabilities, as determined in accordance with sound actuarial principles.

(10) A copy of every contract between the MEWA and any administrator or service company.

(11) Such additional information as the Commissioner may require. (1991, c. 611, s. 1.)

§ 58-49-55. Examinations; deposits; solvency regulation.

(a) The provisions of Articles 2, 5, and 30 of this Chapter regarding examinations, deposits, and supervision and receivership respectively apply to MEWAs. The provisions of Article 62 of this Chapter and of Article 8B of Chapter 105 of the General Statutes do not apply to MEWAs.

(b) An audit or examination of a MEWA shall be conducted only when there are circumstances to support a reasonable belief of a MEWA's noncompliance with this Article. (1991, c. 611, s. 1.)

§ 58-49-60. Annual reports; actuarial certifications; quarterly reports.

(a) Every MEWA shall, within 150 days after the end of each of its fiscal years or within any such extension of time that the Commissioner for good cause grants, file a report with the Commissioner, on forms prescribed by the Commissioner and verified by the oath of a member of the board of trustees and by an administrative executive appointed by the board, showing its financial condition on the last day of the preceding fiscal year. The report shall contain an audited financial statement of the MEWA prepared in accordance with statutory accounting principles, including its balance sheet and a statement of the operations for the preceding fiscal year certified by an independent certified public accountant. The report shall also include an analysis of the adequacy of reserves and contributions or premiums charged, based on a review of past and projected claims and expenses.

(b) In addition to the information called for and furnished in connection with the annual report, if reasonable grounds exist, the Commissioner may request information that summarizes paid and incurred expenses and contributions or premiums received; and may request evidence satisfactory to the Commissioner that the MEWA is actuarially sound. That information and evidence shall be furnished by the MEWA not later than 30 days after the request, unless the Commissioner, for good cause, grants an extension.

(c) Annually, in conjunction with the annual report required in subsection (a) of this section, the MEWA shall submit an actuarial certification prepared by an independent qualified actuary that indicates:

(1) The MEWA is actuarially sound, with the certification considering the rates, benefits, and expenses of, and any other funds available for the payment of obligations of, the MEWA;

(2) The rates being charged and to be charged for contracts are actuarially adequate to the end of the period for which rates have been guaranteed;

(3) Incurred but not reported claims and claims reported but not fully paid have been adequately provided for; and

(4) Such other information relating to the performance of the MEWA that is required by the Commissioner.

(d) If reasonable grounds exist, the Commissioner may require a MEWA to file quarterly, within 45 days after the end of each of its fiscal quarters, an unaudited financial statement on a form prescribed by the Commissioner, verified by the oath of a member of the board of trustees and an administrative executive appointed by the board, showing its financial condition on the last day of the preceding quarter.

(e) Any MEWA that fails to file a report as required by this section is subject to G.S. 58-2-70; and after notice and opportunity for hearing, the Commissioner may suspend the MEWA's authority to enroll new insureds or to do business in this State while the failure continues. (1991, c. 611, s. 1.)

§ 58-49-65. Denial, suspension, or revocation of license.

(a) The Commissioner shall deny, suspend, or revoke a MEWA's license if the Commissioner finds that the MEWA:

(1) Is insolvent;

(2) Is using such methods and practices in the conduct of its business as to render its further transaction of business in this State hazardous or injurious to its participating employers, covered employees and dependents, or to the public;

(3) Has failed to pay any final judgment rendered against it in a court of competent jurisdiction within 60 days after the judgment became final;

(4) Is or has been in violation of or threatens to violate any provision of this Article;

(5) Is no longer actuarially sound; or

(6) Is charging rates that are excessive, inadequate, or unfairly discriminatory.

(b) The Commissioner may deny, suspend, or revoke the license of any MEWA if the Commissioner determines that the MEWA:

(1) Has violated any lawful order or rule of the Commissioner; or any applicable provision of this Article; or

(2) Has refused to produce its accounts, records, or files for examination under G.S. 58-49-55 or through any of its officers has refused to give information with respect to its affairs or to perform any other legal obligation as to an examination.

(c) Whenever the financial condition of the MEWA is such that, if not modified or corrected, its continued operation would result in impairment or insolvency, in addition to any provisions in Article 30 of this Chapter, the Commissioner may order the MEWA to file with the Commissioner and implement a corrective action plan designed to do one or more of the following:

(1) Reduce the total amount of present potential liability for benefits by reinsurance or other means.

(2) Reduce the volume of new business being accepted.

(3) Reduce the expenses of the MEWA by specified methods.

(4) Suspend or limit the writing of new business for a period of time.

If the MEWA fails to submit a plan within the time specified by the Commissioner or submits a plan that is insufficient to correct the MEWA's financial condition, the Commissioner may order the MEWA to implement one or more of the corrective actions listed in this subsection.

(d) The Commissioner shall, in the order suspending the authority of a MEWA to enroll new insureds, specify the period during which the suspension is to be in effect and the conditions, if any, that must be met prior to reinstatement of its authority to enroll new insureds. The order of suspension is subject to rescission or modification by further order of the Commissioner before the expiration of the suspension period. Reinstatement shall not be made unless requested by the MEWA; however, the Commissioner shall not grant reinstatement if it is found that the circumstances for which suspension occurred still exist. (1991, c. 611, s. 1.)

Article 50.

General Accident and Health Insurance Regulations.

Part 1. Miscellaneous Provisions.

§ 58-50-1. Waiver by insurer.

The acknowledgment by any insurer of the receipt of notice given under any policy covered by Articles 49, 50 through 55, 65, or 67 of this Chapter, or the furnishing of forms for filing proofs of loss, or the acceptance of such proofs, or the investigation of any claim under the policy, shall not operate as a waiver of any of the rights of the insurer in defense of any claim arising under the policy. (1913, c. 91, s. 7; C.S., s. 6484; 1991, c. 720, s. 28; 1999-244, s. 10; 2000-140, s. 16.)

§ 58-50-5. Application.

(a)   On and after January 1, 1956, each individual or family accident, health, hospitalization policy, certificate or service plan of hospitalization and medical and/or dental service corporations shall be issued only on application in writing signed by the insured or the head of the household or guardian. Any application or enrollment form that is taken by a resident agent shall also contain the certificate of the agent that he has truly and accurately recorded on the application or enrollment form the information supplied by the insured. Every policy subject to the provisions of this section shall contain as a part of such policy the original or a reproduction of the application required by this section. This section shall not apply to travel or dread disease policies or to policies issued pursuant to a group insurance conversion privilege. If any such policy delivered or issued for delivery to any person in this State shall be reinstated or renewed, and the insured or the beneficiary or assignee of such policy shall make written request to the insurer for a copy of the application, if any, for such reinstatement or renewal, the insurer shall within 15 days after the receipt of such request at his home office or any branch office of the insurer, deliver or mail to the person making such request, a copy of such application. If such copy shall not be so delivered or mailed, the insurer shall be precluded from introducing such application as evidence in any action or proceeding based upon or involving such policy or its reinstatement or renewal.

(b)   No alteration of any written application for any such policy shall be made by any person other than the applicant without his written consent, except that insertions may be made by the insurer, for administrative purposes only, in such manner as to indicate clearly that such insertions are not to be ascribed to the applicant.

(c) The falsity of any statement in the application for any policy covered by Articles 50 through 55 of this Chapter may not bar the right to recover thereunder unless such false statement materially affected either the acceptance of the risk or the hazard assumed by the insurer. (1913, c. 91, s. 8; C.S., s. 6485; 1953, c. 1095, s. 9; 1955, c. 850, s. 6; 1961, c. 1149; 1985, c. 484, s. 4.2; 1991, c. 720, s. 29.)

§ 58-50-10: Repealed by Session Laws 1993, c. 529, s. 4.1.

§ 58-50-15. Conforming to statute.

(a) Other Policy Provisions. - No policy provision which is not subject to G.S. 58-51-15 shall make a policy, or any portion thereof, less favorable in any respect to the insured or the beneficiary than the provisions thereof which are subject to Articles 50 through 55 of this Chapter.

(b) Policy Conflicting with Articles 50 through 55 of this Chapter. - A policy delivered or issued for delivery to any person in this State in violation of Articles 50 through 55 of this Chapter shall be held valid but shall be construed as provided in Articles 50 through 55 of this Chapter. When any provision in a policy subject to Articles 50 through 55 of this Chapter is in conflict with any provision of Articles 50 through 55 of this Chapter, the rights, duties and obligations of the insurer, the insured and the beneficiary shall be governed by the provisions of Articles 50 through 55 of this Chapter. (1913, c. 91, s. 9; C.S., s. 6486; 1953, c. 1095, s. 10; 1991, c. 720, s. 29.)

§ 58-50-20. Age limit.

If any such policy contains a provision establishing, as an age limit or otherwise, a date after which the coverage provided by the policy will not be effective, and if such date falls within a period for which premium is accepted by the insurer or if the insurer accepts a premium after such date, the coverage provided by the policy will continue in force subject to any right of cancellation until the end of the period for which premium has been accepted. In the event the age of the insured has been misstated and if, according to the correct age of the insured, the coverage provided by the policy would not have become effective, or would have ceased prior to the acceptance of such premium or premiums, then the liability of the insurer shall be limited to the refund, upon request, of all premiums paid for the period not covered by the policy. (1953, c. 1095, s. 11.)

§ 58-50-25. Nurses' services.

(a)   No agency, institution or physician providing a service for which payment or reimbursement is required to be made under a policy governed by Articles 1 through 64 of this Chapter shall be denied such payment or reimbursement on account of the fact that such services were rendered through a registered nurse acting under authority of rules and regulations adopted by the North Carolina Medical Board and the Board of Nursing pursuant to G.S. 90-6 and 90-171.23.

(b)   A licensed registered nurse who has successfully completed a program established under G.S. 90-171.38(b) may receive direct payment for conducting medical examinations or medical procedures for the purpose of collecting evidence from victims of offenses described in that subsection if the payment would have otherwise been permitted. (1973, c. 437; 1991, c. 720, s. 37; 1993, c. 347, s. 1; 1995, c. 94, s. 2; 1997-197, s. 1; 1997-375, s. 3.)

§ 58-50-26. Physician services provided by physician assistants.

No agency, institution, or physician providing a service for which payment or reimbursement is required to be made under a policy governed by Articles 1 through 64 of this Chapter shall be denied the payment or reimbursement on account of the fact that the services were rendered through a physician assistant acting under the authority of rules adopted by the North Carolina Medical Board pursuant to G.S. 90-18.1. (1999-210, s. 1.)

§ 58-50-30. Right to choose services of certain providers.

(a) Repealed by Session Laws 2001-297, s. 1, effective January 1, 2001.

(a1) Whenever any health benefit plan, subscriber contract, or policy of insurance issued by a health maintenance organization, hospital or medical service corporation, or insurer governed by Articles 1 through 67 of this Chapter provides for coverage for, payment of, or reimbursement for any service rendered in connection with a condition or complaint that is within the scope of practice of a provider listed in subsection (b) of this section, the insured or other persons entitled to benefits under the policy shall be entitled to coverage of, payment of, or reimbursement for the services, whether the services be performed by a duly licensed physician, or a provider listed in subsection (b) of this section, notwithstanding any provision contained in the plan or policy limiting access to the providers. The policyholder, insured, or beneficiary shall have the right to choose the provider of services notwithstanding any provision to the contrary in any other statute, subject to the utilization review, referral, and prior approval requirements of the plan that apply to all providers for that service; provided that:

(1) In the case of plans that require the use of network providers as a condition of obtaining benefits under the plan or policy, the policyholder, insured, or beneficiary must choose a provider of the services within the network; and

(2) In the case of plans that require the use of network providers as a condition of obtaining a higher level of benefits under the plan or policy, the policyholder, insured, or beneficiary must choose a provider of the services within the network in order to obtain the higher level of benefits.

(a2) Whenever any policy of insurance governed by Articles 1 through 64 of this Chapter provides for certification of disability that is within the scope of practice of a provider listed in subsection (b) of this section, the insured or other persons entitled to benefits under the policy shall be entitled to payment of or reimbursement for the disability whether the disability be certified by a duly licensed physician, or a provider listed in subsection (b) of this section, notwithstanding any provisions contained in the policy. The policyholder, insured, or beneficiary shall have the right to choose the provider of the services notwithstanding any provision to the contrary in any other statute; provided that for plans that require the use of network providers either as a condition of obtaining benefits under the plan or policy or to access a higher level of benefits under the plan or policy, the policyholder, insured, or beneficiary must choose a provider of the services within the network, subject to the requirements of the plan or policy.

(a3) Whenever any health benefit plan, subscriber contract, or policy of insurance issued by a health maintenance organization, hospital or medical service corporation, or insurer governed by Articles 1 through 67 of this Chapter provides coverage for medically necessary treatment, the insurer shall not impose any limitation on treatment or levels of coverage if performed by a duly licensed chiropractor acting within the scope of the chiropractor's practice as defined in G.S. 90-151 unless a comparable limitation is imposed on the medically necessary treatment if performed or authorized by any other duly licensed physician.

(b) This section applies to the following provider types:

(1) A duly licensed optometrist.

(2) A duly licensed dentist.

(3) A duly licensed podiatrist.

(4) A duly licensed chiropractor.

(5) An advanced practice registered nurse, subject to subsection (d) of this section. For purposes of this section, an "advanced practice registered nurse" means only a registered nurse who is duly licensed or certified as a nurse practitioner, clinical specialist in psychiatric and mental health nursing, or nurse midwife.

(6) A psychologist who is one of the following:

a. A licensed psychologist who holds permanent licensure and certification as a health services provider psychologist issued by the North Carolina Psychology Board.

b. A licensed psychological associate who holds permanent licensure.

(7) A licensed clinical social worker, as defined in G.S. 90B-3(2) who is licensed by the North Carolina Social Work Certification and Licensure Board pursuant to Chapter 90B of the General Statutes.

(8) A duly licensed pharmacist, subject to the provisions of subsection (e) of this section.

(9) A fee-based practicing pastoral counselor certified by the North Carolina State Board of Examiners of Fee-Based Practicing Pastoral Counselors pursuant to Article 26 of Chapter 90 of the General Statutes.

(10) A substance abuse professional certified by the North Carolina Substance Abuse Professional Certification Board pursuant to Article 5C of Chapter 90 of the General Statutes.

(11) A physician assistant, as defined by G.S. 90-18.1 and subject to subsection (f) of this section.

(12) A professional counselor licensed by the North Carolina Board of Licensed Professional Counselors pursuant to Article 24 of Chapter 90 of the General Statutes.

(13) A marriage and family therapist licensed by the North Carolina Marriage and Family Therapy Licensure Board pursuant to Article 18C of Chapter 90 of the General Statutes.

(14) A physical therapist licensed by the North Carolina Board of Physical Therapy Examiners pursuant to Article 18B of Chapter 90 of the General Statutes.

(15) A hearing aid specialist licensed by the North Carolina State Hearing Aid Dealers and Fitters Board under Chapter 93D of the General Statutes to engage in fitting or selling hearing aids. For purposes of this subdivision, the term "fitting and selling hearing aids" has the same meaning as defined in G.S. 93D-1.

(c) Recodified as G.S. 58-50-30(b)(7).

(c1) Recodified as G.S. 58-50-30(b)(9).

(c2) Recodified as G.S. 58-50-30(b)(10).

(c3) Recodified as G.S. 58-50-30(b)(12).

(c4) Recodified as G.S. 58-50-30(b)(13).

(c5)   Recodified as G.S. 58-50-30(b)(14).

(d)   Payment or reimbursement is required by this section for a service performed by an advanced practice registered nurse only when:

(1)   The service performed is within the nurse's lawful scope of practice;

(2)   The policy currently provides benefits for identical services performed by other licensed health care providers;

(3)   The service is not performed while the nurse is a regular employee in an office of a licensed physician;

(4)   The service is not performed while the registered nurse is employed by a nursing facility (including a hospital, skilled nursing facility, intermediate care facility, or home care agency); and

(5)   Nothing in this section is intended to authorize payment to more than one provider for the same service.

No lack of signature, referral, or employment by any other health care provider may be asserted to deny benefits under this provision, unless these plan requirements apply to all providers for that service.

(e)   Payment or reimbursement is required by this section for a service performed by a duly licensed pharmacist only when:

(1)   The service performed is within the lawful scope of practice of the pharmacist;

(2)   The service performed is not initial counseling services required under State or federal law or regulation of the North Carolina Board of Pharmacy;

(3)   The policy currently provides reimbursement for identical services performed by other licensed health care providers; and

(4)   The service is identified as a separate service that is performed by other licensed health care providers and is reimbursed by identical payment methods.

Nothing in this subsection authorizes payment to more than one provider for the same service.

(f) Payment or reimbursement is required by this section for a service performed by a duly licensed physician assistant only when:

(1) The service performed is within the lawful scope of practice of the physician assistant in accordance with rules adopted by the North Carolina Medical Board pursuant to G.S. 90-18.1;

(2) The policy currently provides reimbursement for identical services performed by other licensed health care providers; and

(3) The reimbursement is made to the physician, clinic, agency, or institution employing the physician assistant.

Nothing in this subsection is intended to authorize payment to more than one provider for the same service.

(g) A health maintenance organization, hospital or medical service corporation, or insurer governed by Articles 1 through 67 of this Chapter shall not exclude from participation in its provider network or from eligibility to provide particular covered services under the plan or policy any duly licensed physician or provider listed in subsection (b) of this section, acting within the scope of the provider's license or certification under North Carolina law, solely on the basis of the provider's license or certification. Any health maintenance organization, hospital or medical service corporation, or insurer governed by Articles 1 through 67 of this Chapter that offers coverage through a network plan may condition participation in the network on satisfying written participation criteria, including credentialing, quality, and accessibility criteria. The participation criteria shall be developed and applied in a like manner consistent with the licensure and scope of practice for each type of provider. Any health maintenance organization, hospital or medical service corporation, or insurer governed by Articles 1 through 67 of this Chapter that excludes a provider listed in subsection (b) of this section from participation in its network or from eligibility to provide particular covered services under the plan or policy shall provide the affected listed provider with a written explanation of the basis for its decision. A health maintenance organization, hospital or medical service corporation, or insurer governed by Articles 1 through 67 of this Chapter shall not exclude from participation in its provider network a provider listed in subsection (b) of this section acting within the scope of the provider's license or certification under

North Carolina law solely on the basis that the provider lacks hospital privileges, unless use of hospital services by the provider on behalf of a policy holder, insured, or beneficiary reasonably could be expected.

(h) Nothing in this section shall be construed as expanding the scope of practice of any duly licensed physician or provider listed in subsection (b) of this section. (1913, c. 91, s. 11; C.S., s. 6488; 1965, c. 396, s. 2; c. 1169, s. 2; 1967, c. 690, s. 2; 1969, c. 679; 1973, c. 610; 1977, c. 601, ss. 2, 31/2; 1991, c. 720, s. 29; 1993, c. 347, s. 2; c. 375, s. 3; c. 464, s. 2; c. 554, s. 1; 1995, c. 193, s. 41, c. 223, s. 1; c. 406, s. 3; 1997-197, ss. 1, 2; 1999-186, s. 1; 1999-199, s. 1; 1999-210, s. 2; 2001-297, s. 1; 2001-446, s. 1.7; 2001-487, s. 40(g); 2003-117, s. 1; 2003-368, s. 1; 2005-276, s. 6.29; 2005-345, ss. 3(a), 3(b); 2007-24, s. 1; 2012-129, s. 1; 2013-296, s. 1.)

§ 58-50-35. Notice of nonpayment of premium required before forfeiture.

No insurance company doing business in this State and issuing health and/or accident insurance policies, other than contracts of group insurance or disability and/or accidental death benefits in connection with policies of life insurance, the premium for which is to be collected in weekly, monthly, or other periodical installments by authority of a payroll deduction order executed by the assured and delivered to such insurance company or the assured's employer authorizing the deduction of such premium installments from the assured's salary or wages, shall, during the period for which such policy is issued, declare forfeited or lapsed any such policy hereafter issued or renewed until and unless a written or printed notice of the failure of the employer to remit said premium or installment thereof stating the amount or portion thereof due on such policy and to whom it must be paid, has been duly addressed and mailed to the person who is insured under such policy at least 15 days before said policy is canceled or lapsed. (1909, c. 884; C.S., s. 6465; 1929, c. 308, s. 1; 1931, c. 317; 1945, c. 379.)

§ 58-50-40. Willful failure to pay group insurance premiums; willful termination of a group health plan; notice to persons insured; penalty; restitution; examination of insurance transactions.

(a) As used in this section and in G.S. 58-50-45:

(1) "Group health insurance" means any policy described in G.S. 58-51-75, 58-51-80, or 58-51-90; any group insurance certificate or group subscriber contract issued by a service corporation pursuant to Articles 65 and 66 of this Chapter; any health care plan provided or arranged by a health maintenance organization pursuant to Article 67 of this Chapter; or any multiple employer welfare arrangement as defined in G.S. 58-49-30(a).

(2) "Group health plan" means a single employer self-insured group health plan as defined in section 607(1) of the Employee Retirement Income Security Act of 1974, 29 U.S.C. § 1167(1), as amended.

(3) "Insurance fiduciary" means any person, employer, principal, agent, trustee, or third-party administrator who is responsible for the payment of group health or group life insurance premiums or who is responsible for funding a group health plan.

(4) "Premiums" includes contributions to a group health plan or to a multiple employer welfare arrangement.

(b) No insurance fiduciary shall:

(1) Cause the cancellation or nonrenewal of group health or group life insurance and the consequential loss of the coverages of the persons insured by willfully failing to pay such premiums in accordance with the terms of a group health or group life insurance contract; or, in the case of a group health plan to which there are no premiums contributed, terminate the plan by willfully failing to fund the plan; and

(2) Willfully fail to deliver, at least 45 days before the termination of the group health or group life insurance or group health plan, to all persons covered by the group policy or group health plan a written notice of the insurance fiduciary's intention to stop payment of premiums for the group life or health insurance or the insurance fiduciary's intention to cease funding of a group health plan.

(c) Any insurance fiduciary who violates subsection (b) of this section shall be guilty of a Class H felony.

(d) Repealed by Session Laws 1991, c. 644, s. 37.

(e) Upon conviction under subsection (c) of this section the court shall order the insurance fiduciary to make full restitution to persons insured who incurred expenses that would have been covered by the group health insurance or group health plan or full restitution to beneficiaries of the group life insurance for death benefits that would have been paid if the coverage had not been terminated.

(f) Insurance fiduciaries subject to this section shall be subject to the provisions of G.S. 58-2-200 with respect only to transactions involving group health or life insurance.

(g) In the notice required by subsection (b) of this section, the insurance fiduciary shall also notify those persons of their rights to health insurance conversion policies under Article 53 of this Chapter and their rights to purchase individual policies under the federal Health Insurance Portability and Accountability Act of 1996 (HIPAA), Public Law 104-191, as amended, and Article 68 of this Chapter.

(h) In the event of the insolvency of an employer or insurance fiduciary who has violated this section, any person specified in subsection (e) of this section shall have a lien upon the assets of the employer or insurance fiduciary for the expenses or benefits specified in subsection (e) of this section. With respect to personal property within the estate of the insolvent employer or insurance fiduciary, the lien shall have priority over unperfected security interests.

(i) Upon the termination of a group health insurance contract by the insurer, the insurer shall notify every subscriber and certificate holder under the contract of the termination of the contract along with the certification required to be provided under G.S. 58-68-30(e). Upon the termination of a group health insurance contract by the insurance fiduciary, the insurance fiduciary shall notify every subscriber and certificate holder under the contract of the termination of the contract along with the certification required to be provided under G.S. 58-68-30(e).

(j) This section shall not apply to the cessation of individual contributions made by any person covered by a group health or group life insurance policy or group health plan. (1985, c. 507, s. 1; 1989, c. 485, s. 51; 1989 (Reg. Sess., 1990), c. 1055, ss. 2, 3.1; 1991, c. 644, s. 37; 1993, c. 539, s. 1274; 1994, Ex. Sess., c. 24, s. 14(c); 2001-422, s. 1; 2006-105, s. 1.8.)

§ 58-50-45. Group health or life insurers to notify insurance fiduciaries of obligations.

(a) Upon the issuance or renewal of any policy, contract, certificate, or evidence of coverage of group health or life insurance, the insurer, corporation, or health maintenance organization shall give written notice to the insurance fiduciary of the provisions of G.S. 58-50-40.

(b) The notice required by subsection (a) of this section shall be printed in 10 point type and shall read as follows:

"UNDER NORTH CAROLINA GENERAL STATUTE SECTION 58-50-40, NO PERSON, EMPLOYER, PRINCIPAL, AGENT, TRUSTEE, OR THIRD PARTY ADMINISTRATOR, WHO IS RESPONSIBLE FOR THE PAYMENT OF GROUP HEALTH OR LIFE INSURANCE OR GROUP HEALTH PLAN PREMIUMS, SHALL: (1) CAUSE THE CANCELLATION OR NONRENEWAL OF GROUP HEALTH OR LIFE INSURANCE, HOSPITAL, MEDICAL, OR DENTAL SERVICE CORPORATION PLAN, MULTIPLE EMPLOYER WELFARE ARRANGEMENT, OR GROUP HEALTH PLAN COVERAGES AND THE CONSEQUENTIAL LOSS OF THE COVERAGES OF THE PERSONS INSURED, BY WILLFULLY FAILING TO PAY THOSE PREMIUMS IN ACCORDANCE WITH THE TERMS OF THE INSURANCE OR PLAN CONTRACT, AND (2) WILLFULLY FAIL TO DELIVER, AT LEAST 45 DAYS BEFORE THE TERMINATION OF THOSE COVERAGES, TO ALL PERSONS COVERED BY THE GROUP POLICY A WRITTEN NOTICE OF THE PERSON'S INTENTION TO STOP PAYMENT OF PREMIUMS. THIS WRITTEN NOTICE MUST ALSO CONTAIN A NOTICE TO ALL PERSONS COVERED BY THE GROUP POLICY OF THEIR RIGHTS TO HEALTH INSURANCE CONVERSION POLICIES UNDER ARTICLE 53 OF CHAPTER 58 OF THE GENERAL STATUTES AND THEIR RIGHTS TO PURCHASE INDIVIDUAL POLICIES UNDER THE FEDERAL HEALTH INSURANCE PORTABILITY AND ACCOUNTABILITY ACT AND UNDER ARTICLE 68 OF CHAPTER 58 OF THE GENERAL STATUTES. VIOLATION OF THIS LAW IS A FELONY. ANY PERSON VIOLATING THIS LAW IS ALSO SUBJECT TO A COURT ORDER REQUIRING THE PERSON TO COMPENSATE PERSONS INSURED FOR EXPENSES OR LOSSES INCURRED AS A RESULT OF THE TERMINATION OF THE INSURANCE." (1985, c. 507, s. 1; 1989 (Reg. Sess., 1990), c. 1055, s. 3; 1991, c. 644, s. 38; 2001-422, s. 2.)

§ 58-50-46: Recodified as G.S. 108A-55.4 by Session Laws 2006-221, s. 9(a), effective January 1, 2007.

Part 2. PPOs, Utilization Review and Grievances.

§ 58-50-50: Repealed by Session Laws, 1997-519, s. 3.17.

§ 58-50-55: Repealed by Session Laws 1997-519, s. 3.17.

§ 58-50-56. Insurers, preferred provider organizations, and preferred provider benefit plans.

(a) Definitions. - As used in this section:

(1) "Insurer" means an insurer or service corporation subject to this Chapter.

(2) "Preferred provider" means a health care provider who has agreed to accept special reimbursement or other terms for health care services from an insurer for health care services on a fee-for-service basis. A "preferred provider" is not a health care provider participating in any prepaid health service or capitation arrangement implemented or administered by the Department of Health and Human Services or its representatives.

(3) "Preferred provider benefit plan" means a health benefit plan offered by an insurer in which covered services are available from health care providers who are under a contract with the insurer in accordance with this section and in which enrollees are given incentives through differentials in deductibles, coinsurance, or copayments to obtain covered health care services from contracted health care providers.

(4) "Preferred provider organization" or "PPO" means an insurer holding contracts with preferred providers to be used by or offered to insurers offering preferred provider benefit plans.

(b)   Insurers may enter into preferred provider contracts or enter into other cost containment arrangements approved by the Commissioner to reduce the costs of providing health care services. These contracts or arrangements may be entered into with licensed health care providers of all kinds without regard to specialty of services or limitation to a specific type of practice. A preferred provider contract or other cost containment arrangement that is not disapproved by the Commissioner within 90 days of its filing by the insurer shall be deemed to be approved.

(c)   At the initial offering of a preferred provider plan to the public, health care providers may submit proposals for participation in accordance with the terms of the preferred provider plan within 30 days after that offering. After that time period, any health care provider may submit a proposal, and the insurer offering the preferred provider benefit plan shall consider all pending applications for participation and give reasons for any rejections or failure to act on an application on at least an annual basis. Any health care provider seeking to participate in the preferred provider benefit plan, whether upon the initial offering or subsequently, may be permitted to do so in the discretion of the insurer offering the preferred provider benefit plan. G.S. 58-50-30 applies to preferred provider benefit plans.

(d)   Any provision of a contract between an insurer offering a preferred provider benefit plan and a health care provider that restricts the provider's right to enter into preferred provider contracts with other persons is prohibited, is void ab initio, and is not enforceable. The existence of that restriction does not invalidate any other provision of the contract.

(e)   Except where specifically prohibited either by this section or by rules adopted by the Commissioner, the contractual terms and conditions for special reimbursements shall be those that the parties find mutually agreeable.

(f)   Every insurer offering a preferred provider benefit plan and contracting with a PPO shall require by contract that the PPO shall provide all of the preferred providers with whom it holds contracts information about the insurer and the insurer's preferred provider benefit plans. This information shall include for each insurer and preferred provider benefit plan the benefit designs and incentives that are used to encourage insureds to use preferred providers.

(g)   The Commissioner may adopt rules applicable to insurers offering preferred provider benefit plans under this section. These rules shall provide for:

(1) Accessibility of preferred provider services to individuals within the insured group.

(2) The adequacy of the number and locations of health care providers.

(3) The availability of services at reasonable times.

(4) Financial solvency.

(h) Each insurer offering a preferred provider benefit plan shall provide the Commissioner with summary data about the financial reimbursements offered to health care providers. All such insurers shall disclose annually the following information:

(1) The name by which the preferred provider benefit plan is known and its business address.

(2) The name, address, and nature of any PPO or other separate organization that administers the preferred provider benefit plan for the insurer.

(3) The terms of the agreements entered into by the insurer with preferred providers.

(4) Any other information necessary to determine compliance with this section, rules adopted under this section, or other requirements applicable to preferred provider benefit plans.

(i) A person enrolled in a preferred provider benefit plan may obtain covered health care services from a provider who does not participate in the plan. In accordance with rules adopted by the Commissioner and subject to G.S. 58-3-200(d), the preferred provider benefit plan may limit coverage for health care services obtained from a nonparticipating provider. The Commissioner shall adopt rules on product limitations, including payment differentials for services rendered by nonparticipating providers. These rules shall be similar in substance to rules governing HMO point-of-service products.

(j) A list of the current participating providers in the geographic area in which a substantial portion of health care services will be available shall be provided to insureds and contracting parties. The list shall include participating physician assistants and their supervising physician.

(k)   Publications or advertisements of preferred provider benefit plans or organizations shall not refer to the quality or efficiency of the services of nonparticipating providers. (1997-443, s. 11A.122; 1997-519, s. 3.1; 1998-211, s. 2; 1999-210, s. 3; 2001-297, s. 3; 2001-334, s. 2.1.)

§ 58-50-57. Offsets against provider reimbursement for workers' compensation payments forbidden.

(a)   An insurer that provides a health benefit plan as defined in G.S. 58-3-167 shall not offset or reverse a health plan payment against a provider reimbursement for other medical charges unless the health plan payment was for a specific medical charge for which the employee, employer, or carrier is liable or responsible according to a final adjudication of the claim under the Workers' Compensation Act, Article 1 of Chapter 97 of the General Statutes or an order of the North Carolina Industrial Commission approving a settlement agreement entered into under that Article.

(b)   No contract between an insurer that provides a health benefit plan as defined in G.S. 58-3-167 and a medical provider shall contain a provision that authorizes the insurer to offset or reverse a health plan payment against a provider reimbursement for other medical charges unless the health plan payment was for a specific medical charge for which the employee, employer, or carrier is liable or responsible according to a final adjudication of the claim under the Workers' Compensation Act, Article 1 of Chapter 97 of the General Statutes or an order of the North Carolina Industrial Commission approving a settlement agreement entered into under that Article. (2001-216, s. 5; 2001-487, s. 102(b).)

§ 58-50-58. Reserved for future codification purposes.

§ 58-50-59. Reserved for future codification purposes.

§ 58-50-60: Repealed by Session Laws 1997-519, s. 4.4.

§ 58-50-61. Utilization review.

(a) Definitions. - As used in this section, in G.S. 58-50-62, and in Part 4 of this Article, the term:

(1) "Certificate of coverage" includes a policy of insurance issued to an individual person or a franchise policy issued pursuant to G.S. 58-51-90.

(1a) "Clinical peer" means a health care professional who holds an unrestricted license in a state of the United States, in the same or similar specialty, and routinely provides the health care services subject to utilization review.

(2) "Clinical review criteria" means the written screening procedures, decision abstracts, clinical protocols, and practice guidelines used by an insurer to determine medically necessary services and supplies.

(3) "Covered person" means a policyholder, subscriber, enrollee, or other individual covered by a health benefit plan. "Covered person" includes another person, other than the covered person's provider, who is authorized to act on behalf of a covered person.

(4) "Emergency medical condition" means a medical condition manifesting itself by acute symptoms of sufficient severity including, but not limited to, severe pain, or by acute symptoms developing from a chronic medical condition that would lead a prudent layperson, possessing an average knowledge of health and medicine, to reasonably expect the absence of immediate medical attention to result in any of the following:

a. Placing the health of an individual, or with respect to a pregnant woman, the health of the woman or her unborn child, in serious jeopardy.

b. Serious impairment to bodily functions.

c. Serious dysfunction of any bodily organ or part.

(5) "Emergency services" means health care items and services furnished or required to screen for or treat an emergency medical condition until the

condition is stabilized, including prehospital care and ancillary services routinely available to the emergency department.

(6) "Grievance" means a written complaint submitted by a covered person about any of the following:

a. An insurer's decisions, policies, or actions related to availability, delivery, or quality of health care services. A written complaint submitted by a covered person about a decision rendered solely on the basis that the health benefit plan contains a benefits exclusion for the health care service in question is not a grievance if the exclusion of the specific service requested is clearly stated in the certificate of coverage.

b. Claims payment or handling; or reimbursement for services.

c. The contractual relationship between a covered person and an insurer.

d. The outcome of an appeal of a noncertification under this section.

(7) "Health benefit plan" means any of the following if offered by an insurer: an accident and health insurance policy or certificate; a nonprofit hospital or medical service corporation contract; a health maintenance organization subscriber contract; or a plan provided by a multiple employer welfare arrangement. "Health benefit plan" does not mean any plan implemented or administered through the Department of Health and Human Services or its representatives. "Health benefit plan" also does not mean any of the following kinds of insurance:

a. Accident.

b. Credit.

c. Disability income.

d. Long-term or nursing home care.

e. Medicare supplement.

f. Specified disease.

g. Dental or vision.

h. Coverage issued as a supplement to liability insurance.

i. Workers' compensation.

j. Medical payments under automobile or homeowners.

k. Hospital income or indemnity.

l. Insurance under which benefits are payable with or without regard to fault and that is statutorily required to be contained in any liability policy or equivalent self-insurance.

(8) "Health care provider" means any person who is licensed, registered, or certified under Chapter 90 of the General Statutes or the laws of another state to provide health care services in the ordinary care of business or practice or a profession or in an approved education or training program; a health care facility as defined in G.S. 131E-176(9b) or the laws of another state to operate as a health care facility; or a pharmacy.

(9) "Health care services" means services provided for the diagnosis, prevention, treatment, cure, or relief of a health condition, illness, injury, or disease.

(10) "Insurer" means an entity that writes a health benefit plan and that is an insurance company subject to this Chapter, a service corporation under Article 65 of this Chapter, a health maintenance organization under Article 67 of this Chapter, or a multiple employer welfare arrangement under Article 49 of this Chapter.

(11) "Managed care plan" means a health benefit plan in which an insurer either (i) requires a covered person to use or (ii) creates incentives, including financial incentives, for a covered person to use providers that are under contract with or managed, owned, or employed by the insurer.

(12) "Medically necessary services or supplies" means those covered services or supplies that are:

a. Provided for the diagnosis, treatment, cure, or relief of a health condition, illness, injury, or disease.

b. Except as allowed under G.S. 58-3-255, not for experimental, investigational, or cosmetic purposes.

c. Necessary for and appropriate to the diagnosis, treatment, cure, or relief of a health condition, illness, injury, disease, or its symptoms.

d. Within generally accepted standards of medical care in the community.

e. Not solely for the convenience of the insured, the insured's family, or the provider.

For medically necessary services, nothing in this subdivision precludes an insurer from comparing the cost-effectiveness of alternative services or supplies when determining which of the services or supplies will be covered.

(13) "Noncertification" means a determination by an insurer or its designated utilization review organization that an admission, availability of care, continued stay, or other health care service has been reviewed and, based upon the information provided, does not meet the insurer's requirements for medical necessity, appropriateness, health care setting, level of care or effectiveness, or does not meet the prudent layperson standard for coverage of emergency services in G.S. 58-3-190, and the requested service is therefore denied, reduced, or terminated. A "noncertification" is not a decision rendered solely on the basis that the health benefit plan does not provide benefits for the health care service in question, if the exclusion of the specific service requested is clearly stated in the certificate of coverage. A "noncertification" includes any situation in which an insurer or its designated agent makes a decision about a covered person's condition to determine whether a requested treatment is experimental, investigational, or cosmetic, and the extent of coverage under the health benefit plan is affected by that decision.

(14) "Participating provider" means a provider who, under a contract with an insurer or with an insurer's contractor or subcontractor, has agreed to provide health care services to covered persons in return for direct or indirect payment from the insurer, other than coinsurance, copayments, or deductibles.

(15) "Provider" means a health care provider.

(16) "Stabilize" means to provide medical care that is appropriate to prevent a material deterioration of the person's condition, within reasonable medical probability, in accordance with the HCFA (Health Care Financing

Administration) interpretative guidelines, policies, and regulations pertaining to responsibilities of hospitals in emergency cases (as provided under the Emergency Medical Treatment and Labor Act, section 1867 of the Social Security Act, 42 U.S.C.S. § 1395dd), including medically necessary services and supplies to maintain stabilization until the person is transferred.

(17) "Utilization review" means a set of formal techniques designed to monitor the use of or evaluate the clinical necessity, appropriateness, efficacy or efficiency of health care services, procedures, providers, or facilities. These techniques may include:

a. Ambulatory review. - Utilization review of services performed or provided in an outpatient setting.

b. Case management. - A coordinated set of activities conducted for individual patient management of serious, complicated, protracted, or other health conditions.

c. Certification. - A determination by an insurer or its designated URO that an admission, availability of care, continued stay, or other service has been reviewed and, based on the information provided, satisfies the insurer's requirements for medically necessary services and supplies, appropriateness, health care setting, level of care, and effectiveness.

d. Concurrent review. - Utilization review conducted during a patient's hospital stay or course of treatment.

e. Discharge planning. - The formal process for determining, before discharge from a provider facility, the coordination and management of the care that a patient receives after discharge from a provider facility.

f. Prospective review. - Utilization review conducted before an admission or a course of treatment including any required preauthorization or precertification.

g. Retrospective review. - Utilization review of medically necessary services and supplies that is conducted after services have been provided to a patient, but not the review of a claim that is limited to an evaluation of reimbursement levels, veracity of documentation, accuracy of coding, or adjudication for payment. Retrospective review includes the review of claims for emergency services to determine whether the prudent layperson standard in G.S. 58-3-190 has been met.

h. Second opinion. - An opportunity or requirement to obtain a clinical evaluation by a provider other than the provider originally making a recommendation for a proposed service to assess the clinical necessity and appropriateness of the proposed service.

(18) "Utilization review organization" or "URO" means an entity that conducts utilization review under a managed care plan, but does not mean an insurer performing utilization review for its own health benefit plan.

(b) Insurer Oversight. - Every insurer shall monitor all utilization review carried out by or on behalf of the insurer and ensure compliance with this section. An insurer shall ensure that appropriate personnel have operational responsibility for the conduct of the insurer's utilization review program. If an insurer contracts to have a URO perform its utilization review, the insurer shall monitor the URO to ensure compliance with this section, which shall include:

(1) A written description of the URO's activities and responsibilities, including reporting requirements.

(2) Evidence of formal approval of the utilization review organization program by the insurer.

(3) A process by which the insurer evaluates the performance of the URO.

(c) Scope and Content of Program. - Every insurer shall prepare and maintain a utilization review program document that describes all delegated and nondelegated review functions for covered services including:

(1) Procedures to evaluate the clinical necessity, appropriateness, efficacy, or efficiency of health services.

(2) Data sources and clinical review criteria used in decision making.

(3) The process for conducting appeals of noncertifications.

(4) Mechanisms to ensure consistent application of review criteria and compatible decisions.

(5) Data collection processes and analytical methods used in assessing utilization of health care services.

(6) Provisions for assuring confidentiality of clinical and patient information in accordance with State and federal law.

(7) The organizational structure (e.g., utilization review committee, quality assurance, or other committee) that periodically assesses utilization review activities and reports to the insurer's governing body.

(8) The staff position functionally responsible for day-to-day program management.

(9) The methods of collection and assessment of data about underutilization and overutilization of health care services and how the assessment is used to evaluate and improve procedures and criteria for utilization review.

(d) Program Operations. - In every utilization review program, an insurer or URO shall use documented clinical review criteria that are based on sound clinical evidence and that are periodically evaluated to assure ongoing efficacy. An insurer may develop its own clinical review criteria or purchase or license clinical review criteria. Criteria for determining when a patient needs to be placed in a substance abuse treatment program shall be either (i) the diagnostic criteria contained in the most recent revision of the American Society of Addiction Medicine Patient Placement Criteria for the Treatment of Substance-Related Disorders or (ii) criteria adopted by the insurer or its URO. The Department, in consultation with the Department of Health and Human Services, may require proof of compliance with this subsection by a plan or URO.

Qualified health care professionals shall administer the utilization review program and oversee review decisions under the direction of a medical doctor. A medical doctor licensed to practice medicine in this State shall evaluate the clinical appropriateness of noncertifications. Compensation to persons involved in utilization review shall not contain any direct or indirect incentives for them to make any particular review decisions. Compensation to utilization reviewers shall not be directly or indirectly based on the number or type of noncertifications they render. In issuing a utilization review decision, an insurer shall: obtain all information required to make the decision, including pertinent clinical information; employ a process to ensure that utilization reviewers apply clinical review criteria consistently; and issue the decision in a timely manner pursuant to this section.

(e) Insurer Responsibilities. - Every insurer shall:

(1) Routinely assess the effectiveness and efficiency of its utilization review program.

(2) Coordinate the utilization review program with its other medical management activity, including quality assurance, credentialing, provider contracting, data reporting, grievance procedures, processes for assessing satisfaction of covered persons, and risk management.

(3) Provide covered persons and their providers with access to its review staff by a toll-free or collect call telephone number whenever any provider is required to be available to provide services which may require prior certification to any plan enrollee. Every insurer shall establish standards for telephone accessibility and monitor telephone service as indicated by average speed of answer and call abandonment rate, on at least a month-by-month basis, to ensure that telephone service is adequate, and take corrective action when necessary.

(4) Limit its requests for information to only that information that is necessary to certify the admission, procedure or treatment, length of stay, and frequency and duration of health care services.

(5) Have written procedures for making utilization review decisions and for notifying covered persons of those decisions.

(6) Have written procedures to address the failure or inability of a provider or covered person to provide all necessary information for review. If a provider or covered person fails to release necessary information in a timely manner, the insurer may deny certification.

(f) Prospective and Concurrent Reviews. - As used in this subsection, "necessary information" includes the results of any patient examination, clinical evaluation, or second opinion that may be required. Prospective and concurrent determinations shall be communicated to the covered person's provider within three business days after the insurer obtains all necessary information about the admission, procedure, or health care service. If an insurer certifies a health care service, the insurer shall notify the covered person's provider. For a noncertification, the insurer shall notify the covered person's provider and send written or electronic confirmation of the noncertification to the covered person. In concurrent reviews, the insurer shall remain liable for health care services until the covered person has been notified of the noncertification.

(g) Retrospective Reviews. - As used in this subsection, "necessary information" includes the results of any patient examination, clinical evaluation, or second opinion that may be required. For retrospective review determinations, an insurer shall make the determination within 30 days after receiving all necessary information. For a certification, the insurer may give written notification to the covered person's provider. For a noncertification, the insurer shall give written notification to the covered person and the covered person's provider within five business days after making the noncertification.

(h) Notice of Noncertification. - A written notification of a noncertification shall include all reasons for the noncertification, including the clinical rationale, the instructions for initiating a voluntary appeal or reconsideration of the noncertification, and the instructions for requesting a written statement of the clinical review criteria used to make the noncertification. An insurer shall provide the clinical review criteria used to make the noncertification to any person who received the notification of the noncertification and who follows the procedures for a request. An insurer shall also inform the covered person in writing about the availability of assistance from Health Insurance Smart NC, including the telephone number and address of the Program.

(i) Requests for Informal Reconsideration. - An insurer may establish procedures for informal reconsideration of noncertifications and, if established, the procedures shall be in writing. After a written notice of noncertification has been issued in accordance with subsection (h) of this section, the reconsideration shall be conducted between the covered person's provider and a medical doctor licensed to practice medicine in this State designated by the insurer. An insurer shall not require a covered person to participate in an informal reconsideration before the covered person may appeal a noncertification under subsection (j) of this section. If, after informal reconsideration, the insurer upholds the noncertification decision, the insurer shall issue a new notice in accordance with subsection (h) of this section. If the insurer is unable to render an informal reconsideration decision within 10 business days after the date of receipt of the request for an informal reconsideration, it shall treat the request for informal reconsideration as a request for an appeal; provided that the requirements of subsection (k) of this section for acknowledging the request shall apply beginning on the day the insurer determines an informal reconsideration decision cannot be made before the tenth business day after receipt of the request for an informal reconsideration.

(j)   Appeals of Noncertifications. - Every insurer shall have written procedures for appeals of noncertifications by covered persons or their providers acting on their behalves, including expedited review to address a situation where the time frames for the standard review procedures set forth in this section would reasonably appear to seriously jeopardize the life or health of a covered person or jeopardize the covered person's ability to regain maximum function. Each appeal shall be evaluated by a medical doctor licensed to practice medicine in this State who was not involved in the noncertification.

(k)   Nonexpedited Appeals. - Within three business days after receiving a request for a standard, nonexpedited appeal, the insurer shall provide the covered person with the name, address, and telephone number of the coordinator and information on how to submit written material. For standard, nonexpedited appeals, the insurer shall give written notification of the decision, in clear terms, to the covered person and the covered person's provider within 30 days after the insurer receives the request for an appeal. If the decision is not in favor of the covered person, the written decision shall contain:

(1)   The professional qualifications and licensure of the person or persons reviewing the appeal.

(2)   A statement of the reviewers' understanding of the reason for the covered person's appeal.

(3)   The reviewers' decision in clear terms and the medical rationale in sufficient detail for the covered person to respond further to the insurer's position.

(4)   A reference to the evidence or documentation that is the basis for the decision, including the clinical review criteria used to make the determination, and instructions for requesting the clinical review criteria.

(5)   A statement advising the covered person of the covered person's right to request a second-level grievance review and a description of the procedure for submitting a second-level grievance under G.S. 58-50-62.

(6)   Notice of the availability of assistance from Health Insurance Smart NC, including the telephone number and address of the Program.

(l)   Expedited Appeals. - An expedited appeal of a noncertification may be requested by a covered person or his or her provider acting on the covered person's behalf only when a nonexpedited appeal would reasonably appear to seriously jeopardize the life or health of a covered person or jeopardize the covered person's ability to regain maximum function. The insurer may require documentation of the medical justification for the expedited appeal. The insurer shall, in consultation with a medical doctor licensed to practice medicine in this State, provide expedited review, and the insurer shall communicate its decision in writing to the covered person and his or her provider as soon as possible, but not later than four days after receiving the information justifying expedited review. The written decision shall contain the provisions specified in subsection (k) of this section. If the expedited review is a concurrent review determination, the insurer shall remain liable for the coverage of health care services until the covered person has been notified of the determination. An insurer is not required to provide an expedited review for retrospective noncertifications.

(m)   Disclosure Requirements. - In the certificate of coverage and member handbook provided to covered persons, an insurer shall include a clear and comprehensive description of its utilization review procedures, including the procedures for appealing noncertifications and a statement of the rights and responsibilities of covered persons, including the voluntary nature of the appeal process, with respect to those procedures. An insurer shall also include in the certificate of coverage and the member handbook information about the availability of assistance from Health Insurance Smart NC, including the telephone number and address of the Program. An insurer shall include a summary of its utilization review procedures in materials intended for prospective covered persons. An insurer shall print on its membership cards a toll-free telephone number to call for utilization review purposes.

(n)   Maintenance of Records. - Every insurer and URO shall maintain records of each review performed and each appeal received or reviewed, as well as documentation sufficient to demonstrate compliance with this section. The maintenance of these records, including electronic reproduction and storage, shall be governed by rules adopted by the Commissioner that apply to insurers. These records shall be retained by the insurer and URO for a period of five years or, for domestic companies, until the Commissioner has adopted a final report of a general examination that contains a review of these records for that calendar year, whichever is later.

(o) Violation. - A violation of this section subjects an insurer to G.S. 58-2-70. (1997-443, s. 11A.122; 1997-519, s. 4.1; 1999-116, s. 1; 1999-391, ss. 1-4; 2001-417, ss. 2-7; 2001-416, ss. 4.4, 5; 2003-105, s. 1; 2005-223, s. 8; 2008-124, s. 5.1; 2013-199, ss. 13, 14, 15.)

§ 58-50-62. Insurer grievance procedures.

(a) Purpose and Intent. - The purpose of this section is to provide standards for the establishment and maintenance of procedures by insurers to assure that covered persons have the opportunity for appropriate resolutions of their grievances.

(b) Availability of Grievance Process. - Every insurer shall have a grievance process whereby a covered person may voluntarily request a review of any decision, policy, or action of the insurer that affects that covered person. A decision rendered solely on the basis that the health benefit plan does not provide benefits for the health care service in question is not subject to the insurer's grievance procedures, if the exclusion of the specific service requested is clearly stated in the certificate of coverage. The grievance process may provide for an immediate informal consideration by the insurer of a grievance. If the insurer does not have a procedure for informal consideration or if an informal consideration does not resolve the grievance, the grievance process shall provide for first- and second-level reviews of grievances. Appeal of a noncertification that has been reviewed under G.S. 58-50-61 shall be reviewed as a second-level grievance under this section.

(b1) Informal Consideration of Grievances. - If the insurer provides procedures for informal consideration of grievances, the procedures shall be in writing, and the following requirements apply:

(1) If the grievance concerns a clinical issue and the informal consideration decision is not in favor of the covered person, the insurer shall treat the request as a request for a first-level grievance review, except that the requirements of subdivision (e) (1) of this section apply on the day the decision is made or on the tenth business day after receipt of the request for informal consideration, whichever is sooner;

(2) If the grievance concerns a nonclinical issue and the informal consideration decision is not in favor of the covered person, the insurer shall

issue a written decision that includes the information set forth in subsection (c) of this section; or

(3) If the insurer is unable to render an informal consideration decision within 10 business days after receipt of the grievance, the insurer shall treat the request as a request for a first-level grievance review, except that the requirements of subdivision (e) (1) of this section apply beginning on the day the insurer determines an informal consideration decision cannot be made before the tenth business day after receipt of the grievance.

(c) Grievance Procedures. - Every insurer shall have written procedures for receiving and resolving grievances from covered persons. A description of the grievance procedures shall be set forth in or attached to the certificate of coverage and member handbook provided to covered persons. The description shall include a statement informing the covered person that the grievance procedures are voluntary and shall also inform the covered person about the availability of the Commissioner's office for assistance, including the telephone number and address of the office.

(d) Maintenance of Records. - Every insurer shall maintain records of each grievance received and the insurer's review of each grievance, as well as documentation sufficient to demonstrate compliance with this section. The maintenance of these records, including electronic reproduction and storage, shall be governed by rules adopted by the Commissioner that apply to insurers. The insurer shall retain these records for five years or, for domestic companies, until the Commissioner has adopted a final report of a general examination that contains a review of these records for that calendar year, whichever is later.

(e) First-Level Grievance Review. - A covered person or a covered person's provider acting on the covered person's behalf may submit a grievance.

(1) The insurer does not have to allow a covered person to attend the first-level grievance review. A covered person may submit written material. Except as provided in subdivision (3) of this subsection, within three business days after receiving a grievance, the insurer shall provide the covered person with the name, address, and telephone number of the coordinator and information on how to submit written material.

(2) An insurer shall issue a written decision, in clear terms, to the covered person and, if applicable, to the covered person's provider, within 30 days after receiving a grievance. The person or persons reviewing the grievance shall not

be the same person or persons who initially handled the matter that is the subject of the grievance and, if the issue is a clinical one, at least one of whom shall be a medical doctor with appropriate expertise to evaluate the matter. Except as provided in subdivision (3) of this subsection, if the decision is not in favor of the covered person, the written decision issued in a first-level grievance review shall contain:

a. The professional qualifications and licensure of the person or persons reviewing the grievance.

b. A statement of the reviewers' understanding of the grievance.

c. The reviewers' decision in clear terms and the contractual basis or medical rationale in sufficient detail for the covered person to respond further to the insurer's position.

d. A reference to the evidence or documentation used as the basis for the decision.

e. A statement advising the covered person of his or her right to request a second-level grievance review and a description of the procedure for submitting a second-level grievance under this section.

f. Notice of the availability of assistance from Health Insurance Smart NC, including the telephone number and address of the Program.

(3) For grievances concerning the quality of clinical care delivered by the covered person's provider, the insurer shall acknowledge the grievance within 10 business days. The acknowledgement shall advise the covered person that (i) the insurer will refer the grievance to its quality assurance committee for review and consideration or any appropriate action against the provider and (ii) State law does not allow for a second-level grievance review for grievances concerning quality of care.

(f) Second-Level Grievance Review. - An insurer shall establish a second-level grievance review process for covered persons who are dissatisfied with the first-level grievance review decision or a utilization review appeal decision. A covered person or the covered person's provider acting on the covered person's behalf may submit a second-level grievance.

(1) An insurer shall, within 10 business days after receiving a request for a second-level grievance review, make known to the covered person:

a. The name, address, and telephone number of a person designated to coordinate the grievance review for the insurer.

b. A statement of a covered person's rights, which include the right to request and receive from an insurer all information relevant to the case; attend the second-level grievance review; present his or her case to the review panel; submit supporting materials before and at the review meeting; ask questions of any member of the review panel; and be assisted or represented by a person of his or her choice, which person may be without limitation to: a provider, family member, employer representative, or attorney. If the covered person chooses to be represented by an attorney, the insurer may also be represented by an attorney.

c. The availability of assistance from Health Insurance Smart NC, including the telephone number and address of the Program.

(2) An insurer shall convene a second-level grievance review panel for each request. The panel shall comprise persons who were not previously involved in any matter giving rise to the second-level grievance, are not employees of the insurer or URO, and do not have a financial interest in the outcome of the review. A person who was previously involved in the matter may appear before the panel to present information or answer questions. All of the persons reviewing a second-level grievance involving a noncertification or a clinical issue shall be providers who have appropriate expertise, including at least one clinical peer. Provided, however, an insurer that uses a clinical peer on an appeal of a noncertification under G.S. 58-50-61 or on a first-level grievance review panel under this section may use one of the insurer's employees on the second-level grievance review panel in the same matter if the second-level grievance review panel comprises three or more persons.

(g) Second-Level Grievance Review Procedures. - An insurer's procedures for conducting a second-level grievance review shall include:

(1) The review panel shall schedule and hold a review meeting within 45 days after receiving a request for a second-level review.

(2) The covered person shall be notified in writing at least 15 days before the review meeting date.

(3) The covered person's right to a full review shall not be conditioned on the covered person's appearance at the review meeting.

(h) Second-Level Grievance Review Decisions. - An insurer shall issue a written decision to the covered person and, if applicable, to the covered person's provider, within seven business days after completing the review meeting. The decision shall include:

(1) The professional qualifications and licensure of the members of the review panel.

(2) A statement of the review panel's understanding of the nature of the grievance and all pertinent facts.

(3) The review panel's recommendation to the insurer and the rationale behind that recommendation.

(4) A description of or reference to the evidence or documentation considered by the review panel in making the recommendation.

(5) In the review of a noncertification or other clinical matter, a written statement of the clinical rationale, including the clinical review criteria, that was used by the review panel to make the recommendation.

(6) The rationale for the insurer's decision if it differs from the review panel's recommendation.

(7) A statement that the decision is the insurer's final determination in the matter. In cases where the review concerned a noncertification and the insurer's decision on the second-level grievance review is to uphold its initial noncertification, a statement advising the covered person of his or her right to request an external review and a description of the procedure for submitting a request for external review to the Commissioner of Insurance.

(8) Notice of the availability of the Commissioner's office for assistance, including the telephone number and address of the Commissioner's office.

(9) Notice of the availability of assistance from Health Insurance Smart NC, including the telephone number and address of the Program.

(i) Expedited Second-Level Procedures. - An expedited second-level review shall be made available where medically justified as provided in G.S. 58-50-61(l), whether or not the initial review was expedited. The provisions of subsections (f), (g), and (h) of this section apply to this subsection except for the following timetable: When a covered person is eligible for an expedited second-level review, the insurer shall conduct the review proceeding and communicate its decision within four days after receiving all necessary information. The review meeting may take place by way of a telephone conference call or through the exchange of written information.

(j) No insurer shall discriminate against any provider based on any action taken by the provider under this section or G.S. 58-50-61 on behalf of a covered person.

(k) Violation. - A violation of this section subjects an insurer to G.S. 58-2-70. (1997-519, s. 4.2; 2001-417, ss. 8-11; 2001-446, s. 4.6; 2003-105, s. 2(a)-(d); 2008-124, s. 5.2; 2013-199, ss. 16, 17.)

§ 58-50-63: Expired pursuant to Session Laws 2005-453, s. 3, effective July 1, 2005.

§ 58-50-64. Reserved for future codification purposes.

Part 3. Scope and Sanctions.

§ 58-50-65. Certain policies of insurance not affected.

(a) Nothing in Articles 50 through 55 of this Chapter applies to or affects any policy of liability or workers' compensation insurance, except that the provisions of G.S. 58-50-56(g) and (h) apply to policies of workers' compensation insurance and to individual and group self-funded workers' compensation insurance plans. If there is any conflict between managed care provisions of this Chapter and managed care provisions of Chapter 97 of the General Statutes with respect to workers' compensation insurance, the provisions of Chapter 97 govern.

(b) Nothing in Articles 50 through 55 of this Chapter shall apply to or in any way affect contracts supplemental to contracts of life or endowment insurance where such supplemental contracts contain no provisions except such as operate to safeguard such insurance against lapse or to provide special benefits therefor in the event that the insured shall be totally, or totally and permanently disabled by reason of accidental bodily injury or by sickness, nor to contracts issued as supplements to life insurance contracts or contracts of endowment insurance, and intended to increase the amount insured by such life or endowment contracts in the event that the death or disability of the insured shall result from accidental bodily injuries: Provided, that no such supplemental contracts shall be issued or delivered to any person in this State unless and until a copy of the form thereof has been submitted to and approved by the Commissioner under such reasonable rules and regulations as he shall make concerning the provisions in such contracts, and their submission to and approval by him.

(c) Nothing in Articles 50 through 55 of this Chapter shall apply to or in any way affect fraternal benefit societies.

(d) The provisions of G.S. 58-51-5(5) and G.S. 58-51-15(a)(1), (4), and (10) may be omitted from railroad ticket policies sold only at railroad stations or at railroad ticket offices by railroad employees. (1911, c. 209, s. 5; 1913, c. 91, s. 12; C.S., s. 6489; 1921, c. 136, s. 5; 1945, c. 385; 1947, c. 721; 1991, c. 636, s. 3; c. 720, ss. 4, 42; 1993 (Reg. Sess., 1994), c. 679, s. 10.4; 1995, c. 193, s. 42; 1999-219, s. 4.1.)

§ 58-50-70. Punishment for violation.

Any company, association, society, or other insurer or any officer or agent thereof, which or who issues or delivers to any person in this State any policy in willful violation of Articles 50 through 55 of this Chapter, shall be guilty of a Class 3 misdemeanor and, upon conviction, shall be punished only by a fine of not more than five thousand dollars ($5,000) for each offense; and the Commissioner may revoke the license of any company, corporation, association, society, or other insurer of another state or country, or of the agent thereof, which or who willfully violates any provision of Articles 50 through 55 of this Chapter. (1911, c. 209, s. 6; 1913, c. 91, s. 13; C.S., s. 6490; 1985, c. 666,

s. 28; 1991, c. 720, ss. 4, 42; 1993, c. 539, s. 467; 1994, Ex. Sess., c. 24, s. 14(c).)

Part 4. Health Benefit Plan External Review.

§ 58-50-75. Purpose, scope, and definitions.

(a) The purpose of this Part is to provide standards for the establishment and maintenance of external review procedures to assure that covered persons have the opportunity for an independent review of an appeal decision upholding a noncertification or a second-level grievance review decision upholding a noncertification, as defined in this Part.

(b) This Part applies to all insurers that offer a health benefit plan and that provide or perform utilization review pursuant to G.S. 58-50-61, the State Health Plan for Teachers and State Employees, any optional plans or programs operating under Part 2 of Article 3A of Chapter 135 of the General Statutes, the North Carolina Health Insurance Risk Pool, and the Health Insurance Program for Children. With respect to second-level grievance review decisions, this Part applies only to second-level grievance review decisions involving noncertification decisions.

(c) In addition to the definitions in G.S. 58-50-61(a), as used in this Part:

(1) "Covered benefits" or "benefits" means those benefits consisting of medical care, provided directly through insurance or otherwise and including items and services paid for as medical care, under the terms of a health benefit plan.

(2) "Covered person" means a policyholder, subscriber, enrollee, or other individual covered by a health benefit plan. "Covered person" includes another person, including the covered person's health care provider, acting on behalf of the covered person. Nothing in this subdivision shall require the covered person's health care provider to act on behalf of the covered person.

(3) "Independent review organization" or "organization" means an entity that conducts independent external reviews of appeals of noncertifications and second-level grievance review decisions. (2001-446, s. 4.5; 2007-298, s. 8.5; 2007-323, s. 28.22A(o); 2007-345, s. 12; 2009-382, s. 24.)

§ 58-50-76: Reserved for future codification purposes.

§ 58-50-77. Notice of right to external review.

(a) An insurer shall notify the covered person in writing of the covered person's right to request an external review and include the appropriate statements and information set forth in this section at the time the insurer sends written notice of:

(1) A noncertification decision under G.S. 58-50-61;

(2) An appeal decision under G.S. 58-50-61 upholding a noncertification; and

(3) A second-level grievance review decision under G.S. 58-50-62 upholding the original noncertification.

(b) The insurer shall include in the notice required under subsection (a) of this section for a notice related to a noncertification decision under G.S. 58-50-61, a statement informing the covered person that if the covered person has a medical condition where the time frame for completion of an expedited review of an appeal decision involving a noncertification decision under G.S. 58-50-61 would reasonably be expected to seriously jeopardize the life or health of the covered person or jeopardize the covered person's ability to regain maximum function, then the covered person may file a request for an expedited external review under G.S. 58-50-82 at the same time the covered person files a request for an expedited review of an appeal involving a noncertification decision under G.S. 58-50-61, but that the Commissioner will determine whether the covered person shall be required to complete the expedited review of the grievance before conducting the expedited external review.

(c) The insurer shall include in the notice required under subsection (a) of this section for a notice related to an appeal decision under G.S. 58-50-61, a statement informing the covered person that:

(1) If the covered person has a medical condition where the time frame for completion of an expedited review of a grievance involving an appeal decision under G.S. 58-50-61 would reasonably be expected to seriously jeopardize the life or health of the covered person or jeopardize the covered person's ability to regain maximum function, the covered person may file a request for an expedited external review under G.S. 58-50-82 at the same time the covered person files a request for an expedited review of a grievance involving an appeal decision under G.S. 58-50-62, but that the Commissioner will determine whether the covered person shall be required to complete the expedited review of the grievance before conducting the expedited external review.

(2) If the covered person has not received a written decision from the insurer within 60 days after the date the covered person files the second-level grievance with the insurer pursuant to G.S. 58-50-62 and the covered person has not requested or agreed to a delay, the covered person may file a request for external review under G.S. 58-50-80 and shall be considered to have exhausted the insurer's internal grievance process for purposes of G.S. 58-50-79.

(d) The insurer shall include in the notice required under subsection (a) of this section for a notice related to a final second-level grievance review decision under G.S. 58-50-62, a statement informing the covered person that:

(1) If the covered person has a medical condition where the time frame for completion of a standard external review under G.S. 58-50-80 would reasonably be expected to seriously jeopardize the life or health of the covered person or jeopardize the covered person's ability to regain maximum function, the covered person may file a request for an expedited external review under G.S. 58-50-82; or

(2) If the second-level grievance review decision concerns an admission, availability of care, continued stay, or health care service for which the covered person received emergency services but has not been discharged from a facility, the covered person may request an expedited external review under G.S. 58-50-82.

(e) In addition to the information to be provided under this section, the insurer shall include a copy of the description of both the standard and expedited external review procedures the insurer is required to provide under G.S. 58-50-93, including the provisions in the external review procedures that give the covered person the opportunity to submit additional information. (2001-446, s. 4.5.)

§ 58-50-78: Reserved for future codification purposes.

§ 58-50-79. Exhaustion of internal grievance process.

(a) Except as provided in G.S. 58-50-82, a request for an external review under G.S. 58-50-80 or G.S. 58-50-82 shall not be made until the covered person has exhausted the insurer's internal appeal and grievance processes under G.S. 58-50-61 and G.S. 58-50-62.

(b) A covered person shall be considered to have exhausted the insurer's internal grievance process for purposes of this section, if the covered person:

(1) Has filed a second-level grievance involving a noncertification appeal decision under G.S. 58-50-61 and G.S. 58-50-62, and

(2) Except to the extent the covered person requested or agreed to a delay, has not received a written decision on the grievance from the insurer within 60 days since the date the covered person can demonstrate that a grievance was filed with the insurer.

(c) Notwithstanding subsection (b) of this section, a covered person may not make a request for an external review of a noncertification involving a retrospective review determination made under G.S. 58-50-61 until the covered person has exhausted the insurer's internal grievance process.

(d) A request for an external review of a noncertification may be made before the covered person has exhausted the insurer's internal grievance and appeal procedures under G.S. 58-50-61 and G.S. 58-50-62 whenever the insurer agrees to waive the exhaustion requirement. If the requirement to exhaust the insurer's internal grievance procedures is waived, the covered person may file a request in writing for a standard external review as set forth in G.S. 58-50-80 or may make a request for an expedited external review as set forth in G.S. 58-50-82. In addition, the insurer may choose to eliminate the second-level grievance review under G.S. 58-50-62. In such case, the covered person may file a request in writing for a standard external review under G.S. 58-50-80 or may make a request for an expedited external review as set forth in G.S. 58-50-82 within 60 days after receiving notice of an appeal decision upholding a noncertification. (2001-446, s. 4.5; 2009-382, s. 25.)

§ 58-50-80. Standard external review.

(a)   Within 120 days after the date of receipt of a notice under G.S. 58-50-77, a covered person may file a request for an external review with the Commissioner.

(b)   Upon receipt of a request for an external review under subsection (a) of this section, the Commissioner shall, within 10 business days, complete all of the following:

(1)   Notify and send a copy of the request to the insurer that made the decision which is the subject of the request. The notice shall include a request for any information that the Commissioner requires to conduct the preliminary review under subdivision (2) of this subsection and require that the insurer deliver the requested information to the Commissioner within three business days of receipt of the notice.

(2)   Conduct a preliminary review of the request to determine whether:

a.   The individual is or was a covered person in the health benefit plan at the time the health care service was requested or, in the case of a retrospective review, was a covered person in the health benefit plan at the time the health care service was provided.

b.   The health care service that is the subject of the noncertification appeal decision or the second-level grievance review decision upholding a noncertification reasonably appears to be a covered service under the covered person's health benefit plan.

c.   The covered person has exhausted the insurer's internal appeal and grievance processes under G.S. 58-50-61 and G.S. 58-50-62, unless the covered person is considered to have exhausted the insurer's internal appeal or grievance process under G.S. 58-50-79, or unless the insurer has waived its right to conduct an expedited review of the appeal decision.

d. The covered person has provided all the information and forms required by the Commissioner that are necessary to process an external review.

(3) Notify in writing the covered person and the covered person's provider who performed or requested the service whether the request is complete and whether the request has been accepted for external review. If the request is complete and accepted for external review, the notice shall include a copy of the information that the insurer provided to the Commissioner pursuant to subdivision (b)(1) of this section, and inform the covered person that the covered person may submit to the assigned independent review organization in writing, within seven days after the receipt of the notice, additional information and supporting documentation relevant to the initial denial for the organization to consider when conducting the external review. If the covered person chooses to send additional information to the assigned independent review organization, then the covered person shall at the same time and by the same means, send a copy of that information to the insurer. The Commissioner shall also notify the covered person in writing of the availability of assistance from Health Insurance Smart NC, including the telephone number and address of Health Insurance Smart NC.

(4) Notify the insurer in writing whether the request for external review has been accepted. If the request has been accepted, the notice shall direct the insurer or its designee utilization review organization to provide to the assigned organization and to the covered person or authorized representative who made the request for external review on behalf of the covered person, within seven days of receipt of the notice, the documents and any information considered in making the noncertification appeal decision or the second-level grievance review decision.

(5) Assign the review to an independent review organization approved under G.S. 58-50-85. The assignment shall be made using an alphabetical list of the independent review organizations, systematically assigning reviews on a rotating basis to the next independent review organization on that list capable of performing the review to conduct the external review. After the last organization on the list has been assigned a review, the Commissioner shall return to the top of the list to continue assigning reviews.

(6) Forward to the review organization that was assigned by the Commissioner any documents that were received relating to the request for external review.

(c)   If the finding of the preliminary review under subdivision (b)(2) of this section is that the request is not complete, the Commissioner shall request from the covered person the information or materials needed to make the request complete. The covered person shall furnish the Commissioner with the requested information or materials within 150 days after the date of the insurer's decision for which external review is requested.

(d)   If the finding of the preliminary review under subdivision (b)(2) of this section is that the request is not accepted for external review, the Commissioner shall inform the covered person, the covered person's provider who performed or requested the service, and the insurer in writing of the reasons for its nonacceptance.

(e)   Failure by the insurer or its designee utilization review organization to provide the documents and information within the time specified in this subsection shall not delay the conduct of the external review. However, if the insurer or its utilization review organization fails to provide the documents and information within the time specified in subdivision (b)(4) of this section, the assigned organization may terminate the external review and make a decision to reverse the noncertification appeal decision or the second-level grievance review decision. Within one business day of making the decision under this subsection, the organization shall notify the covered person, the insurer, and the Commissioner.

(f)   If the covered person submits additional information to the Commissioner pursuant to subdivision (b)(3) of this section, the Commissioner shall forward the information to the assigned review organization within two business days of receiving it and shall forward a copy of the information to the insurer.

(g)   Upon receipt of the information required to be forwarded under subsection (f) of this section, the insurer may reconsider its noncertification appeal decision or second-level grievance review decision that is the subject of the external review. Reconsideration by the insurer of its noncertification appeal decision or second-level grievance review decision under this subsection shall not delay or terminate the external review. The external review shall be terminated if the insurer decides, upon completion of its reconsideration, to reverse its noncertification appeal decision or second-level grievance review decision and provide coverage or payment for the requested health care service that is the subject of the noncertification appeal decision or second-level grievance review decision.

(h) Upon making the decision to reverse its noncertification appeal decision or second-level grievance review decision under subsection (g) of this section, the insurer shall notify the covered person, the organization, and the Commissioner in writing of its decision. The organization shall terminate the external review upon receipt of the notice from the insurer sent under this subsection.

(i) The assigned organization shall review all of the information and documents received under subsections (b) and (f) of this section that have been forwarded to the organization by the Commissioner and the insurer. In addition, the assigned review organization, to the extent the documents or information are available, shall consider the following in reaching a decision:

(1) The covered person's medical records.

(2) The attending health care provider's recommendation.

(3) Consulting reports from appropriate health care providers and other documents submitted by the insurer, covered person, or the covered person's treating provider.

(4) The most appropriate practice guidelines that are based on sound clinical evidence and that are periodically evaluated to assure ongoing efficacy.

(5) Any applicable clinical review criteria developed and used by the insurer or its designee utilization review organization.

(6) Medical necessity, as defined in G.S. 58-3-200(b).

(7) Any documentation supporting the medical necessity and appropriateness of the provider's recommendation.

The assigned organization shall review the terms of coverage under the covered person's health benefit plan to ensure that the organization's decision shall not be contrary to the terms of coverage under the covered person's health benefit plan with the insurer.

The assigned organization's determination shall be based on the covered person's medical condition at the time of the initial noncertification decision.

(j)   Within 45 days after the date of receipt by the Commissioner of the request for external review, the assigned organization shall provide written notice of its decision to uphold or reverse the noncertification appeal decision or second-level grievance review decision to the covered person, the insurer, the covered person's provider who performed or requested the service, and the Commissioner. In reaching a decision, the assigned review organization is not bound by any decisions or conclusions reached during the insurer's utilization review process or the insurer's internal grievance process under G.S. 58-50-61 and G.S. 58-50-62.

(k)   The organization shall include in the notice sent under subsection (j) of this section:

(1)   A general description of the reason for the request for external review.

(2)   The date the organization received the assignment from the Commissioner to conduct the external review.

(3)   The date the organization received information and documents submitted by the covered person and by the insurer.

(4)   The date the external review was conducted.

(5)   The date of its decision.

(6)   The principal reason or reasons for its decision.

(7)   The clinical rationale for its decision.

(8)   References to the evidence or documentation, including the practice guidelines, considered in reaching its decision.

(9)   The professional qualifications and licensure of the clinical peer reviewers.

(10)   Notice to the covered person that he or she is not liable for the cost of the external review.

(l)   Upon receipt of a notice of a decision under subsection (k) of this section reversing the noncertification appeal decision or second-level grievance review decision, the insurer shall within three business days reverse the noncertification appeal decision or second-level grievance review decision that was the subject of the review and shall provide coverage or payment for the requested health care service or supply that was the subject of the noncertification appeal decision or second-level grievance review decision. In the event the covered person is no longer enrolled in the health benefit plan when the insurer receives notice of a decision under subsection (k) of this section reversing the noncertification appeal decision or second-level grievance review decision, the insurer that made the noncertification appeal decision or second-level grievance review decision shall be responsible under this section only for the costs of those services or supplies the covered person received or would have received prior to disenrollment if the service had not been denied when first requested.

(m)   For the purposes of this section, a person is presumed to have received a written notice two days after the notice has been placed, first-class postage prepaid, in the United States mail addressed to the person. The presumption may be rebutted by sufficient evidence that the notice was received on another day or not received at all. (2001-446, s. 4.5; 2002-187, ss. 3.1, 3.2; 2003-105, s. 3; 2005-223, s. 10(a); 2009-382, ss. 26, 27; 2013-199, s. 18.)

§ 58-50-81: Reserved for future codification purposes.

§ 58-50-82. Expedited external review.

(a)   Except as provided in subsection (g) of this section, a covered person may file a request for an expedited external review with the Commissioner at the time the covered person receives:

(1)   A noncertification decision under G.S. 58-50-61(f) if:

a.   The covered person has a medical condition where the time frame for completion of an expedited review of an appeal involving a noncertification set forth in G.S. 58-50-61(l) would be reasonably expected to seriously jeopardize the life or health of the covered person or would jeopardize the covered person's ability to regain maximum function; and

b. The covered person has filed a request for an expedited appeal under G.S. 58-50-61(l).

(2) An appeal decision under G.S. 58-50-61(k) or (l) upholding a noncertification if:

a. The noncertification appeal decision involves a medical condition of the covered person for which the time frame for completion of an expedited second-level grievance review of a noncertification set forth in G.S. 58-50-62(i) would reasonably be expected to seriously jeopardize the life or health of the covered person or jeopardize the covered person's ability to regain maximum function; and

b. The covered person has filed a request for an expedited second-level review of a noncertification as set forth in G.S. 58-50-61(i); or

(3) A second-level grievance review decision under G.S. 58-60-62(h) or (i) upholding a noncertification:

a. If the covered person has a medical condition where the time frame for completion of a standard external review under G.S. 58-50-80 would reasonably be expected to seriously jeopardize the life or health of the covered person or jeopardize the covered person's ability to regain maximum function; or

b. If the second-level grievance concerns a noncertification of an admission, availability of care, continued stay, or health care service for which the covered person received emergency services, but has not been discharged from a facility.

(b) (Effective until January 1, 2016) Within three business days of receiving a request for an expedited external review, the Commissioner shall complete all of the following:

(1) Notify the insurer that made the noncertification, noncertification appeal decision, or second-level grievance review decision which is the subject of the request that the request has been received and provide a copy of the request. The Commissioner shall also request any information from the insurer necessary to make the preliminary review set forth in G.S. 58-50-80(b)(2) and require the insurer to deliver the information not later than one business day after the request was made.

(2) Determine whether the request is eligible for external review and, if it is eligible, determine whether it is eligible for expedited review.

a. For a request made pursuant to subdivision (a)(1) of this section that the Commissioner has determined meets the reviewability requirements set forth in G.S. 58-50-80(b)(2), determine, based on medical advice from a medical professional who is not affiliated with the organization that will be assigned to conduct the external review of the request, whether the request should be reviewed on an expedited basis because the time frame for completion of an expedited review under G.S. 58-50-61(l) would reasonably be expected to seriously jeopardize the life or health of the covered person or would jeopardize the covered person's ability to regain maximum function. The Commissioner shall then inform the covered person, the covered person's provider who performed or requested the service, and the insurer whether the Commissioner has accepted the covered person's request for an expedited external review. If the Commissioner has accepted the covered person's request for an expedited external review, then the Commissioner shall, in accordance with G.S. 58-50-80, assign an organization to conduct the review within the appropriate time frame. If the Commissioner has not accepted the covered person's request for an expedited external review, then the covered person shall be informed by the Commissioner that the covered person must exhaust, at a minimum, the insurer's internal appeal process under G.S. 58-50-61(l) before making another request for an external review with the Commissioner.

b. For a request made pursuant to subdivision (a)(2) of this section that the Commissioner has determined meets the reviewability requirements set forth in G.S. 58-50-80(b)(2), the Commissioner shall determine, based on medical advice from a medical professional who is not affiliated with the organization that will be assigned to conduct the external review of the request, whether the request should be reviewed on an expedited basis because the time frame for completion of an expedited review under G.S. 58-50-62 would reasonably be expected to seriously jeopardize the life or health of the covered person or would jeopardize the covered person's ability to regain maximum function. The Commissioner shall then inform the covered person, the covered person's provider who performed or requested the service, and the insurer whether the Commissioner has accepted the covered person's request for an expedited external review. If the Commissioner has accepted the covered person's request for an expedited external review, then the Commissioner shall, in accordance with G.S. 58-50-80, assign an organization to conduct the review within the appropriate time frame. If the Commissioner has not accepted the covered person's request for an expedited external review, then the covered person shall be informed by the Commissioner that the covered person must exhaust the insurer's internal grievance process under G.S. 58-50-62 before making another request for an external review with the Commissioner.

c. For a request made pursuant to sub-subdivision (a)(3)a. of this section that the Commissioner has determined meets the reviewability requirements set forth in G.S. 58-50-80(b)(2), the Commissioner shall determine, based on medical advice from a medical professional who is not affiliated with the organization that will be assigned to conduct the external review of the request, whether the request should be reviewed on an expedited basis because the time frame for completion of a standard external review under G.S. 58-50-80 would reasonably be expected to seriously jeopardize the life or health of the covered person or would jeopardize the covered person's ability to regain maximum function. The Commissioner shall then inform the covered person, the covered person's provider who performed or requested the service, and the insurer whether the review will be conducted using an expedited or standard time frame and shall, in accordance with G.S. 58-50-80, assign an organization to conduct the review within the appropriate time frame.

d. For a request made pursuant to sub-subdivision (a)(3)b. of this section, that the Commissioner has determined meets the reviewability requirements set forth in G.S. 58-50-80(b)(2), the Commissioner shall, in accordance with G.S. 58-50-80, assign an organization to conduct the expedited review and inform the covered person, the covered person's provider who performed or requested the service, and the insurer of its decision.

(b) (Effective January 1, 2016) Within two days after receiving a request for an expedited external review, the Commissioner shall complete all of the following:

(1) Notify the insurer that made the noncertification, noncertification appeal decision, or second-level grievance review decision which is the subject of the request that the request has been received and provide a copy of the request. The Commissioner shall also request any information from the insurer necessary to make the preliminary review set forth in G.S. 58-50-80(b)(2) and require the insurer to deliver the information not later than one business day after the request was made.

(2) Determine whether the request is eligible for external review and, if it is eligible, determine whether it is eligible for expedited review.

a. For a request made pursuant to subdivision (a)(1) of this section that the Commissioner has determined meets the reviewability requirements set forth in G.S. 58-50-80(b)(2), determine, based on medical advice from a medical professional who is not affiliated with the organization that will be assigned to conduct the external review of the request, whether the request should be reviewed on an expedited basis because the time frame for completion of an expedited review under G.S. 58-50-61(l) would reasonably be expected to seriously jeopardize the life or health of the covered person or would jeopardize the covered person's ability to regain maximum function. The Commissioner shall then inform the covered person, the covered person's provider who performed or requested the service, and the insurer whether the Commissioner has accepted the covered person's request for an expedited external review. If the Commissioner has accepted the covered person's request for an expedited external review, then the Commissioner shall, in accordance with G.S. 58-50-80, assign an organization to conduct the review within the appropriate time frame. If the Commissioner has not accepted the covered person's request for an expedited external review, then the covered person shall be informed by the Commissioner that the covered person must exhaust, at a minimum, the insurer's internal appeal process under G.S. 58-50-61(l) before making another request for an external review with the Commissioner.

b. For a request made pursuant to subdivision (a)(2) of this section that the Commissioner has determined meets the reviewability requirements set forth in G.S. 58-50-80(b)(2), the Commissioner shall determine, based on medical advice from a medical professional who is not affiliated with the organization that will be assigned to conduct the external review of the request, whether the request should be reviewed on an expedited basis because the time frame for completion of an expedited review under G.S. 58-50-62 would reasonably be expected to seriously jeopardize the life or health of the covered person or would jeopardize the covered person's ability to regain maximum function. The Commissioner shall then inform the covered person, the covered person's provider who performed or requested the service, and the insurer whether the Commissioner has accepted the covered person's request for an expedited external review. If the Commissioner has accepted the covered person's request for an expedited external review, then the Commissioner shall, in accordance with G.S. 58-50-80, assign an organization to conduct the review within the appropriate time frame. If the Commissioner has not accepted the covered person's request for an expedited external review, then the covered person shall be informed by the Commissioner that the covered person must exhaust the insurer's internal grievance process under G.S. 58-50-62 before making another request for an external review with the Commissioner.

c. For a request made pursuant to sub-subdivision (a)(3)a. of this section that the Commissioner has determined meets the reviewability requirements set forth in G.S. 58-50-80(b)(2), the Commissioner shall determine, based on medical advice from a medical professional who is not affiliated with the organization that will be assigned to conduct the external review of the request, whether the request should be reviewed on an expedited basis because the time frame for completion of a standard external review under G.S. 58-50-80 would reasonably be expected to seriously jeopardize the life or health of the covered person or would jeopardize the covered person's ability to regain maximum function. The Commissioner shall then inform the covered person, the covered person's provider who performed or requested the service, and the insurer whether the review will be conducted using an expedited or standard time frame and shall, in accordance with G.S. 58-50-80, assign an organization to conduct the review within the appropriate time frame.

d. For a request made pursuant to sub-subdivision (a)(3)b. of this section, that the Commissioner has determined meets the reviewability requirements set forth in G.S. 58-50-80(b)(2), the Commissioner shall, in accordance with G.S. 58-50-80, assign an organization to conduct the expedited review and inform the covered person, the covered person's provider who performed or requested the service, and the insurer of its decision.

(c) (Effective until January 1, 2016) As soon as possible, but within the same business day of receiving notice under subdivision (b)(2) of this section that the request has been assigned to a review organization, the insurer or its designee utilization review organization shall provide or transmit all documents and information considered in making the noncertification appeal decision or the second-level grievance review decision to the assigned review organization electronically or by telephone or facsimile or any other available expeditious method. A copy of the same information shall be sent by the same means or other expeditious means to the covered person or the covered person's representative who made the request for expedited external review.

(c) (Effective January 1, 2016) As soon as possible, but within the same day after receiving notice under subdivision (b)(2) of this section that the request has been assigned to a review organization, the insurer or its designee utilization review organization shall provide or transmit all documents and information considered in making the noncertification appeal decision or the second-level grievance review decision to the assigned review organization electronically or by telephone or facsimile or any other available expeditious method. A copy of the same information shall be sent by the same means or other expeditious means to the covered person or the covered person's representative who made the request for expedited external review.

(d) In addition to the documents and information provided or transmitted under subsection (c) of this section, the assigned organization, to the extent the information or documents are available, shall consider the following in reaching a decision:

(1) The covered person's pertinent medical records.

(2) The attending health care provider's recommendation.

(3) Consulting reports from appropriate health care providers and other documents submitted by the insurer, covered person, or the covered person's treating provider.

(4) The most appropriate practice guidelines that are based on sound clinical evidence and that are periodically evaluated to assure ongoing efficacy.

(5) Any applicable clinical review criteria developed and used by the insurer or its designee utilization review organization in making noncertification decisions.

(6) Medical necessity, as defined in G.S. 58-3-200(b).

(7) Any documentation supporting the medical necessity and appropriateness of the provider's recommendation.

The assigned organization shall review the terms of coverage under the covered person's health benefit plan to ensure that the organization's decision shall not be contrary to the terms of coverage under the covered person's health benefit plan.

The assigned organization's determination shall be based on the covered person's medical condition at the time of the initial noncertification decision.

(e) (Effective until January 1, 2016) As expeditiously as the covered person's medical condition or circumstances require, but not more than four business days after the date of receipt of the request for an expedited external review, the assigned organization shall make a decision to uphold or reverse the noncertification, noncertification appeal decision, or second-level grievance review decision and notify the covered person, the covered person's provider who performed or requested the service, the insurer, and the Commissioner of the decision. In reaching a decision, the assigned organization is not bound by any decisions or conclusions reached during the insurer's utilization review process or internal grievance process under G.S. 58-50-61 and G.S. 58-50-62.

(e) (Effective January 1, 2016) As expeditiously as the covered person's medical condition or circumstances require, but not more than three days after the date of receipt of the request for an expedited external review, the assigned organization shall make a decision to uphold or reverse the noncertification, noncertification appeal decision, or second-level grievance review decision and notify the covered person, the covered person's provider who performed or requested the service, the insurer, and the Commissioner of the decision. In reaching a decision, the assigned organization is not bound by any decisions or conclusions reached during the insurer's utilization review process or internal grievance process under G.S. 58-50-61 and G.S. 58-50-62.

(f) If the notice provided under subsection (e) of this section was not in writing, within two days after the date of providing that notice, the assigned organization shall provide written confirmation of the decision to the covered person, the covered person's provider who performed or requested the service, the insurer, and the Commissioner and include the information set forth in G.S. 58-50-80(k).

Upon receipt of the notice of a decision under subsection (e) of this section that reverses the noncertification, noncertification appeal decision, or second-level grievance review decision, the insurer shall within one day reverse the noncertification, noncertification appeal decision, or second-level grievance review decision that was the subject of the review and shall provide coverage or payment for the requested health care service or supply that was the subject of the noncertification, noncertification appeal decision, or second-level grievance review decision.

(g) An expedited external review shall not be provided for retrospective noncertifications. (2001-446, s. 4.5; 2005-223, ss. 10(b), 11, 12; 2007-298, ss. 3.1, 3.2; 2009-382, ss. 28-30; 2013-199, s. 10.)

§ 58-50-83: Reserved for future codification purposes.

§ 58-50-84. Binding nature of external review decision.

(a) An external review decision is binding on the insurer.

(b) An external review decision is binding on the covered person except to the extent the covered person has other remedies available under applicable federal or State law.

(c) A covered person may not file a subsequent request for external review involving the same noncertification appeal decision or second-level grievance review decision for which the covered person has already received an external review decision under this Part. (2001-446, s. 4.5.)

§ 58-50-85. Approval of independent review organizations.

(a) The Commissioner shall approve independent review organizations eligible to be assigned to conduct external reviews under this Part to ensure that an organization satisfies the minimum qualifications established under G.S. 58-50-87. The Commissioner shall develop an application form for initially approving and for reapproving organizations to conduct external reviews.

(b) Any organization wishing to be approved to conduct external reviews under this Part shall submit the application form and include with the form all documentation and information necessary for the Commissioner to determine if the organization satisfies the minimum qualifications established under G.S. 58-50-87. Applicants must submit pricing information sufficient to demonstrate that if selected, the applicant's total fee per review will not exceed commercially reasonable fees charged for similar services in the industry. The Commissioner shall not approve any independent review organization that either fails to provide sufficient pricing information or has fees that do not meet the guidelines established under this subsection.

(c) In order to be eligible for approval by the Commissioner, an independent review organization shall be accredited by a nationally recognized private accrediting entity that the Commissioner has determined has independent review organization accreditation standards that are equivalent to or exceed the minimum qualifications established under G.S. 58-50-87. The Commissioner may approve independent review organizations that are not accredited by a nationally recognized private accrediting entity if there are no acceptable nationally recognized private accrediting entities providing independent review organization accreditation.

(d)   An approval is effective for two years, unless the Commissioner determines before expiration of the approval that the independent review organization is not satisfying the minimum qualifications established under G.S. 58-50-87.

(e)   Whenever the Commissioner determines that an independent review organization no longer satisfies the minimum requirements established under G.S. 58-50-87, the Commissioner shall terminate the approval of the independent review organization. (2001-446, s. 4.5; 2009-382, s. 31.)

§ 58-50-86: Reserved for future codification purposes.

§ 58-50-87. Minimum qualifications for independent review organizations.

(a)   As a condition of approval under G.S. 58-50-85 to conduct external reviews, an independent review organization shall have and maintain written policies and procedures that govern all aspects of both the standard external review process and the expedited external review process set forth in G.S. 58-50-80 and G.S. 58-50-82 that include, at a minimum:

(1)   A quality assurance mechanism in place that ensures:

a.   That external reviews are conducted within the specified time frames and required notices are provided in a timely manner.

b.   The selection of qualified and impartial clinical peer reviewers to conduct external reviews on behalf of the independent review organization and suitable matching of reviewers to specific cases.

c.   The confidentiality of medical and treatment records and clinical review criteria.

d. That any person employed by or under contract with the independent review organization adheres to the requirements of this Part.

e. The independence and impartiality of the independent review organization and the external review process and limits the ability of any person to improperly influence the external review decision.

(2) A toll-free telephone service to receive information on a 24-hour-day, seven-day-a-week basis related to external reviews that is capable of accepting or recording inquiries or providing appropriate instruction to incoming telephone callers during other than normal business hours.

(3) An agreement to maintain and provide to the Commissioner the information set out in G.S. 58-50-90.

(4) A program for credentialing clinical peer reviewers.

(5) An agreement to contractual terms or written requirements established by the Commissioner regarding the procedures for handling a review.

(6) That the independent review organization consult with a medical doctor licensed to practice in North Carolina to advise the independent review organization on issues related to the standard of practice, technology, and training of North Carolina physicians with respect to the organization's North Carolina business.

(b) All clinical peer reviewers assigned by an independent review organization to conduct external reviews shall be medical doctors or other appropriate health care providers who meet the following minimum qualifications:

(1) Be an expert in the treatment of the covered person's injury, illness, or medical condition that is the subject of the external review.

(2) Be knowledgeable about the recommended health care service or treatment through recent or current actual clinical experience treating patients with the same or similar injury, illness, or medical condition of the covered person.

(3) If the covered person's treating provider is a medical doctor, hold a nonrestricted license and, if a specialist medical doctor, a current certification by a recognized American medical specialty board in the area or areas appropriate to the subject of the external review.

(4) If the covered person's treating provider is not a medical doctor, hold a nonrestricted license, registration, or certification in the same allied health occupation as the covered person's treating provider.

(5) Have no history of disciplinary actions or sanctions, including loss of staff privileges or participation restrictions, that have been taken or are pending by any hospital, governmental agency or unit, or regulatory body that raise a substantial question as to the clinical peer reviewer's physical, mental, or professional competence or moral character.

(c) In addition to the requirements set forth in subsection (a) of this section, an independent review organization may not own or control, be a subsidiary of, or in any way be owned or controlled by, or exercise control with a health benefit plan, a national, State, or local trade association of health benefit plans, or a national, State, or local trade association of health care providers.

(d) In addition to the requirements set forth in subsections (a), (b), and (c) of this section, to be approved under G.S. 58-50-85 to conduct an external review of a specified case, neither the independent review organization selected to conduct the external review nor any clinical peer reviewer assigned by the independent organization to conduct the external review may have a material professional, familial, or financial conflict of interest with any of the following:

(1) The insurer that is the subject of the external review.

(2) The covered person whose treatment is the subject of the external review or the covered person's authorized representative.

(3) Any officer, director, or management employee of the insurer that is the subject of the external review.

(4) The health care provider, the health care provider's medical group, or independent practice association recommending the health care service or treatment that is the subject of the external review.

(5) The facility at which the recommended health care service or treatment would be provided.

(6) The developer or manufacturer of the principal drug, device, procedure, or other therapy being recommended for the covered person whose treatment is the subject of the external review.

(e) In determining whether an independent review organization or a clinical peer reviewer of the independent review organization has a material professional, familial, or financial conflict of interest for purposes of subsection (d) of this section, the Commissioner shall take into consideration situations where the independent review organization to be assigned to conduct an external review of a specified case or a clinical peer reviewer to be assigned by the independent review organization to conduct an external review of a specified case may have an apparent professional, familial, or financial relationship or connection with a person described in subsection (d) of this section, but that the characteristics of that relationship or connection are such that they are not a material professional, familial, or financial conflict of interest that results in the disapproval of the independent review organization or the clinical peer reviewer from conducting the external review. (2001-446, s. 4.5.)

§ 58-50-88: Reserved for future codification purposes.

§ 58-50-89. Hold harmless for Commissioner, medical professionals, and independent review organizations.

Neither the Commissioner, a medical professional rendering advice to the Commissioner under G.S. 58-50-82(b)(2), an independent review organization, nor a clinical peer reviewer working on behalf of an organization shall be liable for damages to any person for any opinions rendered during or upon completion of an external review conducted under this Part, unless the opinion was rendered in bad faith or involved gross negligence. (2001-446, s. 4.5; 2002-187, s. 3.3.)

§ 58-50-90. External review reporting requirements.

(a) An organization assigned under G.S. 58-50-80 or G.S. 58-50-82 to conduct an external review shall maintain written records in the aggregate and by insurer on all requests for external review for which it conducted an external review during a calendar year and submit a report to the Commissioner, as required under subsection (b) of this section.

(b) Each organization required to maintain written records on all requests for external review under subsection (a) of this section for which it was assigned to conduct an external review shall submit to the Commissioner, upon the Commissioner's request, a report in the format specified by the Commissioner.

(c) The report shall include in the aggregate and for each insurer:

(1) The total number of requests for external review.

(2) The number of requests for external review resolved and, of those resolved, the number resolved upholding the noncertification appeal decision or second-level grievance review decision and the number resolved reversing the noncertification appeal decision or second-level grievance review decision.

(3) The average length of time for resolution.

(4) A summary of the types of coverages or cases for which an external review was sought, as provided in the format required by the Commissioner.

(5) The number of external reviews under G.S. 58-50-80 that were terminated as the result of a reconsideration by the insurer of its noncertification appeal decision or second-level grievance review decision after the receipt of additional information from the covered person.

(6) Any other information the Commissioner may request or require.

(d) The organization shall retain the written records required under this section for at least three years.

(e) Each insurer shall maintain written records in the aggregate and for each type of health benefit plan offered by the insurer on all requests for external review of which the insurer receives notice from the Commissioner under this Part. The insurer shall retain the written records required under this section for at least three years. (2001-446, s. 4.5; 2009-382, s. 32.)

§ 58-50-91: Reserved for future codification purposes.

§ 58-50-92. Funding of external review.

The insurer against which a request for a standard external review or an expedited external review is filed shall reimburse the Department of Insurance for the fees charged by the organization in conducting the external review, including work actually performed by the organization for a case that was terminated due to the insurer's decision to reconsider a request and reverse its noncertification decision, prior to the insurer notifying the organization of the reversal pursuant to G.S. 58-50-80(j), or when a review is terminated pursuant to G.S. 58-50-80(h) because the insurer failed to provide information to the review organization. (2001-446, s. 4.5.)

§ 58-50-93. Disclosure requirements.

(a) Each insurer shall include a description of the external review procedures in or attached to the policy, certificate, membership booklet, outline of coverage, or other evidence of coverage it provides to covered persons.

(b) The description required under subsection (a) of this section shall include a statement that informs the covered person of the right of the covered person to file a request for an external review of a noncertification, noncertification appeal decision or a second-level grievance review decision upholding a noncertification with the Commissioner. The statement shall include the telephone number and address of the Commissioner.

(c) In addition to subsection (b) of this section, the statement shall inform the covered person that, when filing a request for an external review, the covered person will be required to authorize the release of any medical records of the covered person that may be required to be reviewed for the purpose of reaching a decision on the external review. (2001-446, s. 4.5.)

§ 58-50-94. Selection of independent review organizations.

(a) At least every two years, or more frequently if the Commissioner determines is needed to secure adequate selection of independent review organizations, the Commissioner shall prepare and publish requests for proposals from independent review organizations that want to be approved under G.S. 58-50-85. All proposals shall be sealed. The Commissioner shall open all proposals in public.

(b) After the public opening, the Commissioner shall review the proposals, examining the quality of the services offered by the independent review organizations, the reputation and capabilities of the independent review organizations submitting the proposals, and the provisions in G.S. 58-50-85 and G.S. 58-50-87. The Commissioner shall determine which proposal or proposals would satisfy the provisions of this Part. The Commissioner shall make his determination in consultation with an evaluation committee whose membership includes representatives of insurers subject to Part 4 of Article 50 of Chapter 58 of the General Statutes, health care providers, and insureds. In selecting the review organizations, in addition to considering cost, quality, and adherence to the requirements of the request for proposals, the Commissioner shall consider the desirability and feasibility of contracting with multiple review organizations and shall ensure that, for any given type of case involving highly specialized services and treatments, at least one review organization is available and capable of reviewing the case.

(c) An independent review organization may seek to modify or withdraw a proposal only after the public opening and only on the basis that the proposal contains an unintentional clerical error as opposed to an error in judgment. An independent review organization seeking to modify or withdraw a proposal shall submit to the Commissioner a written request, with facts and evidence in support of its position, before the determination made by the Commissioner under subsection (b) of this section, but not later than two days after the public opening of the proposals. The Commissioner shall promptly review the request, examine the nature of the error, and determine whether to permit or deny the request.

(d) The provisions of Article 3C of Chapter 143 of the General Statutes do not apply to this Part. (2001-446, s. 4.5; 2009-382, s. 33.)

§ 58-50-95. Report by Commissioner.

The Commissioner shall report annually to the Joint Legislative Oversight Committee on Health and Human Services regarding the nature and appropriateness of reviews conducted under this Part. The report, which shall be provided to the public upon request, should include the number of reviews, underlying issues in dispute, character of the reviews, dollar amounts in question, whether the review was decided in favor of the covered person or the health benefit plan, the cost of review, and any other information relevant to the evaluation of the effectiveness of this Part. (2001-446, s. 4.5; 2007-298, s. 3.3; 2011-291, s. 2.6.)

Part 5. Small Employer Group Health Insurance Reform.

§ 58-50-100. Title and reference.

This section and G.S. 58-50-105 through G.S. 58-50-156 are known and may be cited as the North Carolina Small Employer Group Health Coverage Reform Act, referred to in those sections as "this Act". (1991, c. 630, s. 1; 2006-105, s. 1.9.)

§ 58-50-105. Purpose and intent.

The purpose and intent of this Act is to promote the availability of accident and health insurance coverage to small employers, to prevent abusive rating practices, to require disclosure of rating practices to purchasers, to establish rules for continuity of coverage for employers and covered individuals, and to improve the efficiency and fairness of the small group accident and health insurance marketplace. (1991, c. 630, s. 1.)

§ 58-50-110. Definitions.

As used in this Act:

(1) Repealed by Session Laws 2001-334, s. 12.1, effective August 3, 2001.

(1a) "Actuarial certification" means a written statement by a member of the American Academy of Actuaries or other individual acceptable to the Commissioner that a small employer carrier is in compliance with the provisions of G.S. 58-50-130, and to the extent applicable, the provisions of Article 68 of this Chapter, based upon the person's examination, including a review of the appropriate records and of the actuarial assumptions and methods used by the small employer carrier in establishing premium rates for applicable health benefit plans.

(1b) "Adjusted community rating" means a method used to develop carrier premiums which spreads financial risk across a large population and allows adjustments for the following demographic factors: age, gender, family composition, and geographic areas, as determined pursuant to G.S. 58-50-130(b).

(2) Repealed by Session Laws 1993, c. 529, s. 3.3.

(3) "Basic health care plan" means a health care plan for small employers that is lower in cost than a standard health care plan and is required to be offered by all small employer carriers pursuant to G.S. 58-50-125 and approved by the Commissioner in accordance with G.S. 58-50-125.

(4) "Board" means the board of directors of the Pool.

(5) "Carrier" means any person that provides one or more health benefit plans in this State, including a licensed insurance company, a prepaid hospital or medical service plan, a health maintenance organization (HMO), and a multiple employer welfare arrangement.

(5a) "Case characteristics" means the demographic factors age, gender, family size, geographic location, and industry.

(6), (7) Repealed by Session Laws 1993, c. 529, s. 3.3.

(8) "Committee" means the Small Employer Carrier Committee as created by G.S. 58-50-120.

(9) "Dependent" means the spouse or child of an eligible employee, subject to applicable terms of the health care plan covering the employee.

(10) "Eligible employee" means an employee who works for a small employer on a full-time basis, with a normal work week of 30 or more hours, including a sole proprietor, a partner or a partnership, or an independent contractor, if included as an employee under a health care plan of a small employer; but does not include employees who work on a part-time, temporary, or substitute basis.

(10a) "Grandfathered health plan" means a health benefit plan providing coverage considered grandfathered health coverage described in 45 C.F.R. § 147.140(a).

(11) "Health benefit plan" means any accident and health insurance policy or certificate; nonprofit hospital or medical service corporation contract; health, hospital, or medical service corporation plan contract; HMO subscriber contract; plan provided by a MEWA or plan provided by another benefit arrangement, to the extent permitted by ERISA, subject to G.S. 58-50-115. Health benefit plan does not include benefits described in G.S. 58-68-25(b).

(12) "Impaired insurer" has the same meaning as prescribed in G.S. 58-62-20(6) or G.S. 58-62-16(8).

(12a) "Industry" means a demographic factor used to reflect the financial risk associated with a specific industry.

(13) Repealed by Session Laws 1993, c. 529, s. 3.3.

(14) "Late enrollee" has the same meaning as defined in G.S. 58-68-30(b)(2); provided that the initial enrollment period shall be a period of at least 30 consecutive calendar days. In addition to the special enrollment provisions in G.S. 58-68-30(f), an eligible employee or dependent shall not be considered a late enrollee under a small employer health benefit plan if:

a. Repealed by Session Laws 1998-211, s. 9, effective November 1, 1998.

1, 2. Repealed by Session Laws 1998-211, s. 9, effective November 1, 1998.

3, 4. Repealed by Session Laws 1993, c. 529, s. 3.3.

b. The individual elects a different health benefit plan offered by the small employer during an open enrollment period;

c. Repealed by Session Laws 1998-211, s. 9, effective November 1, 1998.

d. A court has ordered coverage be provided for a spouse or minor child under a covered employee's health benefit plan and the request for enrollment for a spouse is made within 30 days after issuance of the court order. A minor child shall be enrolled in accordance with the requirements of G.S. 58-51-120; or

e. Repealed by Session Laws 1998-211, s. 9, effective November 1, 1998.

(15) Repealed by Session Laws 1993, c. 529, s. 3.3.

(16) "Pool" means the North Carolina Small Employer Health Reinsurance Pool created in G.S. 58-50-150.

(17) "Preexisting-conditions provision" means a preexisting-condition provision as defined in G.S. 58-68-30.

(18) "Premium" includes insurance premiums or other fees charged for a health benefit plan, including the costs of benefits paid or reimbursements made to or on behalf of persons covered by the plan.

(19) "Rating period" means the calendar period for which premium rates established by a small employer carrier are assumed to be in effect, as determined by the small employer carrier.

(20) "Risk-assuming carrier" means a small employer carrier electing to comply with the requirements set forth in G.S. 58-50-140.

(21) "Reinsuring carrier" means a small employer carrier electing to comply with the requirements set forth in G.S. 58-50-145.

(21a) "Self-employed individual" means an individual or sole proprietor who derives a majority of his or her income from a trade or business carried on by the individual or sole proprietor which results in taxable income as indicated on IRS form 1040, Schedule C or F and which generated taxable income in one of the two previous years.

(22) "Small employer" means any individual actively engaged in business that, on at least fifty percent (50%) of its working days during the preceding calendar quarter, employed no more than 50 eligible employees, the majority of whom are employed within this State, and is not formed primarily for purposes of buying health insurance and in which a bona fide employer-employee relationship exists. In determining the number of eligible employees, companies that are affiliated companies, or that are eligible to file a combined tax return for purposes of taxation by this State, shall be considered one employer. Subsequent to the issuance of a health benefit plan to a small employer and for the purpose of determining eligibility, the size of a small employer shall be determined annually. Except as otherwise specifically provided, the provisions of this Act that apply to a small employer shall continue to apply until the plan anniversary following the date the small employer no longer meets the requirements of this definition. For purposes of this subdivision, the term small employer includes self-employed individuals. Effective January 1, 2014, this definition shall apply only to grandfathered group health plans subject to this Act.

(22a) (Repealed effective January 1, 2016 - see note) "Small employer" means, in connection with a nongrandfathered group health plan with respect to a calendar year and a plan year, an employer that employed an average of at least one but not more than 50 employees on business days during the preceding calendar year and that employs at least one employee on the first day of the plan year. The number of employees shall be determined using the method set forth in section 4980H(c)(2) of the Internal Revenue Code.

(22b) (Effective January 1, 2016 - see note) "Small employer" means, in connection with a nongrandfathered group health plan with respect to a calendar year and a plan year, an employer who employed an average of at least one but not more than 100 employees on business days during the preceding calendar year and who employs at least one employee on the first day of the plan year. The number of employees shall be determined using the method set forth in section 4980H(c)(2) of the Internal Revenue Code.

(23) "Small employer carrier" means any carrier that offers health benefit plans covering eligible employees of one or more small employers.

(24) "Standard health care plan" means a health care plan for small employers required to be offered by all small employer carriers under G.S. 58-50-125 and approved by the Commissioner in accordance with G.S. 58-50-125. (1991, c. 630, s. 1; 1993, c. 408, ss. 1, 2; c. 529, s. 3.3; 1993 (Reg. Sess.,

1994), c. 569, s. 6; 1997-259, s. 2; 1998-211, s. 9; 2001-334, ss. 12.1, 12.2; 2006-154, ss. 5, 6; 2013-357, ss. 2(b), 4(a), (b).)

§ 58-50-112. Affiliated companies; HMOs.

For the purposes of this Act, companies that are affiliated companies or that are eligible to file a consolidated tax return shall be treated as one carrier except that any insurance company, hospital service plan, or medical service plan that is an affiliate of an HMO located in North Carolina or any HMO located in North Carolina that is an affiliate of an insurance company, a health service corporation, or a medical service corporation may treat the HMO as a separate carrier and each HMO that operates only one HMO in a service area of North Carolina may be considered a separate carrier. (1991, c. 630, s. 1.)

§ 58-50-113: Repealed by Session Laws 1993, c. 529, s. 3.4.

§ 58-50-115. Health benefit plans subject to Act.

(a) A health benefit plan is subject to this Act if it provides health benefits for small employers and if any of the following conditions are met:

(1) Any part of the premiums or benefits is paid by a small employer or any covered individual is reimbursed, whether through wage or adjustments or otherwise, by a small employer for any portion of the premium;

(2) The health benefit plan is treated by the employer as part of a plan or program for the purpose of sections 106, 125, or 162 of the United States Internal Revenue Code; or

(3) The small employer has permitted payroll deductions for the eligible enrollees for the health benefit plans.

(b) Repealed by Session Laws 1993, c. 529, s. 3.5, effective January 1, 1995. (1991, c. 630, s. 1; 1993, c. 529, s. 3.5; 2013-357, s. 2(c).)

§ 58-50-120: Repealed by Session Laws 2006-154, s. 9, effective July 23, 2006.

§ 58-50-125. Health care plans; formation; approval; offerings.

(a) (Repealed effective January 1, 2015 - see note) To improve the availability and affordability of health benefits coverage for small employers, the Committee shall recommend to the Commissioner two plans of coverage, one of which shall be a basic health care plan and the second of which shall be a standard health care plan. Each plan of coverage shall be in two forms, one of which shall be in the form of insurance and the second of which shall be consistent with the basic method of operation and benefit plans of HMOs, including federally qualified HMOs. On or before January 1, 1992, the Committee shall file a progress report with the Commissioner. The Committee shall submit the recommended plans to the Commissioner for approval within 180 days after the appointment of the Committee under G.S. 58-50-120. The Committee shall take into consideration the levels of health benefit plans provided in North Carolina, and appropriate medical and economic factors, and shall establish benefit levels, cost sharing, exclusions, and limitations. Notwithstanding subsection (c) of this section, in developing and approving the plans, the Committee and the Commissioner shall give due consideration to cost-effective and life-saving health care services and to cost-effective health care providers. The Committee shall file with the Commissioner its findings and recommendations, and reasons for the findings and recommendations, if it does not provide for coverage by any type of health care provider specified in G.S. 58-50-30. The recommended plans may include cost containment features such as, but not limited to: preferred provider provisions; utilization review of medical necessity of hospital and physician services; case management benefit alternatives; or other managed care provisions.

(a1) (Repealed effective January 1, 2015 - see note) Both the basic health care plan and the standard health care plan provided for in subsection (a) of this section may have optional deductible and co-payment levels as may be determined by the small employer carrier, including high deductible options. A small employer carrier shall file any changes in deductibles or co-payment levels with the Commissioner for the Commissioner's approval prior to implementing the changes in this State. The Commissioner may periodically review and update the benefits provided by these plans to address trends in the small group market. The Commissioner shall consult with small employer carriers and representatives of the insurance agent and small employer communities as part of that periodic review.

(b)　　Repealed by Session Laws 2006-154, s. 9, effective July 23, 2006.

(c)　　Except as provided under Article 68 of this Chapter, the plans developed under this section are not required to provide coverage that meets the requirements of other provisions of this Chapter that mandate either coverage or the offer of coverage by the type or level of health care services or health care provider.

(d)　　If a small employer carrier offers coverage to a small employer, the small employer carrier shall offer coverage to all eligible employees of a small employer and their dependents. A small employer carrier shall not offer coverage to only certain individuals in a small employer group except in the case of late enrollees as provided in G.S. 58-50-130(a)(4b). A small employer carrier shall not modify any health benefit plan with respect to a small employer, any eligible employee, or dependent through riders, endorsements, or otherwise, in order to restrict or exclude coverage for certain diseases or medical conditions otherwise covered by the health benefit plan. In the case of an eligible employee or dependent of an eligible employee who, before the effective date of the plan, was excluded from coverage or denied coverage by a small employer carrier in the process of providing a health benefit plan to an eligible small employer, the small employer carrier shall provide an opportunity for the eligible employee or dependent of an eligible employee to enroll in the health benefit plan currently held by the small employer.

(e)　　Repealed by Session Laws 2006-154, s. 9, effective July 23, 2006.

(f)　　To the extent it is required under this section and G.S. 58-68-40, every small employer carrier shall fairly market all of its small group health benefit plans it offers on a guaranteed issue basis to all small employers in the geographic areas in which the carrier makes coverage available or provides benefits.

(g)　　Repealed by Session Laws 2006-154, s. 9, effective July 23, 2006.

(h)　　The provisions of subsection (d) of this section apply to every health benefit plan delivered, issued for delivery, renewed, or continued in this State or covering persons residing in this State on or after the date the plan becomes operational, as determined by the Commissioner. For purposes of this subsection, the date a health benefit plan is continued is the anniversary date of the issuance of the health benefit plan. (1991, c. 630, s. 1; c. 761, s. 10; 1993, c. 529, s. 3.6; 1997-259, ss. 3, 4; 2006-154, ss. 1, 2, 9, 10, 14; 2013-357, ss. 2(d), (e).)

§§ 58-50-126, 58-50-127: Repealed by Session Laws 2013-357, s. 2(a), effective January 1, 2014.

§ 58-50-130. Required health care plan provisions.

(a) Health benefit plans covering small employers are subject to the following provisions:

(1) to (4) Repealed by Session Laws 1997-259, s. 5, effective July 14, 1997.

(4a) A carrier may continue to enforce reasonable employer participation and contribution requirements on small employers applying for coverage; however, participation and contribution requirements may vary among small employers only by the size of the small employer group and shall not differ because of the health benefit plan involved. In applying minimum participation requirements to a small employer, a small employer carrier shall not consider employees or dependents who have qualifying existing coverage in determining whether an applicable participation level is met. "Qualifying existing coverage" means benefits or coverage provided under: (i) Medicare, Medicaid, and other government funded programs; or (ii) an employer-based health insurance or health benefit arrangement, including a self-insured plan, that provides benefits similar to or in excess of benefits provided under the basic health care plan.

(4b) Late enrollees may only be excluded from coverage for the greater of 18 months or an 18-month preexisting-condition exclusion; however, if both a period of exclusion from coverage and a preexisting-condition exclusion are applicable to a late enrollee, the combined period shall not exceed 18 months. If a period of exclusion from coverage is applied, a late enrollee shall be enrolled at the end of that period in the health benefit plan held at the time by the small employer.

(5) No small employer carrier, insurer, subsidiary of an insurer, or controlled individual of an insurance holding company shall provide stop loss, catastrophic, or reinsurance coverage to small employers who employ fewer than 26 eligible employees that does not comply with the underwriting, rating, and other applicable standards in this Act. An insurer shall not issue a stop loss health insurance policy to any person, firm, corporation, partnership, or association defined as a small employer that does any of the following:

a. Provides direct coverage of health expenses payable to an individual.

b. Has an annual attachment point for claims incurred per individual that is lower than twenty thousand dollars ($20,000) for plan years beginning in 2013. For subsequent policy years, the amount shall be indexed using the Consumer Price Index for Medical Services for All Urban Consumers for the South Region and shall be rounded to the nearest whole thousand dollars. The index factor shall be the index as of July of the year preceding the change divided by the index as of July 2012.

c. Has an annual aggregate attachment point lower than the greater of one of the following:

1. One hundred twenty percent (120%) of expected claims.

2. Twenty thousand dollars ($20,000) for plan years beginning in 2013. For subsequent policy years, the amount shall be indexed using the Consumer Price Index for Medical Services for All Urban Consumers for the South Region and shall be rounded to the nearest whole thousand dollars. The index factor shall be the index as of July of the year preceding the change divided by the index as of July 2012.

Nothing in this subsection prohibits an insurer from providing additional incentives to small employers with benefits promoting a medical home or benefits that provide health care screenings, are focused on outcomes and key performance indicators, or are reimbursed on an outcomes basis rather than a fee-for-service basis.

(6) If a small employer carrier offers coverage to a small employer, the small employer carrier shall offer coverage to all eligible employees of a small employer and their dependents. A small employer carrier shall not offer coverage to only certain individuals in a small employer group except in the case of late enrollees as provided in G.S. 58-50-130(a)(4).

(7), (8) Repealed by Session Laws 1997-259, s. 5.

(9) The health benefit plan must meet the applicable requirements of Article 68 of this Chapter.

(b) For all small employer health benefit plans that are grandfathered health benefit plans and that are subject to this section, the premium rates are subject to all of the following provisions:

(1) Small employer carriers shall use an adjusted-community rating methodology in which the premium for each small employer can vary only on the basis of the eligible employee's or dependent's age as determined under subdivision (6) of this subsection, the gender of the eligible employee or dependent, number of family members covered, or geographic area as determined under subdivision (7) of this subsection, or industry as determined under subdivision (9) of this subsection. Premium rates charged during a rating period to small employers with similar case characteristics for same coverage shall not vary from the adjusted community rate by more than twenty-five percent (25%) for any reason, including differences in administrative costs and claims experience.

(2) Rating factors related to age, gender, number of family members covered, geographic location, or industry may be developed by each carrier to reflect the carrier's experience. The factors used by carriers are subject to the Commissioner's review.

(3) A small employer carrier shall not modify the premium rate charged to a small employer or a small employer group member, including changes in rates related to the increasing age of a group member, for 12 months from the initial issue date or renewal date, unless the group is composite rated and composition of the group changed by twenty percent (20%) or more or benefits are changed. The percentage increase in the premium rate charged to a small employer for a new rating period shall not exceed the sum of all of the following:

a. The percentage change in the adjusted community rate as measured from the first day of the prior rating period to the first day of the new rating period.

b. Any adjustment, not to exceed fifteen percent (15%) annually, due to claim experience, health status, or duration of coverage of the employees or dependents of the small employer.

c. Any adjustment because of change in coverage or change in case characteristics of the small employer group.

(4), (5) Repealed by Session Laws 1995, c. 238, s. 1.

(6) Unless the small employer carrier uses composite rating, the small employer carrier shall use the following age brackets:

a. Younger than 15 years;

b. 15 to 19 years;

c. 20 to 24 years;

d. 25 to 29 years;

e. 30 to 34 years;

f. 35 to 39 years;

g. 40 to 44 years;

h. 45 to 49 years;

i. 50 to 54 years;

j. 55 to 59 years;

k. 60 to 64 years;

l. 65 years.

Carriers may combine, but shall not split, complete age brackets for the purposes of determining rates under this subsection. Small employer carriers shall be permitted to develop separate rates for individuals aged 65 years and older for coverage for which Medicare is the primary payor and coverage for which Medicare is not the primary payor.

(7) A carrier shall define geographic area to mean medical care system. Medical care system factors shall reflect the relative differences in expected costs, shall produce rates that are not excessive, inadequate, or unfairly discriminatory in the medical care system areas, and shall be revenue neutral to the small employer carrier.

(8) The Department may adopt rules to administer this subsection and to assure that rating practices used by small employer carriers are consistent with the purposes of this subsection. Those rules shall include consideration of differences based on all of the following:

a. Health benefit plans that use different provider network arrangements may be considered separate plans for the purposes of determining the rating in subdivision (1) of this subsection, provided that the different arrangements are expected to result in substantial differences in claims costs.

b. Except as provided for in sub-subdivision a. of this subdivision, differences in rates charged for different health benefit plans shall be reasonable and reflect objective differences in plan design, but shall not permit differences in premium rates because of the case characteristics of groups assumed to select particular health benefit plans.

c. Small employer carriers shall apply allowable rating factors consistently with respect to all small employers.

(9) In any case where the small employer carrier uses industry as a case characteristic in establishing premium rates, the rate factor associated with any industry classification divided by the lowest rate factor associated with any other industry classification shall not exceed 1.2.

(b1) For all small employer health benefit plans that are not grandfathered health benefit plans and that are subject to this section, the premium rates are subject to all of the following provisions:

(1) A small employer carrier shall use a method to develop premiums for small employer group health benefit plans that are not grandfathered health plans which spreads financial risk across a large population and allows adjustments for only the following factors:

a. Age, except that the rate shall not vary by more than the ratio of three to one (3:1) for adults.

b. Whether the plan or coverage covers individual or family.

c. Geographic rating areas.

d. Tobacco use, except that the rate shall not vary by more than the ratio of one and two-tenths to one (1.2:1) due to tobacco use.

With respect to family coverage under a health benefit plan, the rating variations for age and tobacco use shall be applied based on the portion of premium that is attributable to each family member covered under the plan.

(2) A small employer carrier shall consider the claims experience of all enrollees in all small employer group health benefit plans that are not grandfathered health plans offered by the insurer in the small employer group market in this State to be members of a single risk pool. No small employer carrier shall consider claims experience of grandfathered health plans in developing the single risk pool.

(c) Repealed by Session Laws 1993, c. 529, s. 3.7.

(d) In connection with the offering for sale of any health benefit plan to a small employer, each small employer carrier shall make a reasonable disclosure, as part of its solicitation and sales materials, of the following and shall provide this information to the small employer upon request:

(1) Repealed by Session Laws 1993, c. 529, s. 3.7.

(2) Provisions concerning the small employer carrier's right to change premium rates and the factors other than claims experience that affect changes in premium rates.

(3) Provisions relating to renewability of policies and contracts.

(4) Provisions affecting any preexisting conditions provision.

(5) The benefits available and premiums charged under all health benefit plans for which the small employer is eligible.

(e) Each small employer carrier shall maintain at its principal place of business a complete and detailed description of its rating practices and renewal underwriting practices, including information and documentation that demonstrate that its rating methods and practices are based upon commonly accepted actuarial assumptions and are in accordance with sound actuarial principles.

(f) Each small employer carrier shall file with the Commissioner annually on or before March 15 an actuarial certification certifying that it is in compliance with this Act and that its rating methods are actuarially sound. The small employer carrier shall retain a copy of the certification at its principal place of business.

(g) A small employer carrier shall make the information and documentation described in subsection (e) of this section available to the Commissioner upon request. Except in cases of violations of this Act, the information is proprietary and trade secret information and is not subject to disclosure by the Commissioner to persons outside of the Department except as agreed to by the small employer carrier or as ordered by a court of competent jurisdiction. Nothing in this section affects the Commissioner's authority to approve rates before their use under G.S. 58-65-60(e) or G.S. 58-67-50(c).

(h) The provisions of subdivisions (a)(1), (3), and (5) and subsections (b) through (g) of this section apply to health benefit plans delivered, issued for delivery, renewed, or continued in this State or covering persons residing in this State on or after January 1, 1992. The provisions of subdivisions (a)(2) and (4) of this section apply to health benefit plans delivered, issued for delivery, renewed, or continued in this State or covering persons residing in this State on or after the date the plan becomes operational, as designated by the Commissioner. For purposes of this subsection, the date a health benefit plan is continued is the anniversary date of the issuance of the health benefit plan.

(i) A small employer carrier shall not modify the premium rate charged to a small group nongrandfathered health benefit plan or a small employer group member, including changes in rates related to the increasing age of a group member, for 12 months from the initial issue date or renewal date. (1991, c. 630, s. 1; 1993, c. 408, s. 6; c. 529, ss. 3.2, 3.7; 1993 (Reg. Sess., 1994), c. 569, ss. 7, 8; c. 678, ss. 24, 25; 1995, c. 238, s. 1; c. 507, s. 23A.1(b); 1995 (Reg. Sess., 1996), c. 669, s. 1; 1997-259, ss. 5, 6; 1998-211, ss. 9.1, 10; 1999-132, s. 4.1; 2001-334, ss. 3, 12.3; 2006-154, s. 7; 2013-357, ss. 2(f), (g), 3.)

§ 58-50-131. Premium rates for health benefit plans; approval authority; hearing.

(a)   No schedule of premium rates for coverage for a health benefit plan subject to this act, or any amendment to the schedule, shall be used in conjunction with any such health benefit plan until a copy of the schedule of premium rates or premium rate amendment has been filed with and approved by the Commissioner. Any schedule of premium rates or premium rate amendment filed under this section shall be established in accordance with G.S. 58-50-130(b). The schedule of premium rates shall not be excessive, unjustified, inadequate, or unfairly discriminatory and shall exhibit a reasonable relationship to the benefits provided by the contract of insurance. Each filing shall include a certification by an actuary who is a member of the American Academy of Actuaries and qualified to provide such certifications as described in the U.S. Qualifications Standards promulgated by the American Academy of Actuaries pursuant to its Code of Professional Conduct.

(b)   The Commissioner shall approve or disapprove a schedule of premium rates within 60 days of receipt of a complete filing. It shall be unlawful to use a schedule of premium rates until approved. If the Commissioner disapproves the filing, the Commissioner shall notify the filer, shall specify the reasons for disapproval, and shall provide an opportunity for refiling.

(c)   The Commissioner shall adopt rules as necessary or proper (i) to prevent the federal preemption of health insurance regulation in the State, (ii) to implement the provisions of this section, and (iii) to establish minimum standards for loss ratios of policies subject to this section in accordance with accepted actuarial principles and practices to assure that the benefits are reasonable in relation to the premium charged. The Commissioner shall adopt rules to require the submission of supporting data and any information that the Commissioner considers necessary or proper to determine whether the filed schedule of premium rates meets the standards set forth in this section. (2011-196, s. 4; 2013-199, s. 9.)

§ 58-50-135: Repealed by Session Laws 2013-357, s. 2(a), effective January 1, 2014.

§ 58-50-140: Repealed by Session Laws 2006-154, s. 9, effective July 23, 2006.

§ 58-50-145: Repealed by Session Laws 2006-154, s. 9, effective July 23, 2006.

§ 58-50-149. Limit on cessions to the Reinsurance Pool.

In addition to any individual or group previously reinsured in accordance with G.S. 58-50-150(g)(1), the Pool shall only reinsure a health benefit plan issued or delivered for original issue by a reinsuring carrier on or after October 1, 1995, if the health benefit plan provides coverage to a small employer with no more than 25 eligible employees, including self-employed individuals. Notwithstanding any other provision of law, the Pool shall cease to reinsure any individual or group on January 1, 2007. Reinsuring carriers as of that date shall continue to be governed by G.S. 58-50-135(b) and G.S. 58-50-150 until and through the termination of the Pool. (1995, c. 517, s. 29; 2006-154, s. 8.)

§ 58-50-150. North Carolina Small Employer Health Reinsurance Pool.

(a)   There is created a nonprofit entity to be known as the North Carolina Small Employer Health Reinsurance Pool. All carriers issuing or providing health benefit plans in this State from January 1, 1992, until the termination of the Pool, except any small employer carrier electing to be a risk-assuming carrier, are members of the Pool.

(b)   The members shall select the initial Board, subject to the Commissioner's approval. The Board shall consist of five members. There shall be no more than two members of the Board representing any one carrier. In determining voting rights at the organizational meeting, each member shall be entitled to vote in person or by proxy. Voting rights shall be based on net group health benefit plan premium derived from small employer business. The Board shall at all times, to the extent possible, include at least one domestic insurance company licensed to transact accident and health insurance, one HMO, one nonprofit hospital or medical service plan. Four of the members of the Board shall be small employer carriers. In approving selection of the Board, the Commissioner shall assure that all members are fairly represented.

(c)   If the initial Board is not elected at the organizational meeting, the Commissioner shall appoint the initial Board within 30 days of the organizational meeting.

(d)   As used in this section, "plan of operation" includes articles, bylaws, and operating rules of the Pool. Within 180 days after the appointment of the initial Board, the Board shall submit to the Commissioner a plan of operation and any amendments necessary or suitable to assume the fair, reasonable, and equitable administration of the Pool. The Commissioner shall approve the plan of operation if it assures the fair, reasonable, and equitable administration of the Pool and provides for the proportionate basis in accordance with the provisions of subsections (h) through (o) of this section. The plan of operation shall become effective upon approval in writing by the Commissioner consistent with the date on which the coverage under this section shall be made available. If the Board fails to submit a suitable plan of operation within 180 days after its appointment, or at any time thereafter fails to submit suitable amendments to the plan of operation, the Commissioner shall adopt and promulgate a plan of operation or amendment, as appropriate. The Commissioner shall amend any plan of operation he adopts, as necessary, after a plan of operation is submitted by the Board and approved by the Commissioner.

(e)   The plan of operation shall establish procedures for, among other things:

(1)   Handling and accounting of assets and moneys of the Pool, and for an annual financial reporting to the Commissioner.

(2)   Filling vacancies on the Board, subject to the Commissioner's approval.

(3)   Selecting an administering carrier and setting forth the powers and duties of the administering carrier.

(4)   Reinsuring risks in accordance with the provisions of this Act.

(5)   Collecting assessments from members subject to assessment to provide for claims reinsured by the Pool and for administrative expenses incurred or estimated to be incurred during the period for which the assessment is made.

(6) Any additional matters in the Board's discretion.

(f) The Pool has the general powers and authority granted under the laws of this State to insurance companies licensed to transact accident and health insurance except the power to issue coverage directly to enrollees, and, in addition, the specific authority to do all of the following:

(1) Enter into contracts that are necessary or proper to carry out the provisions and purposes of this Act, including the authority, with the Commissioner's approval, to enter into contracts with similar pools of other states for the joint performance of common administrative functions, or with persons or other organizations for the performance of administrative functions.

(2) Sue or be sued, including taking any legal actions necessary or proper for recovery of any assessments for, on behalf of, or against members.

(3) Take any legal action necessary to avoid the payment of improper, incorrect, or fraudulent claims against the Pool or the coverage reinsured by the Pool.

(4) Issue various reinsurance policies in accordance with the requirements of this section.

(5) Establish rules, conditions, and procedures pertaining to the reinsurance of members' risks by the Pool.

(6) Establish appropriate rates, rate schedules, rate adjustments, rate classifications, and any other actuarial functions appropriate to the Pool's operation.

(7) Assess members in accordance with the provisions of subsections (h) through (o) of this section; and make advance interim assessments that are reasonable and necessary for organizational and interim operating expenses. Any interim assessments shall be credited as offsets against any regular assessments due following the close of the Pool's fiscal year.

(8) Appoint from among members appropriate legal, actuarial, and other committees that are necessary to provide technical assistance in the operation of the Pool, policy, and other contract design, and any other function within the Pool's authority.

(9) Borrow money to effect the purposes of the Pool. Any notes or other evidence of indebtedness of the Pool not in default are legal investments for members and may be carried as admitted assets.

(g) Any member that elects to be a reinsuring carrier may cede, and the Pool shall reinsure the reinsuring carrier, subject to all of the following:

(1) The Pool shall reinsure any basic and standard health care plan originally issued or delivered for original issue by a reinsuring carrier on or after January 1, 1992, under the requirements in G.S. 58-50-125(d). With respect to a basic or standard health care plan, the Pool shall reinsure the level of coverage provided and, with respect to other plans, the Pool shall reinsure the level of coverage provided in the basic or standard health care plan up to, but not exceeding, the level of coverage provided under either the basic or standard health care plans. Small group business of reinsuring carriers in force before January 1, 1992, may not be ceded to the Pool until January 1, 1995, and then only if and when the Board determines that sufficient funding sources are available.

(2) The Pool shall reinsure eligible employees or their dependents or entire small employer groups according to the following:

a. With respect to eligible employees and their dependents who either (i) are employed by a small employer as of the date such employer's coverage by the member begins or (ii) are hired after the beginning of the employer's coverage by the member: The coverage may be reinsured within 60 days after the beginning of the eligible employees' or dependents' coverage under the plan.

b. With respect to eligible employees and their dependents, when the entire employer group is eligible for reinsurance: A small employer carrier may reinsure the entire employer group within 60 days after the beginning of the group's coverage under the plan.

c. With respect to any person reinsured, no reinsurance may be provided for a reinsured employee or dependent until five thousand dollars ($5,000) in benefit payments have been made for services provided during a calendar year for that reinsured employee or dependent, which payments would have been reimbursed through the reinsurance in the absence of the five thousand dollar ($5,000) deductible. The Boards shall review periodically the amount of the deductible and adjust it for inflation. In addition, the member shall retain ten percent (10%) of the next fifty thousand dollars ($50,000) of benefit payments during a calendar year and the Pool shall reinsure the remainder; provided that the members' liability under this section shall not exceed ten thousand dollars ($10,000) in any one calendar year with respect to any one person reinsured. The amount of the member's maximum liability shall be periodically reviewed by the Board and adjusted for inflation, as determined by the Board.

d. Reinsurance may be terminated for each reinsured employee or dependent on any plan anniversary.

e. Premium rates charged for reinsurance by the program to an HMO that is approved by the Secretary of Health and Human Services as a federally qualified health maintenance organization under 42 U.S.C. § 300 et seq., shall be reduced to reflect the restrictions and requirements of 42 U.S.C. § 300 et seq.

f. Every carrier subject to G.S. 58-50-130 shall apply its case management and claims handling techniques, including but not limited to utilization review, individual case management, preferred provider provisions, other managed care provisions or methods of operation, consistently with both reinsured and nonreinsured business.

g. Except as otherwise provided in this section, premium rates charged by the Pool for coverage reinsured by the Pool for that classification or group with similar case characteristics and coverage shall be established as follows:

1. One and one-half times the rate established by the Pool with respect to the eligible employees and their dependents of a small employer, all of whose coverage is reinsured with the Pool and who are reinsured in accordance with this section.

2. Five times the rate established by the Pool with respect to an eligible employee or dependent who is reinsured in accordance with this section.

(3) The Pool shall reinsure no more than the level of benefits provided in either the basic or standard health care plan established in accordance with G.S. 58-50-125.

(4) The Pool may issue different types and levels of reinsurance coverage, including stop-loss coverage; and the reinsurance premium shall be adjusted to reflect the type and level of reinsurance coverage issued.

(5) The reinsurance premium shall also be adjusted to reflect cost containment features of the plan of operation that have proven to be effective including, but not limited to: preferred provider provisions, utilization review of medical necessity of hospital and physician services, case management benefit alternatives, and other managed care provisions or methods of operation.

(h) Following the close of each fiscal year, the administering carrier shall determine the net premiums, the Pool expenses of administration, and the incurred losses for the year, taking into account investment income and other appropriate gains and losses. Health benefit plan premiums and benefits paid by a member that are less than an amount determined by the Board to justify the cost of collection shall not be considered for purposes of determining assessments. As used in this section, "net premiums" means health benefit plan premiums for insured plans but does not mean premiums or revenue received by a carrier for Medicare and Medicaid contracts.

(i) Any net losses for the year shall be recouped by assessments of members as follows:

(1) The Board shall determine an equitable assessment formula to recoup assessments of members that takes into consideration both overall market share of small employer carriers that are members of the Pool and the share of new business of the small employer carriers assumed during the preceding calendar year. For the first three years of operation of the Pool, if an assessment is based on an adjustment made, the assessment shall not be less than fifty percent (50%) nor more than one hundred fifty percent (150%) of the amount it would have been if the assessment were based on the proportional relationship of the small employer carrier's total premiums for small employer coverage written in the year to the total premiums of small employer coverage written by all small employer carriers in this State in the year. The Board shall also determine whether the assessment base used to determine assessments shall be made on a transitional basis or shall be permanent. In no event shall assessments exceed four percent (4%) of the total health benefit plan premium earned in this State from health benefit plans covering small employers of members during the calendar year coinciding or ending during the fiscal year of the Pool. The Board may change the assessment formula, including an assessment adjustment formula, if applicable, from time to time as appropriate.

(2) Health benefit plan premiums and benefits paid by a member that are less than an amount determined by the Board to justify the cost of collection

shall not be considered for purposes of determining assessments. For the purposes of this section, health benefit plan premiums earned by MEWAs and other benefit arrangements, to the extent permitted by ERISA, shall be established by adding paid health losses and administrative expenses.

(j) If the assessment level is inadequate, the Board may adjust reinsurance thresholds, retention levels, or consider other forms of reinsurance. After the first three full years of operations the Board shall report to the Commissioner on its experience, the effect on reinsurance and small group rates of individual ceding, and recommendations on additional funding sources, if needed. If legislative or other broader funding alternatives are not found, the Board may enter into negotiations with representatives of health care providers to resolve any deficit through reductions in future years' payment levels for reinsured plans. Any such recommendations shall take into account the findings of the actuarial study provided for in this subsection. An actuarial study shall be undertaken within the first three years of the Pool's operation to evaluate and measure the relative risks being assumed by differing types of small employer carriers as a result of this Act. The study shall be developed by three actuaries appointed by the Commissioner, with one representing risk assuming carriers, one representing reinsuring carriers, and one from within the Department.

(k) Subject to the approval of the Commissioner, the Board may make an adjustment to the assessment formula for any reinsuring carrier that is an HMO approved as a federally qualified HMO by the Secretary of Health and Human Services under 42 U.S.C. § 300 for restrictions placed on them other than those for which an adjustment has already been made in subsection (b)(2) or (b)(5) of this section that are not imposed on other small group carriers.

(l) If assessments exceed actual losses and administrative expenses of the Pool, the excess shall be held at interest and used by the Board to offset future losses or to reduce Pool premiums. As used in this subsection, "future losses" includes reserves for incurred but not reported claims.

(m) The Board shall determine annually each member's proportion of participation in the Pool based on financial statements and other reports that the Board considers to be necessary and requires that the member files with the Board. All carriers shall report, to the Board, claims payments made and administrative expenses incurred in this State on an annual basis and on a form prescribed by the Commissioner.

(n) The plan of operation shall provide for the imposition of an interest penalty for late payment of assessments.

(o) The Board may abate or defer, in whole or in part, the assessment of a member if, in the Board's opinion, payment of the assessment would endanger the member's ability to fulfill its contractual obligations. In the event an assessment against a member is abated or deferred in whole or in part, the amount by which the assessment is abated or deferred may be assessed against the other members in a manner consistent with the basis for assessments set forth in this section. The member receiving the abatement or deferment shall remain liable to the Pool for the deficiency.

(p) Neither the participation in the Pool as members, the establishment of rates, forms, or procedures, nor any other joint or collective action required by this Act shall be the basis of any legal action, criminal or civil liability, or penalty against the Pool or any of its members.

(q) Any person or member made a party to any action, suit, or proceeding because the person or member serves or served on the Board or on a committee or is or was an officer or employee of the Pool shall be held harmless and be indemnified by the Pool against all liability and costs, including the amounts of judgments, settlements, fines, or penalties, and expenses and reasonable attorneys' fees incurred in connection with the action, suit, or proceeding. However, the indemnification shall not be provided on any matter in which the person or member is finally adjudged in the action, suit, or proceeding to have committed a breach of duty involving gross negligence, dishonesty, willful misfeasance, or reckless disregard of the responsibilities of service or office. Costs and expenses of the indemnification shall be prorated among and paid for by all members.

(r) The Pool is exempt from the taxes imposed by Article 8B of Chapter 105 of the General Statutes. (1991, c. 630, s. 1; 1993, c. 408, s. 7; 2005-223, s. 5; 2006-154, s. 12.)

§ 58-50-151. (Recodified as § 58-51-116 effective July 1, 2002) ERISA plans may not require Medicaid to pay first.

An employee benefit plan as defined in ERISA shall not include any provision which, because an individual is provided or is eligible for benefits or service pursuant to a State plan under Title XIX of the Social Security Act (Medicaid), has the effect of limiting or excluding coverage or payment for any health care for that individual under the terms of the employee benefit plan, provided that the individual is one who would otherwise be covered or entitled to benefits or services under the employee benefit plan. (1993, c. 321, s. 238.1.)

§§ 58-50-155, 58-50-156: Repealed by Session Laws 2013-357, s. 2(a), effective January 1, 2014.

Part 6. North Carolina Health Insurance Risk Pool.

§ 58-50-175. (Repealed effective January 1, 2017 - see note) Definitions.

The following definitions apply to this Part:

(1) "Administrator" - The Pool Administrator selected by the Executive Director in accordance with this Part.

(2) "Benefit plan" - The coverage offered by the Pool to eligible individuals.

(3) "Board" - The Board of Directors of the Pool.

(4) "Commissioner" - The Commissioner of Insurance of North Carolina or the Commissioner's authorized designee.

(5) "Covered person" - Any individual resident of this State, excluding dependents, who is receiving or is eligible to receive medical care benefits from any insurer.

(6) "Creditable coverage" - The same meaning as defined in G.S. 58-68-30(c)(1).

(7) "Dependent" - A resident spouse, an unmarried child under the age of 19 years, a child who is a full-time student under the age of 23 years and who is financially dependent upon the parent or guardian, a child who is over 18 years of age and for whom a person may be obligated to pay child support, or a child of any age who is disabled and dependent upon the parent or guardian.

(8) "Executive Director" - The individual selected by a majority vote of the Board members and hired to serve as the Executive Director of the Pool.

(9) "Federally defined eligible individual" - The same meaning as the defined term "eligible individual" in G.S. 58-68-60(b).

(9a) "Fund." - The North Carolina Health Insurance Risk Pool Fund.

(10) "Health insurance coverage" - The same meaning as defined in G.S. 58-68-25(a)(5) but does not include benefits described in G.S. 58-68-25(b).

(11) "Insurance arrangement" - The plan, program, contract, or other arrangement through which medical care is provided by an employer to its officers or employees but does not include medical care covered through an insurer.

(12) "Insured" - An individual who is eligible to receive benefits from the Pool.

(13) "Insurer" - Any entity, other than the Pool, that provides medical care benefits, including excess or stop-loss insurance, that covers medical care or administers medical care on any individual in this State. For the purposes of this Part, insurer includes:

a. An insurance company;

b. A hospital or medical service corporation;

c. A health maintenance organization;

d. A multiple employer welfare arrangement;

e. A third-party administrator or claims processor; and

f. Any other nongovernmental entity providing a health benefit plan subject to State insurance regulation.

Insurer does not include an entity to the extent the entity provides excepted benefits as defined in G.S. 58-68-25(b).

(14) "Medical care" - All of the following:

a. The diagnosis, cure, mitigation, treatment, or prevention of disease, or amounts paid for the purpose of affecting any structure or function of the body;

b. Transportation primarily for and essential to medical care referred to in sub-subdivision a. of this subdivision; and

c. Insurance covering medical care referred to in sub-subdivisions a. and b. of this subdivision.

(15) "Plan of Operation" - The articles, bylaws, and operating rules and procedures adopted by the Board in accordance with this Part.

(16) "Pool" - The North Carolina Health Insurance Risk Pool.

(17) "Provider" - An individual or entity that provides medical care to individuals residing in this State.

(18) "Resident" - An individual who has legal status in the United States and who:

a. Has been legally domiciled in this State for a period of at least 30 days, except that for a federally defined eligible individual, there shall not be a 30-day requirement;

b. Is legally domiciled in this State on the date of application to the Pool and who is eligible for enrollment in the Pool as a result of the Health Insurance Portability and Accountability Act of 1996; or

c. Is legally domiciled in this State on the date of application to the Pool and is eligible for the credit for health insurance costs under section 35 of the Internal Revenue Code of 1986.

(19) Recodified as G.S. 58-50-175(9a).

(20) "Trade Adjustment Assistance Program" (TAA) - Title II of the Trade Act of 2002, P.L. 107-210. (2007-532, s. 1.1; 2008-118, s. 3.2(a); 2013-410, s. 28.5(d).)

§ 58-50-180. (Repealed effective January 1, 2017 - see note) Risk Pool established; board of directors; plan of operation.

(a) There is hereby created a nonprofit entity to be known as the North Carolina Health Insurance Risk Pool. Notwithstanding that the Pool may be supported in whole or in part from State funds, the Pool is not an instrumentality of the State. The Pool shall operate under the supervision and control of the Board.

(b) The Board of the North Carolina Health Insurance Risk Pool shall consist of the Commissioner, who shall serve as an ex officio nonvoting member of the Board, and 11 members appointed as follows:

(1) One member who represents an insurer, as appointed by the Governor.

(2) Two members of the general public who are not employed by or affiliated with an insurance company or plan, group hospital, or other health care provider and can reasonably be expected to qualify for coverage in the Pool. Members of the general public include individuals whose only affiliation with health insurance or health care coverage is as a covered member. The two members of the general public shall be appointed by the General Assembly, as follows:

a. One member upon the recommendation of the President Pro Tempore of the Senate.

b. One member upon the recommendation of the Speaker of the House of Representatives.

(3) Eight members appointed by the Commissioner, as follows:

a. One insurer who sells individual health insurance policies.

b. One who represents the insurance industry, as recommended by the insurer who covers the largest number of persons in the State.

c. One who is licensed to sell health insurance in this State.

d. Two who represent the medical provider community, one as recommended by the North Carolina Medical Society, and one as recommended by the North Carolina Hospital Association.

e. One who represents business, as recommended by the North Carolina Chamber.

f. One who represents small business, as recommended by the National Federation of Independent Business.

g. One who is either a health policy researcher or a health economist with experience relating to the operation of health insurance risk pools.

(c) The initial appointments by the Governor and the General Assembly upon the recommendation of the Speaker of the House of Representatives and the President Pro Tempore of the Senate shall serve a term of three years. The initial appointments by the Commissioner under sub-subdivisions a., b., and d. of subdivision (b)(3) of this section shall be for a term of two years. The initial appointments by the Commissioner under sub-subdivisions c., e., f., and g. of subdivision (b)(3) of this section shall be for a term of one year. All succeeding appointments shall be for terms of three years. Members shall not serve for more than three successive terms.

A Board member's term shall continue until the member's successor is appointed by the original appointing authority. Vacancies shall be filled by the appointing authority for the unexpired portion of the term in which they occur. A Board member may be removed by the appointing authority for cause.

The Board shall meet at least quarterly upon the call of the chair. A majority of the total membership of the Board shall constitute a quorum.

The Commissioner shall appoint a chair to serve for the initial two years of the Plan's operation. Subsequent chairs shall be elected by a majority vote of the Board members and shall serve for two-year terms. Board members shall receive travel allowances under G.S. 138-5 when traveling to and from meetings of the Board or for official business of the Pool, but shall not receive any per diem under subdivision (a)(1) of that section.

(d) The Board shall submit to the Commissioner a Plan of Operation for the Pool and any amendments necessary or suitable to assure the fair, reasonable, and equitable administration of the Plan of Operation. The Plan of Operation shall become effective upon approval in writing by the Commissioner consistent with the date on which the coverage under this Part must be made available. If the Board fails to submit a suitable Plan of Operation within 180 days after the appointment of the Board, or at any time thereafter fails to submit suitable amendments to the Plan of Operation, the Commissioner shall adopt temporary rules necessary or advisable to effectuate the provisions of this section. The rules shall continue in force until modified by the Commissioner or superseded by a Plan of Operation submitted by the Board and approved by the Commissioner. The Plan of Operation shall:

(1)   Establish procedures for operation of the Pool.

(2)   Establish procedures for selecting a Pool Administrator in accordance with G.S. 58-50-185.

(3)   Establish procedures to create a fund for administrative expenses, which shall be managed by the Board.

(4)   Establish procedures for the collection, handling, disbursing, accounting, and auditing of assets, monies, and claims of the Pool and the Pool Administrator.

(5)   Develop and implement a program to publicize the existence of the Pool, the eligibility requirements, procedures for enrollment, and availability of State premium subsidies and to maintain public awareness of the Pool.

(6)   Establish procedures under which applicants and participants may have grievances reviewed by a grievance committee appointed by the Executive Director in accordance with G.S. 58-50-230.

(7)   Establish procedures for identifying and confirming income levels of applicants for Pool coverage who are eligible to receive a State premium subsidy, if a State premium subsidy is available.

(8)   Provide for other matters as may be necessary and proper for the execution of the Executive Director's powers, duties, and obligations under this Part.

(e)   The Pool shall have the general powers and authority granted under the laws of this State to health insurers and the specific authority to do all of the following:

(1)   Enter into contracts as are necessary or proper to carry out the provisions and purposes of this Part, including the authority, with the approval of

the Executive Director acting upon the approval or authorization of the Board, to enter into contracts with similar plans of other states for the joint performance of common administrative functions or with persons or other organizations for the performance of administrative functions.

(2) Sue or be sued.

(3) Take legal action as necessary to:

a. Avoid the payment of improper claims against the Pool or the coverage provided by or through the Plan.

b. Recover any amounts erroneously or improperly paid by the Plan.

c. Recover any amounts paid by the Pool as a result of mistake of fact or law.

d. Recover other amounts due the Pool.

(4) Establish rates and rate schedules in accordance with this Part.

(4a) Provide premium subsidies for individuals with incomes up to three hundred percent (300%) of the federal poverty guidelines where the Board deems it is fiscally prudent to do so. Premium subsidies may come from the following sources:

a. Federal grants made to the Pool for premium subsidies.

b. The Pool's own funds, not to exceed the amount of the most recent year for which the Pool received a federal grant award under sub-subdivision a. of this subdivision.

(5) Issue policies of insurance in accordance with the requirements of this Part.

(6) Appoint appropriate legal, actuarial, and other committees as necessary to provide technical assistance in the operation of the Pool, policy, and other contract design, and any other function within the Pool's authority.

(7) Establish policies, conditions, and procedures for reinsuring risks of participating health insurers, as defined in G.S. 58-68-25(a), desiring to issue

Pool coverage in their own name. Provision of reinsurance shall not subject the Pool to any of the capital or surplus requirements, if any, otherwise applicable to reinsurers.

(8)   Employ and fix the compensation of employees.

(9)   Prepare and distribute certificate of eligibility forms and enrollment instruction forms to insurance producers and to the general public.

(10)   Provide for reinsurance for the Pool.

(11)   Issue additional types of health insurance policies to provide optional coverage, including Medicare supplemental insurance coverage.

(12)   Provide for and employ cost containment measures and requirements including preadmission screening, second surgical opinion, concurrent utilization review, disease management, individual case management, health and wellness programs including a smoking cessation initiative, and other commonly used benefit plan design features for the purpose of making health insurance coverage offered by the Pool more cost-effective.

(13)   Design, utilize, contract, or otherwise arrange for the delivery of cost-effective health care services, including establishing or contracting with preferred provider organizations, health maintenance organizations, and other limited network provider arrangements.

(14)   Adopt bylaws, policies, and procedures as may be necessary or convenient for the implementation of this Part and the operation of the Pool.

(15)   Enter into contracts with the United States Department of Health and Human Services as is necessary or proper to administer the federal high risk health insurance pool established by the United States Congress in Public Law 111-148, the Patient Protection and Affordable Care Act, as amended.

(f)   The Executive Director, with the approval of the Board, shall operate the Pool in a manner so that the estimated cost of providing the benefit plans offered during any calendar year is not anticipated to exceed the total income the Pool expects to receive from policy premiums and other revenue available to the Pool. The Board may impose a cap on enrollment or may suspend enrollment for an indefinite period if the Board finds that estimated costs are anticipated to exceed income, except that any enrollment cap or suspension shall not apply to federally defined eligible individuals who are eligible to enroll in the Pool pursuant to G.S. 58-50-195(a)(5).

(g) The Executive Director shall make an annual report to the Speaker of the House of Representatives, the President Pro Tempore of the Senate, the Commissioner, the Joint Legislative Oversight Committee on Health and Human Services, and the Committee on Employee Hospital and Medical Benefits. The report shall summarize the activities of the Pool in the preceding calendar year, including the net written and earned premiums, benefit plan enrollment, the expense of administration, and the paid and incurred losses.

(h) Neither the Board nor the employees of the Pool are liable for any obligations of the Pool. There shall be no liability on the part of, and no cause of action of any nature shall arise against, the Pool or its agents or employees, the Board, the Executive Director, or the Commissioner or the Commissioner's representatives for any action taken by them in good faith in the performance of their powers and duties under this Part.

(i) The members of the Board are public servants under G.S. 138A-3(30) and are subject to the provisions of Chapter 138A of the General Statutes. (2007-532, s. 1.1; 2008-124, ss. 6.1, 6.2; 2009-286, s. 1; 2009-570, s. 8(a); 2010-31, s. 24.3; 2011-58, ss. 1, 2; 2011-291, s. 2.7; 2013-410, s. 28.5(d).)

§ 58-50-185. (Repealed effective January 1, 2017 - see note) Administrator.

(a) The Executive Director, with the approval or authorization of the Board, shall select through a competitive bidding process one or more insurers to administer the Pool. The Executive Director shall evaluate bids submitted based on criteria established by the Board. The criteria shall allow for the comparison of information about each bidding administrator and selection of a Pool Administrator based on at least the following:

(1) Proven ability to handle health insurance coverage to individuals.

(2) Efficiency and timeliness of the claim processing procedures.

(3) Estimated total charges for administering the Pool.

(4) Ability to apply effective cost containment programs and procedures and to administer the Pool in a cost-efficient manner.

(5) Financial condition and stability.

(6) Evidence of authority to provide third-party administrative services in North Carolina.

(b) The Administrator shall serve for a period specified in the contract between the Pool and the Administrator subject to removal for cause and subject to any terms, conditions, and limitations of the contract between the Pool and the Administrator. At least one year before the expiration of each period of service by an Administrator, the Executive Director shall invite eligible entities, including the current Administrator, unless the current Administrator was removed for cause, to submit bids to serve as the Administrator. Selection of the Administrator for the succeeding period shall be made at least six months before the end of the current period.

(c) The Administrator shall perform such functions relating to the Pool as may be assigned to it, including:

(1) Verification of eligibility.

(2) Payment of claims.

(3) Establishment of a premium billing procedure for collection of premiums from individuals covered under the Pool.

(4) Other necessary functions to assure timely payment of benefits to covered persons under the Pool.

(d) The Administrator shall submit regular reports to the Executive Director and the Board regarding the operation of the Pool. The contract between the Pool and the Administrator shall specify the frequency, content, and form of the report.

(e) Following the close of each calendar year, the Administrator shall determine net written and earned premiums, the expense of administration, and the paid and incurred losses for the year and report this information to the Executive Director and the Board on a form prescribed by the Executive Director.

(f)   The Administrator shall be paid as provided in the contract between the Pool and the Administrator. (2007-532, s. 1.1; 2008-124, s. 6.3; 2013-410, s. 28.5(d).)

§ 58-50-190. (Repealed effective January 1, 2017 - see note) Risk Pool rates and policy forms.

(a)   The Pool shall adopt and modify, as appropriate, rates, rate schedules, rate adjustments, expense allowances, agent referral fees, claim reserve formulas, and any other actuarial function appropriate to the operation of the Pool. Rates and rate schedules may be adjusted for appropriate factors such as age, sex, and geographic variation in claim cost and shall take into consideration appropriate rating factors in accordance with established actuarial and underwriting practices.

(b)   The Pool shall determine the standard risk rate by considering the premium rates charged by other insurers offering health insurance coverage to individuals. The standard risk rate shall be established using reasonable actuarial techniques and shall reflect anticipated experience and expenses for the coverage. Pool rates shall be one hundred thirty-five percent (135%) to one hundred seventy-five percent (175%) of rates established as applicable for individual standard rates and shall be adjusted annually, at the time of annual renewal.

(c)   The Executive Director, with the approval of the Board and the Commissioner, may develop incentive programs with premium discounts. The Pool may provide for premium surcharges for covered individuals who are smokers. Premium surcharge rates shall be established by the Executive Director, in collaboration with the Board, subject to the approval of the Commissioner.

(d)   Provider reimbursement rates under Pool coverage shall be limited to the rates allowed for providers under the Medicare Program for those services covered by Medicare. The Board shall establish reimbursement rates for services for which Medicare has not established an allowed rate. Providers rendering medical care to an insured shall accept payment of the amount established under this subsection, including any applicable deductible, coinsurance, or co-payment amounts, as payment in full for services rendered.

(e) The Pool shall submit all premium rates and premium rate schedules and amendments to the Commissioner for approval. The Pool shall not use any premium rates, premium rate schedules, or amendments to the rates and schedules unless the Commissioner has approved them. The Commissioner, in evaluating the premium rates and premium rate schedules, shall consider the factors provided in this section. The Pool shall provide all individuals enrolled in the Pool with at least 45 days' notice of any change in Pool premium rates or premium rate schedules.

(f) The Pool shall submit all policy forms, riders, endorsements, and applications for coverage to the Commissioner for approval. The Pool shall not use any policy forms, riders, endorsements, or applications for coverages unless the Commissioner has approved them. Except for any provisions that are specifically treated otherwise under this Part, the provisions of this Chapter that apply to benefit plans and policy forms of health insurers generally shall apply to the benefit plans offered and policy forms used by the Pool. (2007-532, s. 1.1; 2011-58, s. 3; 2013-410, s. 28.5(d).)

§ 58-50-195. (Repealed effective January 1, 2017 - see note) Eligibility for Pool coverage.

(a) Any individual who is and continues to be a resident of this State is eligible for Pool coverage if the individual provides evidence of any of the following:

(1) A notice of rejection or refusal to issue substantially similar health insurance coverage for health reasons by an insurer. A rejection or refusal by an insurer offering only stop-loss, excess loss, or reinsurance coverage with respect to the applicant is not sufficient evidence of eligibility.

(2) An offer to issue health insurance coverage only with a conditional rider that limits coverage for the individual's high-risk medical condition.

(3) A refusal by an insurer to issue health insurance coverage except at a rate exceeding the Pool rate.

(4) A diagnosis of the individual with one of the medical or health conditions listed by the Board in accordance with this section. An individual diagnosed with

one or more of these conditions is eligible for Pool coverage without applying for other health insurance coverage.

(5) Qualification as a federally defined eligible individual, whether or not currently covered by an insurer under that qualification.

(6) An individual who is legally domiciled in this State and is eligible for the credit for health insurance costs under the Trade Adjustment Assistance Reform Act of 2002, section 35 of the Internal Revenue Code of 1986. Each dependent of an individual who is eligible for Pool coverage under this subdivision shall also be eligible for Pool coverage.

(7) The individual has current individual health insurance coverage at a rate exceeding the Pool rate.

(8) The individual is eligible for and has not exhausted current COBRA health insurance coverage at a rate exceeding the Pool rate and provides evidence of eligibility for Pool coverage under any of the subdivisions (1) through (4) of this subsection.

(b) The Board, upon recommendation of the Executive Director, shall adopt a list of medical or health conditions for which a person shall be eligible for Pool coverage under subdivision (a)(4) of this section. The Board may amend the list as the Board considers appropriate.

(c) An individual is not eligible for coverage under the Pool if:

(1) The individual has or obtains medical care benefits substantially similar to or more comprehensive than the benefit plan offered by the Pool, or would be eligible to have coverage if the person elected to obtain it, except that:

a. An individual may maintain other coverage for the period of time the individual is satisfying any preexisting condition waiting period under a Pool policy; and

b. An individual may maintain Pool coverage for the period of time the individual is satisfying a preexisting condition waiting period under another health insurance policy intended to replace the Pool policy.

(2) The individual is determined to be eligible for enrollment in the State Medical Assistance Plan or in Medicare, unless the Pool offers Medicare supplemental insurance coverage.

(3) The individual has previously terminated Pool coverage unless 12 months have lapsed since the termination, except that this subdivision shall not apply with respect to an applicant who is a federally defined eligible individual or to an applicant eligible for or receiving benefits under the Trade Adjustment Assistance Program.

(4) The individual is an inmate or resident of a public institution, except that this subdivision shall not apply with respect to an applicant who is a federally defined eligible individual.

(5) The individual's premiums are paid for or reimbursed under any government-sponsored program or by any government agency or health care provider, except as an otherwise qualifying full-time employee, or dependent thereof, of a government agency or health care provider. This subdivision shall not apply for individuals receiving benefits under the Trade Adjustment Assistance Program or to individuals receiving premium subsidies made available by the State based on individual income levels.

(6) The individual has in effect on the date Pool coverage takes effect health insurance coverage from an insurer or insurance arrangement.

(d) Coverage under the Pool shall cease:

(1) On the date an individual is no longer a resident of this State.

(2) On the date an individual requests coverage to end.

(3) Upon the death of the covered individual.

(4) On the date State law requires cancellation of the Pool policy.

(5) At the option of the Pool, 30 days after the Pool makes any inquiry concerning the individual's eligibility or residence to which the individual does not reply.

(6) Because the individual has failed to make the payments required under this Part.

(7) Because the individual has performed an act or practice that constitutes fraud or made an intentional misrepresentation of material fact under the terms of the coverage.

(e) Except as provided in subsection (d) of this section, an individual who ceases to meet the eligibility requirements of this section may be terminated at the end of the Pool policy period for which the necessary premiums have been paid. (2007-532, s. 1.1; 2008-124, s. 6.4; 2011-58, s. 4; 2013-410, s. 28.5(d).)

§ 58-50-200. (Repealed effective January 1, 2017 - see note) Unfair referral to Pool.

It is an unfair trade practice under Article 63 of this Chapter and under Chapter 75 of the General Statutes for an employer, an insurer, an insurance producer, as defined in G.S. 58-33-10(7), or a third-party administrator to refer an individual employee to the Pool or arrange for an individual employee to apply to the Pool for the purpose of separating that employee from a group medical care benefit plan provided in connection with the employee's employment. This section shall not prohibit an insurer or insurance producer from informing an individual of other coverage options, including coverage provided by the Pool. (2007-532, s. 1.1; 2013-410, s. 28.5(d).)

§ 58-50-205. (Repealed effective January 1, 2017 - note) Minimum Pool benefits.

(a) The Pool shall offer at least two types of benefit plans for individuals eligible under G.S. 58-50-195, including preferred provider organizations with different levels of deductibles and cost-sharing, and at least one choice of a health savings account. The covered services and benefit levels may vary between the types of benefit plans, but at least two types of benefit plans must, at a minimum, cover the benefits and services outlined in the National Association of Insurance Commissioners' (NAIC) Model Health Pool for Uninsurable Individuals Act and be consistent with comprehensive coverage generally available to persons who are eligible for individual health insurance other than Medicare. All benefit plans offered by the Pool shall include disease or case management services.

(b) The Board, upon the recommendation of the Executive Director, shall adopt rules regarding the lifetime limits and per individual combined coinsurance and deductibles for the health insurance products offered by the Pool. The initial rules shall include not less than one million dollars ($1,000,000) lifetime limit and a combined annual limit of up to five thousand dollars ($5,000) per individual on coinsurance and deductibles. The Board, upon recommendation of the Executive Director, shall adopt rules adjusting these limitations at least once every five years to reflect changes in the medical component of the Consumer Price Index. When adopting or adjusting lifetime limits the Board may establish categories of diseases that may be more seriously impacted by the lifetime limits than other diseases covered under the Pool. (2007-532, s. 1.1; 2013-410, s. 28.5(d).)

§ 58-50-210. (Repealed effective January 1, 2017 - see note) Preexisting conditions.

(a) Except as otherwise provided by law, Pool coverage shall exclude charges or expenses incurred during the first six months following the effective date of coverage as to any condition for which medical advice, care, or treatment was recommended or received as to such conditions during the 12-month period immediately preceding the effective date of coverage, except that no preexisting condition exclusion shall be applied to a federally defined eligible individual or an individual who is eligible for the Pool because of his or her eligibility for the credit for health insurance costs under the Trade Adjustment Assistance Reform Act of 2002, section 35 of the Internal Revenue Code of 1986, pursuant to G.S. 58-50-195(a)(6).

(b) Repealed by Session Laws 2008-124, s. 6.5, effective October 1, 2008.

(c) The period of any preexisting condition exclusion shall be reduced by the aggregate of the periods of creditable coverage, if any, applicable as of the enrollment date. Credit for having satisfied some or all of the preexisting condition waiting period under previous creditable coverage, as defined in G.S. 58-51-17(a)(1), shall be provided in accordance with G.S. 58-51-17. (2007-532, s. 1.1; 2008-124, s. 6.5; 2011-58, s. 5; 2013-410, s. 28.5(d).)

§ 58-50-215. (Repealed effective January 1, 2017 - see note) Nonduplication of benefits.

(a) The Pool shall be payor of last resort of benefits whenever any other benefit or source of third-party payment is available. Benefits otherwise payable under coverage shall be reduced by all amounts paid or payable through any other medical care benefits and by all hospital and medical expenses paid or payable under any workers' compensation coverage notwithstanding any provision of law to the contrary, automobile medical payment, or liability insurance, whether provided on the basis of fault or no-fault, and by any hospital or medical benefits paid or payable under or provided pursuant to any State or federal law or program.

(b) The Pool shall have a cause of action against an eligible person for the recovery of the amount of benefits paid that are not for covered expenses. Benefits due from the Pool may be reduced or refused as a setoff against any amount recoverable under this subsection. (2007-532, s. 1.1; 2013-410, s. 28.5(d).)

§ 58-50-220: Reserved for future codification purposes.

§ 58-50-225. (Repealed effective January 1, 2017 - see note) North Carolina Health Insurance Risk Pool Fund.

(a) The North Carolina Health Insurance Risk Pool Fund is established and consists of the following revenue:

(1) Premiums, fees, charges, rebates, refunds, and any other receipts occurring or arising in connection with the Pool.

(2) The revenue transferred to the Fund under G.S. 105-228.5B.

(3) Gifts, grants, and other appropriations.

(4) Any interest earned by the Fund.

(b)   Disbursements from the Fund shall include the amounts required to pay the claims, benefits, and administrative costs as may be determined by the Executive Director and the Board.

(c)   (Repealed effective January 1, 2015) For the purposes of providing the funds necessary to carry out the powers and duties of the Pool, effective July 1, 2008, the Teachers' and State Employees' Comprehensive Major Medical Plan and any successor Plan shall pay an annual surcharge to the North Carolina Health Insurance Risk Pool Fund in the amount of one dollar and fifty cents ($1.50) per member per year based on enrollment of active employee Plan members and their dependents covered under the Plan. The final surcharge shall be paid to the Pool Fund for the 2013-2014 State fiscal year and shall be paid in quarterly installments rather than in one annual payment. Such installments shall be paid to the Pool Fund 60 days after the close of each quarter and shall be due on December 1, 2013, March 1, 2014, June 1, 2014, and September 1, 2014. The Pool shall transfer to the General Fund any funds in excess of the reserve amount established under G.S. 58-50-260(d)(9) that remain in the Pool Fund following the final dissolution of the Pool. (2007-532, ss. 1.1, 6; 2008-118, ss. 3.2(b), (g); 2013-410, ss. 28.5(b), (c),(d).)

§ 58-50-230. (Repealed effective January 1, 2017 - see note) Complaint procedures.

An applicant or participant in coverage from the Pool is entitled to have complaints against the Pool reviewed by a grievance committee appointed by the Executive Director. Members of the Board shall not serve on the grievance committee. The grievance process shall comply with G.S. 58-50-62. The grievance committee shall report to the Board after completion of the review of each complaint. The Executive Director shall retain all written complaints regarding the Pool at least until the third anniversary of the date the Pool received the complaint. Independent review of an appeal decision upholding a noncertification or a second-level grievance review decision upholding a noncertification shall be subject to review pursuant to Part 4 of this Article. (2007-532, s. 1.1; 2013-410, s. 28.5(d).)

§ 58-50-235. (Repealed effective January 1, 2017 - see note) Audit.

An audit of the Pool shall be conducted annually under the oversight of the State Auditor. The cost of the audit shall be reimbursed to the State Auditor from the Fund. (2007-532, s. 1.1; 2008-118, s. 3.2(c) ; 2013-410, s. 28.5(d).)

§ 58-50-240. (Repealed effective January 1, 2017 - see note) Taxation.

The Pool established under this Part is exempt from any and all State taxes. (2007-532, s. 1.1; 2013-410, s. 28.5(d).)

§ 58-50-245. (Repealed effective January 1, 2017 - see note) Rules.

The Board and the Commissioner may adopt rules pursuant to Chapter 150B of the General Statutes, including temporary rules, to implement this Part. (2007-532, s. 1.1; 2013-410, s. 28.5(d).)

§ 58-50-250. (Repealed effective January 1, 2017 - see note) Collective action.

The establishment of rates, forms, or procedures and any other joint or collective action required by this Part may not be the basis of any legal action or criminal or civil liability or penalty against the Pool or any insurer. (2007-532, s. 1.1; 2013-410, s. 28.5(d).)

§ 58-50-255. (Repealed effective January 1, 2017 - see note) Pool financing; Board reporting.

(a) The Board shall monitor methods of financing the Pool to ensure a stable funding source and allow for its continued operation. This monitoring shall include supplementary sources of funding, such as funds obtained from public and private not-for-profit foundations, or other appropriate and available State or non-State funds. The Board shall also review on a regular basis:

(1) The number of individuals in this State who are uninsured as of a date certain because of high-risk conditions.

(2) The number of uninsured individuals who would qualify for coverage under the Pool based on G.S. 58-50-195 and its Plan of Operation.

(3) The cost of coverage under each of the health insurance plans developed by the Board, including administrative costs.

(4) The status of a request by the State to the Centers for Medicare and Medicaid Services for approval of the North Carolina Health Insurance Risk Pool to be considered an acceptable "alternative mechanism" under the federal Health Insurance Portability and Accountability Act in accordance with 45 C.F.R. § 148.128(e).

(5) Methods for providing a premium subsidy on a sliding scale basis for individuals with incomes up to three hundred percent (300%) of the federal poverty guidelines.

(b) The Board shall report its findings and recommendations to the General Assembly on March 1, 2008, and annually thereafter. (2007-532, s. 1.1; 2013-410, s. 28.5(d).)

§ 58-50-260. (Repealed effective January 1, 2017 - see note) Dissolution of Pool.

(a) Insurance operations of the Pool under this Part shall sunset on January 1, 2014.

(b) In order to be handled in the regular course of business, rather than under subsection (f) of this section, all invoices for medical, pharmacy, and any other services provided under this Part must be submitted no later than 90 days after the sunset of insurance operations of the Pool under subsection (a) of this section.

(c) In order to be handled in the regular course of business, rather than under subsection (f) of this section, all appeals and grievances under this Part must be submitted no later than 90 days after the sunset of insurance operations of the Pool under subsection (a) of this section.

(d) On or before September 1, 2013, the Pool shall submit to the Commissioner a plan for dissolution of the Pool. The plan shall address the following:

(1) Continuity of care for those participants in the Pool that are inpatient at the time of sunset of insurance operations of the Pool under subsection (a) of this section.

(2) Continuation of administrative services following the sunset of the Pool's insurance operations.

(3) Closing the Pool's bank and investment accounts.

(4) Cessation of premium subsidy programs.

(5) Performance and completion by June 30, 2014, of a final audit by the State Auditor and submission of the Pool's annual report to the State.

(6) A plan for maintenance of the Pool's books and records pursuant to G.S. 58-56-16 by the Pool's final third-party administrator.

(7) Efforts to secure contingency funding should the Pool's operations so require.

(8) Final dissolution of the Pool.

(9) The deposit and management of funding held in reserve following final dissolution of the Pool to be used in connection with actions by or against the Pool that are timely filed, as provided in subsection (f) of this section.

(10) Other matters that the Commissioner may reasonably require.

(e) The plan of dissolution for the Pool shall become effective upon approval in writing by the Commissioner. The Commissioner shall approve the plan of dissolution if he or she determines that the plan is suitable to assure the fair, reasonable, and equitable dissolution of the Pool and that the plan complies with subsection (d) of this section.

(f) Notwithstanding any longer statute of limitations provided under law for an action, all actions by or against the Pool must be filed on or before one year following the sunset of insurance operations of the Pool under subsection (a) of this section. After final dissolution of the Pool, the Pool's liability for insurance benefits, provider or vendor invoices, and all other matters shall be limited to the reserve amount established under subdivision (9) of subsection (d) of this section, less the costs of resolving the claims by or against the Pool.

(g) Any funds in excess of the reserve amount established under subdivision (9) of subsection (d) of this section that remain in the North Carolina Health Insurance Risk Pool Fund at the time of final dissolution shall be paid into the General Fund. After the resolution of timely filed actions against the Pool, any reserve funds remaining in the Risk Pool Fund shall be paid into the General Fund. (2013-410, ss. 28.5(a), (d).)

§ 58-50-261: Reserved for future codification purposes.

§ 58-50-262: Reserved for future codification purposes.

§ 58-50-263: Reserved for future codification purposes.

§ 58-50-264: Reserved for future codification purposes.

§ 58-50-265: Reserved for future codification purposes.

Part 7. Contracts Between Health Benefit Plans and Health Care Providers.

§ 58-50-270. Definitions.

Unless the context clearly requires otherwise, the following definitions apply in this Part.

(1) "Amendment" - Any change to the terms of a contract, including terms incorporated by reference, that modifies fee schedules. A change required by federal or State law, rule, regulation, administrative hearing, or court order is not an amendment.

(2) "Contract" - An agreement between an insurer and a health care provider for the provision of health care services by the provider on a preferred or in-network basis.

(3) "Health benefit plan" - A policy, certificate, contract, or plan as defined in G.S. 58-3-167.

(3a) "Health care provider" - An individual who is licensed, certified, or otherwise authorized under Chapter 90 or Chapter 90B of the General Statutes or under the laws of another state to provide health care services in the ordinary course of business or practice of a profession or in an approved education or training program and a facility that is licensed under Chapter 131E or Chapter 122C of the General Statutes or is owned or operated by the State of North Carolina in which health care services are provided to patients.

(4) "Insurer" - An entity as defined in G.S. 58-3-227(a)(4). (2009-352, s. 1; 2009-487, s. 2(a).)

§ 58-50-275. Notice contact provisions.

(a) All contracts shall contain a "notice contact" provision listing the name or title and address of the person to whom all correspondence, including proposed amendments and other notices, pertaining to the contractual relationship between parties shall be provided. Each party to a contract shall designate its notice contact under such contract.

(b) Means for sending all notices provided under a contract shall be one or more of the following, calculated as (i) five business days following the date the notice is placed, first-class postage prepaid, in the United States mail; (ii) on the day the notice is hand delivered; (iii) for certified or registered mail, the date on the return receipt; or (iv) for commercial courier service, the date of delivery. Nothing in this section prohibits the use of an electronic medium for a communication other than an amendment if agreed to by the insurer and the provider. (2009-352, s. 1; 2009-487, s. 2(b).)

§ 58-50-280. Contract amendments.

(a) A health benefit plan or insurer shall send any proposed contract amendment to the notice contact of a health care provider pursuant to G.S. 58-50-275. The proposed amendment shall be dated, labeled "Amendment," signed by the health benefit plan or insurer, and include an effective date for the proposed amendment.

(b) A health care provider receiving a proposed amendment shall be given at least 60 days from the date of receipt to object to the proposed amendment. The proposed amendment shall be effective upon the health care provider failing to object in writing within 60 days.

(c) If a health care provider objects to a proposed amendment, then the proposed amendment is not effective and the initiating health benefit plan or insurer shall be entitled to terminate the contract upon 60 days written notice to the health care provider.

(d) Nothing in this Part prohibits a health care provider and insurer from negotiating contract terms that provide for mutual consent to an amendment, a process for reaching mutual consent, or alternative notice contacts. (2009-352, s. 1; 2009-487, s. 2(c).)

§ 58-50-285. Policies and procedures.

(a) A health benefit plan or insurer shall provide a copy of its policies and procedures to a health care provider prior to execution of a new or amended contract and annually to all contracted health care providers. Such policies and procedures may be provided to the health care provider in hard copy, CD, or other electronic format, and may also be provided by posting the policies and procedures on the Web site of the health plan or insurer.

(b) The policies and procedures of a health benefit plan or insurer shall not conflict with or override any term of a contract, including contract fee schedules. In the event of a conflict between a policy or procedure and the language in a contract, the contract language shall prevail. (2009-352, s. 1.)

§ 58-50-290. Health benefit plans or insurers contracting for provision of dental services; no limitation on fees for noncovered services.

(a) No agreement between an insurer or an entity that writes stand-alone dental insurance and a dentist for the provision of dental services on a preferred or in-network basis to plan members or insurance subscribers in connection with coverage under a stand-alone dental plan, but not in connection with or incidental to coverage under a medical plan or health insurance policy, may require that a dentist provide services at a fee limited or set by the plan or insurer, unless the services are reimbursed as covered services under the contract.

(b) For purposes of this section, "covered services" means a service for which reimbursement is available under an insurer's policy, without regard to contractual limitations by a deductible, copayment, coinsurance, waiting period, annual or lifetime maximum, frequency limitation, alternative benefit payment, or other limitation. (2010-138, s. 1.)

§ 58-50-295. Prohibited contract provisions related to reimbursement rates.

No contract with a health care provider shall do any of the following:

(1) Prohibit, or grant a health insurance carrier an option to prohibit, the provider from contracting with another health insurance carrier to provide health care services at a rate that is equal to or lower than the payment specified in the contract.

(2) Require the provider to accept a lower payment rate in the event that the provider agrees to provide health care services to any other health insurance carrier at a rate that is equal to or lower than the payment specified in the contract.

(3) Require, or grant a health insurance carrier an option to require, termination or renegotiation of an existing health care contract in the event that the provider agrees to provide health care services to any other health

insurance carrier at a rate that is equal to or lower than the payment specified in the contract.

(4)   Require, or grant a health insurance carrier an option to require, the provider to disclose, directly or indirectly, the provider's contractual rates with another health insurance carrier.

(5)   Require, or grant a health insurance carrier an option to require, the nonnegotiated adjustment by the issuer of the provider's contractual rate to equal the lowest rate the provider has agreed to charge any other health insurance carrier.

(6)   Require, or grant a health insurance carrier an option to require, the provider to charge another health insurance carrier a rate that is equal to or more than the reimbursement rate specified in the contract. (2013-46, s. 1.)

Article 51.

Nature of Policies.

§ 58-51-1. Form, classification and rates to be approved by Commissioner.

No policy of insurance against loss or damage from the sickness or the bodily injury or death of the insured by accident shall be issued or delivered to any person in this State until a copy of the form thereof and of the classification of risks and the premium rates pertaining thereto have been filed with, and the forms approved by, the Commissioner. If the Commissioner shall notify, in writing, the company or other insurer which has filed such form that it does not comply with the requirements of law, specifying the reasons for his opinion, it shall be unlawful thereafter for any such insurer to issue any policy in such form. The action of the Commissioner in this regard shall be subject to review by any court of competent jurisdiction; but nothing in this Article shall be construed to give jurisdiction to any court not already having jurisdiction. (1911, c. 209, s. 1; 1913, c. 91, s. 1; C.S., s. 6477; 1945, c. 385; 1991, c. 720, s. 4.)

§ 58-51-5. Form of policy.

(a) No policy of accident and health insurance shall be delivered or issued for delivery to any person in this State unless:

(1) The entire money and other considerations therefor are expressed therein; and

(2) The time at which the insurance takes effect and terminates is expressed therein; and

(3) It purports to insure only one person, except that a policy may insure, originally or by subsequent amendment, upon the application of an adult member of a family who shall be deemed the policyholder, any two or more eligible members of that family, including husband, wife, dependent children or any children under a specified age which shall not exceed 19 years and any other persons dependent upon the policyholder; and

(4) The style, arrangement, and overall appearance of the policy, any endorsements, or attached papers give no undue prominence to any portion of the text. For the purpose of this subdivision, "text" includes all printed matter except the name and address of the insurer, the name or title of the policy, and captions and subcaptions.

(5) The exceptions and reductions of indemnity are set forth in the policy and, except those which are set forth in G.S. 58-51-15, are printed, at the insurer's option, either included with the benefit provision to which they apply, or under an appropriate caption such as "EXCEPTIONS," or "EXCEPTIONS AND REDUCTIONS," provided that if an exception or reduction specifically applies only to a particular benefit of the policy, a statement of such exception or reduction shall be included with the benefit provision to which it applies; and

(6) Each such form, including riders and endorsements, shall be identified by a form number in the lower left-hand corner of the first page thereof; and

(7) It contains no provision purporting to make any portion of the charter, rules, constitution, or bylaws of the insurer a part of the policy unless such portion is set forth in full in the policy, except in the case of the incorporation of, or reference to, a statement of rates or classification of risks, or short-rate table filed with the Commissioner.

(8) It contains no provision excluding from coverage claims that are subject to the Workers' Compensation Act, Article 1 of Chapter 97 of the General Statutes, unless the exclusion extends to only specific medical charges for which the employee, employer, or carrier is liable or responsible according to a final adjudication of the claim under that Article or an order of the North Carolina Industrial Commission approving a settlement agreement entered into under that Article.

(b) If any policy is issued by an insurer domiciled in this State for delivery to a person residing in another state, and if the official having responsibility for the administration of the insurance laws of such other state shall have advised the Commissioner that any such policy is not subject to approval or disapproval by such official, the Commissioner may by ruling require that such policy meet the standards set forth in subsection (a) of this section and in G.S. 58-51-15. (1913, c. 91, s. 2; C.S., s. 6478; 1945, c. 385; 1953, c. 1095, s. 1; 1979, c. 755, s. 8; 2001-216, s. 4; 2001-487, s. 102(b).)

§ 58-51-10. Right to return policy and have premium refunded.

Every individual or family hospitalization policy, certificate, contract or plan issued for delivery in the State of North Carolina on and after July 1, 1961, must have printed thereon or attached thereto a notice stating substantially: "YOUR POLICY MAY NOT BE IN FORCE WHEN YOU HAVE A CLAIM! PLEASE READ! Your policy was issued based on the information entered in your application, a copy of which is attached to the policy. If, to the best of your knowledge and belief, there is any misstatement in your application or if any information concerning the medical history of any insured person has been omitted, you should advise the Company immediately regarding the incorrect or omitted information; otherwise, your policy may not be a valid contract. RIGHT TO RETURN POLICY WITHIN 10 DAYS. If for any reason you are not satisfied with your policy, you may return it to the Company within 10 days of the date you received it and the premium you paid will be promptly refunded." If a policyholder or certificate holder or purchaser of a contract or plan returns same pursuant to such notice, coverage under such policy, certificate, contract or plan shall become void immediately upon the mailing or delivery of the contract, certificate, policy or plan to the insurance company at its home or branch office or to the agent through whom it was purchased. Coverage shall exist under such policy, certificate, contract or plan within said 10-day period until said mailing or delivery of the contract. (1955, c. 850, s. 10; 1961, c. 962.)

§ 58-51-15. Accident and health policy provisions.

(a) Required Provisions. - Except as provided in subsection (c) of this section each such policy delivered or issued for delivery to any person in this State shall contain the provisions specified in this subsection in the substance of the words that appear in this section. Such provisions shall be preceded individually by the caption appearing in this subsection or, at the option of the insurer, by such appropriate individual or group captions or subcaptions as the Commissioner may approve.

(1) A provision in the substance of the following language:

ENTIRE CONTRACT; CHANGES: This policy, including the endorsements and the attached papers, if any, constitutes the entire contract of insurance. No change in this policy shall be valid until approved by an executive officer of the insurer and unless such approval be endorsed hereon or attached hereto. No agent has authority to change this policy or waive any of its provisions.

(2) A provision in the substance of the following language:

TIME LIMIT ON CERTAIN DEFENSES:

a. After two years from the date of issue or reinstatement of this policy no misstatements except fraudulent misstatements made by the applicant in the application for such policy shall be used to void the policy or deny a claim for loss incurred or disability (as defined in the policy) commencing after the expiration of such two-year period.

The foregoing policy provision may be used in its entirety only in major or catastrophe hospitalization policies and major medical policies each affording benefits of five thousand dollars ($5,000) or more for any one sickness or injury; disability income policies affording benefits of one hundred dollars ($100.00) or more per month for not less than 12 months; and franchise policies. Other policies to which this section applies must delete the words "except fraudulent misstatements."

(The foregoing policy provision shall not be so construed as to affect any legal requirement for avoidance of a policy or denial of a claim during such initial two-year period, nor to limit the application of G.S. 58-51-15(b), (1), (2), (3), (4) and (5) in the event of misstatement with respect to age or occupation or other insurance.)

(A policy which the insured has the right to continue in force subject to its terms by the timely payment of premium:

1. Until at least age 50 or,

2. In the case of a policy issued after age 44, for at least five years from its date of issue, may contain in lieu of the foregoing the following provisions (from which the clause in parentheses may be omitted at the insurer's option) under the caption "INCONTESTABLE."

After this policy has been in force for a period of two years during the lifetime of the insured (excluding any period during which the insured is disabled), it shall become incontestable as to the statements contained in the application.)

b. This policy contains a provision limiting coverage for preexisting conditions. Preexisting conditions are covered under this policy _____ (insert number of months or days, not to exceed one year) after the effective date of coverage. Preexisting conditions mean "those conditions for which medical advice, diagnosis, care, or treatment was received or recommended within the one-year period immediately preceding the effective date of the person's coverage." Credit for having satisfied some or all of the preexisting condition waiting periods under previous health benefits coverage shall be given in accordance with G.S. 58-51-17. The excepted benefits described in G.S. 58-68-25(b) are not subject to this requirement for giving credit.

(3) A provision in the substance of the following language:

GRACE PERIOD: A grace period of _____ (insert a number not less than "7" for weekly premium policies, "10" for monthly premium policies and "31" for all other policies) days will be granted for the payment of each premium falling due after the first premium, during which grace period the policy shall continue in force.

(A policy which contains a cancellation provision may add, at the end of the above provision, subject to the right of the insurer to cancel in accordance with the cancellation provision hereof.

A policy in which the insurer reserves the right to refuse any renewal shall have, at the beginning of the above provision,

Unless not less than five days prior to the premium due date the insurer has delivered to the insured or has mailed to his last address as shown by the record of the insurer written notice of its intention not to renew this policy beyond the period for which the premium has been accepted.)

(4)   A provision in the substance of the following language:

REINSTATEMENT: If any renewal premium be not paid within the time granted the insured for payment, a subsequent acceptance of premium by the insurer or by any agent duly authorized by the insurer to accept such premium, without requiring in connection therewith an application for reinstatement, shall reinstate the policy; provided, however, that if the insurer or such agent requires an application for reinstatement and issues a conditional receipt for the premium tendered, the policy will be reinstated upon approval of such application by the insurer, or, lacking such approval, upon the forty-fifth day following the date of such conditional receipt unless the insurer has previously notified the insured in writing of its disapproval of such application. The reinstated policy shall cover only loss resulting from such accidental injury as may be sustained after the date of reinstatement and loss due to such sickness as may begin more than 10 days after such date. In all other respects the insured and insurer shall have the same rights thereunder as they had under the policy immediately before the due date of the defaulted premium, subject to any provisions endorsed hereon or attached hereto in connection with the reinstatement. Any premium accepted in connection with a reinstatement shall be applied to a period for which premium has not been previously paid, but not to any period more than 60 days prior to the date of reinstatement.

(The last sentence of the above provision may be omitted from any policy which the insured has the right to continue in force subject to its terms by the timely payment of premiums:

a.   Until at least age 50 or,

b.   In the case of a policy issued after age 44, for at least five years from its date of issue.)

(5)   A provision in the substance of the following language:

NOTICE OF CLAIM: Written notice of claim must be given to the insurer within 20 days after the occurrence or commencement of any loss covered by the policy, or as soon thereafter as is reasonably possible. Notice given by or on behalf of the insured or the beneficiary to the insurer at _____ (insert the location of such office as the insurer may designate for the purpose), or to any authorized agent of the insurer, with information sufficient to identify the insured, shall be deemed notice to the insurer.

(In a policy providing a loss-of-time benefit which may be payable for at least two years, an insurer may at its option insert the following between the first and second sentences of the above provision:

Subject to the qualifications set forth below, if the insured suffers loss of time on account of disability for which indemnity may be payable for at least two years, he shall, at least once in every six months after having given notice of claim, give to the insurer notice of continuance of said disability, except in the event of legal incapacity. The period of six months following any filing of proof by the insured or any payment by the insurer on account of such claim or any denial of liability in whole or in part by the insurer shall be excluded in applying this provision. Delay in the giving of such notice shall not impair the insured's right to any indemnity which would otherwise have accrued during the period of six months preceding the date on which such notice is actually given.)

(6)   A provision in the substance of the following language:

CLAIM FORMS: The insurer, upon receipt of a notice of claim, will furnish to the claimant such forms as are usually furnished by it for filing proofs of loss. If such forms are not furnished within 15 days after the giving of such notice the claimant shall be deemed to have complied with the requirements of this policy as to proof of loss upon submitting, within the time fixed in the policy for filing proofs of loss, written proof covering the occurrence, the character and the extent of the loss for which claim is made.

(7)   A provision in the substance of the following language:

PROOFS OF LOSS: Written proof of loss must be furnished to the insurer at its said office in the case of a claim for loss for which this policy provides any periodic payment contingent upon continuing loss within 180 days after the termination of the period for which the insurer is liable and in case of a claim for any other loss within 180 days after the date of such loss. Failure to furnish such proof within the time required shall not invalidate nor reduce any claim if it was not reasonably possible to give proof within such time, provided such proof is furnished as soon as reasonably possible and in no event, except in the absence of legal capacity of the insured, later than one year from the time proof is otherwise required.

(8)   A provision in the substance of the following language:

TIME OF PAYMENT OF CLAIMS: Indemnities payable under this policy for any loss other than loss for which this policy provides any period payment will be paid immediately upon receipt of due written proof of such loss. Subject to due written proof of loss, all accrued indemnities for loss for which this policy provides periodic payment will be paid _____ (insert period for payment which must not be less frequently than monthly) and any balance remaining unpaid upon the termination of liability will be paid immediately upon receipt of due written proof.

(9)   A provision in the substance of the following language:

PAYMENT OF CLAIMS: Indemnity for loss of life will be payable in accordance with the beneficiary designation and the provisions respecting such payment which may be prescribed herein and effective at the time of payment. If no such designation or provision is then effective, such indemnity shall be payable to the estate of the insured. Any other accrued indemnities unpaid at the insured's death may, at the option of the insurer, be paid either to such beneficiary or to such estate. All other indemnities will be payable to the insured.

(The following provisions, or either of them, may be included with the foregoing provision at the option of the insurer:

If any indemnity of this policy shall be payable to the estate of the insured, or to an insured or beneficiary who is a minor or otherwise not competent to give a valid release, the insurer may pay such indemnity, up to an amount not exceeding $ _____ (insert an amount which shall not exceed three thousand dollars ($3,000)), to any relative by blood or connection by marriage of the insured or beneficiary who is deemed by the insurer to be equitably entitled thereto. Any payment made by the insurer in good faith pursuant to this provision shall fully discharge the insurer to the extent of such payment.

Subject to any written direction of the insured in the application or otherwise all or a portion of any indemnities provided by this policy on account of hospital, nursing, medical, or surgical services, may at the insurer's option and unless the insured requests otherwise in writing not later than the time of filing proofs of such loss, be paid directly to the hospital or person rendering such services; but it is not required that the service be rendered by a particular hospital or person.)

(10)   A provision in the substance of the following language:

PHYSICAL EXAMINATIONS AND AUTOPSY: The insurer at its own expense shall have the right and opportunity to examine the person of the insured when and as often as it may reasonably require during the pendency of a claim hereunder and to make an autopsy in case of death where it is not forbidden by law.

(11)   A provision in the substance of the following language:

LEGAL ACTIONS: No action at law or in equity shall be brought to recover on this policy prior to the expiration of 60 days after written proof of loss has been furnished in accordance with the requirements of this policy. No such action shall be brought after the expiration of three years after the time written proof of loss is required to be furnished.

(12)   A provision in the substance of the following language:

CHANGE OF BENEFICIARY: Unless the insured makes an irrevocable designation of beneficiary, the right to change of beneficiary is reserved to the insured and the consent of the beneficiary or beneficiaries shall not be requisite to surrender or assignment of this policy or to any change of beneficiary or beneficiaries, or to any other changes in this policy.

(The first clause of this provision, relating to the irrevocable designation of beneficiary, may be omitted at the insurer's option.)

(b)   Other Provisions. - Except as provided in subsection (c) of this section, no such policy delivered or issued for delivery to any person in this State shall contain provisions respecting the matters set forth below unless such provisions are in the substance of the words that appear in this section. Any such provision contained in the policy shall be preceded individually by the appropriate caption appearing in this subsection or, at the option of the insurer, by such appropriate individual or group captions or subcaptions as the Commissioner may approve.

(1)   A provision in the substance of the following language:

CHANGE OF OCCUPATION: If the insured be injured or contract sickness after having changed his occupation to one classified by the insurer as more hazardous than that stated in this policy or while doing for compensation anything pertaining to an occupation so classified, the insurer will pay only such portion of the indemnities provided in this policy as the premium paid would have purchased at the rates and within the limits fixed by the insurer for such more hazardous occupation. If the insured changes his occupation to one classified by the insurer as less hazardous than that stated in this policy, the insurer, upon receipt of proof of such change of occupation, will reduce the premium rate accordingly, and will return the excess pro rata unearned premium from the date of change of occupation or from the policy anniversary date immediately preceding receipt of such proof, whichever is the more recent. In applying this provision, the classification of occupational risk and the premium rates shall be such as have been last filed by the insurer prior to the occurrence of the loss for which the insurer is liable or prior to date of proof of change in occupation with the state official having supervision of insurance in the state where the insured resided at the time this policy was issued; but if such filing was not required, then the classification of occupational risk and the premium rates shall be those last made effective by the insurer in such state prior to the occurrence of the loss or prior to the date of proof of change in occupation.

(2)   A provision in the substance of the following language:

MISSTATEMENT OF AGE: If the age of the insured has been misstated, all amounts payable under this policy shall be such as the premium paid would have purchased at the correct age.

(3)   A provision in the substance of the following language:

OTHER INSURANCE IN THIS INSURER: If an accident or health or accident and health policy or policies previously issued by the insurer to the insured be in force concurrently herewith, making the aggregate indemnity for ____ (insert type of coverage or coverages) in excess of $ _____ (insert maximum limit of indemnity or indemnities) the excess insurance shall be void and all premiums paid for such excess shall be returned to the insured or to his estate.

Or, in lieu thereof:

Insurance effective at any one time on the insured under a like policy or policies in this insurer is limited to the one such policy elected by the insured, his beneficiary or his estate, as the case may be, and the insurer will return all premiums paid for all other such policies.

(4)   A provision in the substance of the following language:

INSURANCE WITH OTHER INSURERS: If there be other valid coverage, not with this insurer, providing benefits for the same loss on a provision of service basis or on an expense incurred basis and of which this insurer has not been given written notice prior to the occurrence or commencement of loss, the only liability under any expense incurred coverage of this policy shall be for such proportion of the loss as the amount which would otherwise have been payable hereunder plus the total of the like amounts under all such other valid coverages for the same loss of which this insurer had notice bears to the total like amounts under all valid coverages for such loss, and for the return of such portion of the premiums paid as shall exceed the pro rata portion for the amount so determined. For the purpose of applying this provision when other coverage is on a provision of service basis, the "like amount" of such other coverage shall be taken as the amount which the services rendered would have cost in the absence of such coverage.

(If the foregoing policy provision is included in a policy which also contains the next following policy provision there shall be added to the caption of the foregoing provision the phrase "____ EXPENSE INCURRED BENEFITS." The insurer may, at its option, include in this provision a definition of "other valid coverage," approved as to form by the Commissioner, which definition shall be limited in subject matter to coverage provided by organizations subject to regulation by insurance law or by insurance authorities of this or any other state of the United States or any province of Canada, and by hospital or medical service organizations, and to any other coverage the inclusion of which may be approved by the Commissioner. In the absence of such definition such term shall not include group insurance, automobile medical payments insurance, or coverage provided by hospital or medical service organizations or by union welfare plans or employer or employee benefit organizations. For the purpose of applying the foregoing policy provision with respect to any insured, any amount of benefit provided for such insured pursuant to any compulsory benefit statute (including any workers' compensation or employer's liability statute) whether provided by a governmental agency or otherwise shall in all cases be deemed to be "other valid coverage" of which the insurer has had notice. In applying the foregoing policy provisions no third-party liability coverage shall be included as "other valid coverage.")

(5) A provision in the substance of the following language:

INSURANCE WITH OTHER INSURERS: If there be other valid coverage, not with this insurer, providing benefits for the same loss on other than an expense incurred basis and of which this insurer has not been given written notice prior to the occurrence or commencement of loss, the only liability for such benefits under this policy shall be for such proportion of the indemnities otherwise provided hereunder for such loss as the like indemnities of which the insurer had notice (including the indemnities under this policy) bear to the total amount of all like indemnities for such loss, and for the return of such portion of the premium paid as shall exceed the pro rata portion for the indemnities thus determined.

(If the foregoing policy provision is included in a policy which also contains the next preceding policy provision there shall be added to the caption of the foregoing provision the phrase "____ OTHER BENEFITS." The insurer may, at its option, include in this provision a definition of "other valid coverage," approved as to form by the Commissioner, which definition shall be limited in subject matter to coverage provided by organizations subject to regulation by insurance law or by insurance authorities of this or any other state of the United States or any province of Canada, and to any other coverage the inclusion of which may be approved by the Commissioner. In the absence of such definition such term shall not include group insurance, or benefits provided by union welfare plans or by employer or employee benefit organizations. For the purpose of applying the foregoing policy provision with respect to any insured, any amount of benefit provided for such insured pursuant to any compulsory benefit statute (including any workers' compensation or employer's liability statute) whether provided by a governmental agency or otherwise shall in all cases be deemed to be "other valid coverage" of which the insurer has had notice. In applying the foregoing policy provision no third-party liability coverage shall be included as "other valid coverage.")

(6) A provision in the substance of the following language:

RELATION OF EARNINGS TO INSURANCE: If the total monthly amount of loss of time benefits promised for the same loss under all valid loss of time coverage upon the insured, whether payable on a weekly or monthly basis, shall exceed the monthly earnings of the insured at the time disability commenced or his average monthly earnings for the period of two years immediately preceding a disability for which claim is made, whichever is the greater, the insurer will be liable only for such proportionate amount of such benefits under this policy as the amount of such monthly earnings or such average monthly earnings of the insured bears to the total amount of monthly benefits for the same loss under all such coverage upon the insured at the time such disability commences and for the return of such part of the premiums paid during such two years as shall exceed the pro rata amount of the premiums for the benefits actually paid hereunder; but this shall not operate to reduce the total monthly amount of benefits payable under all such coverage upon the insured below the sum of two hundred dollars ($200.00) or the sum of the monthly benefits specified in such coverages, whichever is the lesser, nor shall it operate to reduce benefits other than those payable for loss of time.

(The foregoing policy provision may be inserted only in a policy which the insured has the right to continue in force subject to its terms by the timely payment of premiums:

a. Until at least age 50 or,

b. In the case of a policy issued after age 44, for at least five years from its date of issue.

The insurer may, at its option, include in this provision a definition of "valid loss of time coverage," approved as to form by the Commissioner, which definition shall be limited in subject matter to coverage provided by governmental agencies or by organizations subject to regulation by insurance law or by insurance authorities of this or any other state of the United States or any province of Canada, or to any other coverage the inclusion of which may be approved by the Commissioner or any combination of such coverages. In the absence of such definition such term shall not include any coverage provided for such insured pursuant to any compulsory benefit statute (including any workers' compensation or employer's liability statute), or benefits provided by union welfare plans or by employer or employee benefit organizations.)

(7) A provision in the substance of the following language:

UNPAID PREMIUM: Upon the payment of a claim under this policy, any premium then due and unpaid or covered by any note or written order may be deducted therefrom.

(8) Repealed by Session Laws 1955, c. 886, s. 1.

(9) A provision in the substance of the following language:

CONFORMITY WITH STATE STATUTES: Any provision of this policy which, on its effective date, is in conflict with the statutes of the state in which the insured resides on such date is hereby amended to conform to the minimum requirements of such statutes.

(10) A provision in the substance of the following language:

ILLEGAL OCCUPATION: The insurer shall not be liable for any loss to which a contributing cause was the insured's commission of or attempt to commit a felony or to which a contributing cause was the insured's being engaged in an illegal occupation.

(11) Repealed by Session Laws 2001-334, s. 4.1, effective October 1, 2001.

(c) Inapplicable or Inconsistent Provisions. - If any provision of this section is in whole or in part inapplicable to or inconsistent with the coverage provided by a particular form of policy the insurer, with the approval of the Commissioner, shall omit from such policy any inapplicable provision or part of a provision, and shall modify any inconsistent provision or part of the provision in such manner as to make the provision as contained in the policy consistent with the coverage provided by the policy.

(d) Order of Certain Policy Provisions. - The provisions which are the subject of subsections (a) and (b) of this section, or any corresponding provisions which are used in lieu thereof in accordance with such subsections, shall be printed in the consecutive order of the provisions in such subsections or, at the option of the insurer, any such provision may appear as a unit in any part of the policy, with other provisions to which it may be logically related, provided the resulting policy shall not be in whole or in part unintelligible, uncertain, ambiguous, abstruse, or likely to mislead a person to whom the policy is offered, delivered or issued.

(e) Third-Party Ownership. - The word "insured," as used in Articles 50 through 55 of this Chapter shall not be construed as preventing a person other than the insured with a proper insurable interest from making application for and owning a policy covering the insured or from being entitled under such a policy to any indemnities, benefits and rights provided therein.

(f) Requirements of Other Jurisdictions.

(1) Any policy of a foreign or alien insurer, when delivered or issued for delivery to any person in this State, may contain any provision which is not less favorable to the insured or the beneficiary than the provisions of Articles 50 through 55 of this Chapter and which is prescribed or required by the law of the state under which the insurer is organized.

(2) Any policy of a domestic insurer may, when issued for delivery in any other state or country, contain any provision permitted or required by the laws of such other state or country.

(g) Filing Procedure. - The Commissioner may make such reasonable rules and regulations concerning the procedure for the filing or submission of policies subject to Articles 50 through 55 of this Chapter as are necessary, proper or advisable to the administration of Articles 50 through 55 of this Chapter. This provision shall not abridge any other authority granted the Commissioner by law.

(h) Preexisting Condition Exclusion Clarification. - Sub-subdivision (a)(2)b. of this section does not apply to policies issued to eligible individuals under G.S. 58-68-60.

(i) Applicability. - This section applies to all accident and health insurance policies delivered or issued for delivery in this State, including certificates issued under group policies that are delivered or issued for delivery in this State. This section also applies to certificates issued under a policy issued and delivered to a trust or association outside this State and covering persons residing in this State. (1953, c. 1095, s. 2; 1955, c. 850, s. 8; c. 886, s. 1; 1961, c. 432; 1979, c. 755, ss. 9-12; 1983 (Reg. Sess., 1984), c. 1110, s. 13; 1987, c. 864, s. 42; 1987 (Reg. Sess., 1988), c. 975, s. 2; 1991, c. 636, s. 3; c. 720, s. 35; 1993, c. 506, s. 4; c. 553, s. 17; 1995, c. 507, s. 23A.1(g); 1995 (Reg. Sess., 1996), c. 742, s. 27; 1997-259, ss. 7, 7.1; 1999-351, s. 1; 2000-162, s. 4(d); 2001-334, s. 4.1; 2002-187, s. 5.2; 2005-223, ss. 4(a), 4(b); 2007-298, s. 2.1; 2009-382, s. 8.)

§ 58-51-16. Intoxicants and narcotics.

(a) Except for the payment of benefits for the necessary care and treatment of chemical dependency as provided by law, an accident and health insurer shall not be liable for any loss sustained or contracted in consequence of the insured's being intoxicated or under the influence of any narcotic unless administered on the advice of a physician.

(b) The provision in subsection (a) of this section may not be used with respect to a medical expense policy.

(c) For purposes of this section, "medical expense policy" means an accident and health insurance policy that provides hospital, medical, and surgical expense coverage. (2001-334, s. 4.2.)

§ 58-51-17. Portability for accident and health insurance.

(a) Rules Relating to Crediting Previous Coverage.

(1) Creditable coverage defined. - For the purposes of this section, "creditable coverage" means, with respect to an individual, coverage of the individual under any of the following:

a. A group health plan as defined in G.S. 58-68-25(a)(4b).

b. Health insurance coverage without regard to whether the coverage is offered in the group market, the individual market, or otherwise.

c. Part A or part B of title XVIII of the Social Security Act.

d. Title XIX of the Social Security Act, other than coverage consisting solely of benefits under section 1928.

e. Chapter 55 of title 10, United States Code.

f. A medical care program of the Indian Health Service or of a tribal organization.

g. A State health benefits risk pool.

h. A health plan offered under chapter 89 of title 5, United States Code.

i. A public health plan (as defined in federal regulations).

j. A health benefit plan under section 5(e) of the Peace Corps Act (22 U.S.C. § 2504(e)).

k. Title XXI of the Social Security Act (State Children's Health Insurance Program).

"Creditable coverage" does not include coverage consisting solely of coverage of excepted benefits as described in G.S. 58-68-25(b). However, short-term limited-duration health insurance coverage shall be considered creditable coverage for purposes of this section.

(2) Not counting periods before significant breaks in coverage.

a. In general. - A period of creditable coverage shall not be counted, with respect to enrollment of an individual under an individual health insurance plan, if, after the period and before the enrollment date, there was a 63-day period during all of which the individual was not covered under any creditable coverage.

b. Waiting period not treated as a break in coverage. - For the purposes of sub-subdivision a. of this subdivision and subdivision (b)(3) of this section, any period that an individual is in a waiting period, as defined in G.S. 58-68-30(b)(4)c., for any coverage under an individual health insurance plan shall not be taken into account in determining the continuous period under sub-subdivision a. of this subdivision.

c. For an individual who elects COBRA continuation coverage during the second election period provided under the Trade Act of 2002, the days between the date the individual lost group health plan coverage and the first day of the second COBRA election period shall not be considered when determining whether a significant break in coverage has occurred.

(3) Method of crediting coverage. - An individual health insurer shall count a period of creditable coverage without regard to the specific benefits covered during the period.

(4) Establishment of period. - Periods of creditable coverage for an individual shall be established through presentation of certifications described in subsection (c) of this section or in another manner that is specified in regulations.

(5) Determination of creditable coverage.

a. Determination within reasonable time. - If an individual health insurer receives creditable coverage information under subsection (c) of this section, the insurer shall, within a reasonable time following receipt of the information, make a determination regarding the amount of the individual's creditable coverage and the length of any exclusion that remains. Whether this determination is made within a reasonable time depends on the relevant facts and circumstances. Relevant facts and circumstances include whether a plan's application of a preexisting condition exclusion would prevent an individual from having access to urgent medical care.

b. No time limit on presenting evidence of creditable coverage. - An individual health insurer shall not impose any limit on the amount of time that an individual has to present a certificate or other evidence of creditable coverage.

(b) Exceptions.

(1) Exclusion not applicable to certain newborns. - Subject to subdivision (3) of this subsection, an individual health insurer shall not impose any preexisting condition exclusion in the case of an individual who, as of the last day of the 30-day period beginning with the individual's date of birth, is covered under creditable coverage.

(2) Exclusion not applicable to certain adopted children. - Subject to subdivision (3) of this subsection, an individual health insurer shall not impose any preexisting condition exclusion in the case of a child who is adopted or placed for adoption before attaining 18 years of age and who, as of the last day of the 30-day period beginning on the date of the adoption or placement for adoption, is covered under creditable coverage. The previous sentence does not apply to coverage before the date of the adoption or placement for adoption.

(3) Loss if break in coverage. - Subdivisions (1) and (2) of this subsection shall no longer apply to an individual after the end of the first 63-day period during all of which the individual was not covered under any creditable coverage.

(c) Certifications and Disclosure of Coverage.

(1) In general. - An individual health insurer shall provide the certification described in this subdivision (i) at the time an individual ceases to be covered under the plan, and (ii) on the request on behalf of an individual made not later

than 24 months after the date of cessation of the coverage described in clause (i) of this subdivision, whichever is later.

(2)   Certification. - The certification described in this subdivision is a written certification of (i) the period of creditable coverage of the individual under the plan and (ii) any waiting period and affiliation period, if applicable, imposed with respect to the individual for any coverage under the plan.

(d)   Applicability. - This section applies to all health benefit plans of individual health insurance coverage delivered or issued for delivery in this State, including certificates issued under group policies that are delivered or issued for delivery in this State. This section also applies to certificates issued under a policy issued and delivered to a trust or association outside this State and covering persons residing in this State. (2007-298, s. 2.2; 2009-382, ss. 1, 9, 10.)

§ 58-51-20. Renewability of individual and blanket hospitalization and accident and health insurance policies.

(a)   Every individual or blanket family hospitalization policy and accident and health policy, other than noncancelable or nonrenewable policies but including group, blanket and franchise policies, as defined in Articles 1 through 64 of this Chapter, covering less than 10 persons, issued in North Carolina after January 1, 1956, shall include in substance the following provision:

Renewability: This policy is renewable at the option of the policyholder unless sufficient notice of nonrenewal is given the policyholder in writing by the insurer.

Sufficient notice shall be, during the first year of any policy, or during the first year following any lapse and reinstatement, a period of 30 days before the premium due date. After one continuous year of coverage and acceptance of premium for any portion of the second or subsequent year sufficient notice shall be a number of full months most nearly equivalent to one fourth the number of months of continuous coverage from the inception date of the policy, to the date of mailing of the notice: Provided no period of required notice shall exceed two years.

(b)   No insurance company issuing individual or blanket family hospitalization or accident and health policies of insurance shall have the right to unilaterally restrict coverage, reduce benefits or increase rates upon any contract of hospitalization or accident and health insurance which is subject to the provisions of this section except as provided herein.

(c)   Any hospitalization or accident and health policy reissued or renewed in the name of the insured during the grace period shall be construed to be a continuation of the policy first issued.

(d)   The requirements of this section do not apply to a refusal or renewal because of a change of occupation of an insured to one classified by the insurer as uninsurable nor to an increase in rate due to a change of occupation of an insured to a more hazardous occupation. (1955, c. 886, s. 2; 1957, c. 1085, s. 2; 1979, c. 755, s. 13; 1985, c. 666, s. 71; 1989, c. 485, s. 55; 1991, c. 644, s. 27.)

§ 58-51-25. Policy coverage to continue as to mentally retarded or physically handicapped children; coverage of dependent students on medically necessary leave of absence.

(a)   An individual or group accident and health insurance policy, hospital service plan policy, or medical service plan policy that provides that coverage of a dependent child shall terminate upon attainment of the limiting age for dependent children specified in the policy or contract, shall also provide in substance that attainment of such limiting age shall not operate or terminate the coverage of such child while the child is and continues to be (i) incapable of self-sustaining employment by reason of mental retardation or physical handicap; and (ii) chiefly dependent upon the policyholder or subscriber for support and maintenance: Provided, proof of such incapacity and dependency is furnished to the insurer, hospital service plan corporation, or medical service plan corporation by the policyholder or subscriber within 31 days of the child's attainment of the limiting age and subsequently as may be required by the insurer or corporation, but not more frequently than annually after the child's attainment of the limiting age.

(b)   All health benefit plans, as defined in G.S. 58-3-167, that provide that coverage of a dependent child shall terminate upon a change in enrollment of the child in a postsecondary educational institution shall provide for the continued eligibility of the dependent child during a medically necessary leave of absence from the postsecondary educational institution in accordance with all applicable requirements of Public Law 110-381, known as Michelle's Law. (1969, c. 745, s. 1; 1971, c. 1126, s. 1; 2009-382, s. 17.)

§ 58-51-30. Policies to cover newborn infants, foster children, and adopted children.

(a) As used in this section:

(1) "Foster child" means a minor (i) over whom a guardian has been appointed by the clerk of superior court of any county in North Carolina; or (ii) the primary or sole custody of whom has been assigned by order of a court of competent jurisdiction;

(2) "Placement in the foster home" means physically residing with a person appointed as guardian or custodian of a foster child as long as that guardian or custodian has assumed the legal obligation for total or partial support of the foster child with the intent that the foster child reside with the guardian or custodian on more than a temporary or short-term basis.

(3) "Placement for adoption" has the same meaning as defined in G.S. 58-51-125(a)(2).

(b) Every health benefit plan, as defined in G.S. 58-51-115(a)(1), that provides benefits for any sickness, illness, or disability of any minor child or that provides benefits for any medical treatment or service furnished by a health care provider or institution to any minor child shall provide the benefits for those occurrences beginning with the moment of the child's birth if the birth occurs while the plan is in force. Every health benefit plan shall extend coverage to a newborn child without requirements for prior notification unless an additional premium charge to add the dependent is due. If an additional premium charge is due to cover the dependent, the health benefit plan shall cover the newborn child from the moment of birth if the newborn is enrolled within 30 days after the date of birth. Foster children and adopted children shall be treated the same as newborn infants and eligible for coverage on the same basis upon placement in the foster home or placement for adoption. Every health benefit plan shall extend coverage to a foster child or adopted child without requirements for prior notification unless an additional premium charge to add the foster child or adopted child is due. If an additional premium charge is due to cover the foster child or adopted child, the health benefit plan shall cover the foster child or adopted child upon placement in the foster home or placement for adoption if the foster child or adopted child is enrolled within 30 days after the placement in the foster home or placement for adoption.

(c)   Benefits in such plans shall be the same for congenital defects or anomalies as are provided for most sicknesses or illnesses suffered by minor children that are covered by the plans. Benefits for congenital defects or anomalies shall specifically include, but not be limited to, all necessary treatment and care needed by individuals born with cleft lip or cleft palate.

(d)   No plan shall be approved by the Commissioner under this Chapter that does not comply with this section.

(e)   This section applies to insurers governed by Articles 1 through 63 of this Chapter and to corporations governed by Articles 65, 66, and 67 of this Chapter.

(f)   This section and G.S. 58-51-125 shall be construed in pari materia. (1973, c. 345, ss. 1, 2; 1981 (Reg. Sess., 1982), c. 1349; 1991, c. 644, s. 12; 1993, c. 504, s. 32; c. 553, s. 18; 1993 (Reg. Sess., 1994), c. 644, s. 2; 2001-334, s. 5; 2005-223, s. 3.)

§ 58-51-35. Insurers and others to afford coverage to mentally retarded and physically handicapped children.

(a)   No insurance company licensed in this State pursuant to the provisions of Articles 1 through 64 of this Chapter and no corporation governed by the provisions of Articles 65 and 66 of this Chapter shall refuse to issue or deliver any individual or group accident and health insurance policy of hospital or medical service plan policy in this State which it is currently issuing for delivery in this State and which affords benefits or coverage for minor children of the applicant, by reason of the physical handicap or mental retardation of any minor children of the applicant; nor shall any such policy issued and delivered in this State carry a higher premium rate or charge or restrict or exclude coverage or benefits by reason of said mental retardation or physical handicap. Provided, however, such policy may exclude benefits, otherwise payable for disability, hospitalization, or medical or other therapeutic expense directly and solely attributable to such mental retardation or such physical handicap.

(b) The Commissioner shall revoke the license of any insurer or any corporation governed by the provisions of Articles 65 and 66 of this Chapter if it fails to comply with the provisions of this section.

(c) The provisions of this section shall apply to corporations governed by the provisions of Articles 65 and 66 of this Chapter. (1973, c. 754, ss. 1, 2; 1991, c. 720, s. 4.)

§ 58-51-37. Pharmacy of choice.

(a) This section shall apply to all health benefit plans providing pharmaceutical services benefits, including prescription drugs, to any resident of North Carolina. This section shall also apply to insurance companies and health maintenance organizations that provide or administer coverages and benefits for prescription drugs. This section shall not apply to any entity that has its own facility, employs or contracts with physicians, pharmacists, nurses, and other health care personnel, and that dispenses prescription drugs from its own pharmacy to its employees and to enrollees of its health benefit plan; provided, however, this section shall apply to an entity otherwise excluded that contracts with an outside pharmacy or group of pharmacies to provide prescription drugs and services. This section shall not apply to any federal program, clinical trial program, hospital or other health care facility licensed pursuant to Chapter 131E or Chapter 122C of the General Statutes, when dispensing prescription drugs to its patients.

(b) As used in this section:

(1) "Copayment" means a type of cost sharing whereby insured or covered persons pay a specified predetermined amount per unit of service with their insurer paying the remainder of the charge. The copayment is incurred at the time the service is used. The copayment may be a fixed or variable amount.

(2) "Contract provider" means a pharmacy granted the right to provide prescription drugs and pharmacy services according to the terms of the insurer.

(3) "Health benefit plan" is as that term is defined in G.S. 58-50-110(11).

(4) "Insurer" means any entity that provides or offers a health benefit plan.

(5) "Pharmacy" means a pharmacy registered with the North Carolina Board of Pharmacy.

(c) The terms of a health benefit plan shall not:

(1) Prohibit or limit a resident of this State, who is eligible for reimbursement for pharmacy services as a participant or beneficiary of a health benefit plan, from selecting a pharmacy of his or her choice when the pharmacy has agreed to participate in the health benefit plan according to the terms offered by the insurer;

(2) Deny a pharmacy the opportunity to participate as a contract provider under a health benefit plan if the pharmacy agrees to provide pharmacy services that meet the terms and requirements, including terms of reimbursement, of the insurer under a health benefit plan, provided that if the pharmacy is offered the opportunity to participate, it must participate or no provisions of G.S. 58-51-37 shall apply;

(3) Impose upon a beneficiary of pharmacy services under a health benefit plan any copayment, fee, or condition that is not equally imposed upon all beneficiaries in the same benefit category, class, or copayment level under the health benefit plan when receiving services from a contract provider;

(4) Impose a monetary advantage or penalty under a health benefit plan that would affect a beneficiary's choice of pharmacy. Monetary advantage or penalty includes higher copayment, a reduction in reimbursement for services, or promotion of one participating pharmacy over another by these methods.

(5) Reduce allowable reimbursement for pharmacy services to a beneficiary under a health benefit plan because the beneficiary selects a pharmacy of his or her choice, so long as that pharmacy has enrolled with the health benefit plan under the terms offered to all pharmacies in the plan coverage area; or

(6) Require a beneficiary, as a condition of payment or reimbursement, to purchase pharmacy services, including prescription drugs, exclusively through a mail-order pharmacy.

(d) A pharmacy, by or through a pharmacist acting on its behalf as its employee, agent, or owner, may not waive, discount, rebate, or distort a copayment of any insurer, policy, or plan, or a beneficiary's coinsurance portion of a prescription drug coverage or reimbursement and if a pharmacy, by or through a pharmacist's acting on its behalf as its employee, agent or owner, provides a pharmacy service to an enrollee of a health benefit plan that meets the terms and requirements of the insurer under a health benefit plan, the pharmacy shall provide its pharmacy services to all enrollees of that health benefit plan on the same terms and requirements of the insurer. A violation of this subsection shall be a violation of the Pharmacy Practice Act subjecting the pharmacist as a licensee to disciplinary authority of the North Carolina Board of Pharmacy pursuant to G.S. 90-85.38.

(e) At least 60 days before the effective date of any health benefit plan providing reimbursement to North Carolina residents for prescription drugs, which restricts pharmacy participation, the entity providing the health benefit plan shall notify, in writing, all pharmacies within the geographical coverage area of the health benefit plan, and offer to the pharmacies the opportunity to participate in the health benefit plan. All pharmacies in the geographical coverage area of the plan shall be eligible to participate under identical reimbursement terms for providing pharmacy services, including prescription drugs. The entity providing the health benefit plan shall, through reasonable means, on a timely basis, and on regular intervals in order to effectuate the purposes of this section, inform the beneficiaries of the plan of the names and locations of pharmacies that are participating in the plan as providers of pharmacy services and prescription drugs. Additionally, participating pharmacies shall be entitled to announce their participation to their customers through a means acceptable to the pharmacy and the entity providing the health benefit plans. The pharmacy notification provisions of this section shall not apply when an individual or group is enrolled, but when the plan enters a particular county of the State.

(f) If rebates or marketing incentives are allowed to pharmacies or other dispensing entities providing services or benefits under a health benefit plan, these rebates or marketing incentives shall be offered on an equal basis to all pharmacies and other dispensing entities providing services or benefits under a health benefit plan when pharmacy services, including prescription drugs, are purchased in the same volume and under the same terms of payment. Nothing in this section shall prevent a pharmaceutical manufacturer or wholesale distributor of pharmaceutical products from providing special prices, marketing incentives, rebates, or discounts to different purchasers not prohibited by federal and State antitrust laws.

(g) Any entity or insurer providing a health benefit plan is subject to G.S. 58-2-70. A violation of this section shall subject the entity providing a health benefit plan to the sanctions of revocation, suspension, or refusal to renew license in the discretion of the Commissioner pursuant to G.S. 58-3-100.

(h) A violation of this section creates a civil cause of action for damages or injunctive relief in favor of any person or pharmacy aggrieved by the violation.

(i) The Commissioner shall not approve any health benefit plan providing pharmaceutical services which does not conform to this section.

(j) Any provision in a health benefit plan which is executed, delivered, or renewed, or otherwise contracted for in this State that is contrary to any provision of this section shall, to the extent of the conflict, be void.

(k) It shall be a violation of this section for any insurer or any person to provide any health benefit plan providing for pharmaceutical services to residents of this State that does not conform to the provisions of this section. (1993, c. 293, s. 1.)

§ 58-51-38. Direct access to obstetrician-gynecologists.

(a) Each health benefit plan shall allow each female plan participant or beneficiary age 13 or older direct access within the health benefit plan, without prior referral, to the health care services of an obstetrician-gynecologist participating in the health benefit plan, within the benefits provided under that health benefit plan pertaining to obstetrician-gynecologist services.

For purposes of this section:

(1) "Health benefit plan" means an HMO subscriber contract or any preferred provider, exclusive provider, or other managed care arrangement offered under a health benefit plan, as defined in G.S. 58-50-110(11).

(2) "Health care services" means the full scope of medically necessary services provided by the participating obstetrician-gynecologist in the care of or related to the female reproductive system and breasts, and in performing annual screening, counseling, and immunization for disorders and diseases in accordance with the most current published recommendations of the American College of Obstetricians and Gynecologists, and includes services provided by nurse practitioners, physician's assistants, and certified nurse midwives in

collaboration with the obstetrician-gynecologist in the care of the participant or beneficiary.

(3) "Benefits" are those medical services or other items to which an individual is entitled under the terms of her contract with a health benefit plan, as approved by the Department of Insurance.

(b) Each health benefit plan shall inform female participants and beneficiaries in writing of the provisions of this section. The information shall be provided in benefit handbooks and materials and enrollment materials. (1995, c. 63, s. 1.)

§ 58-51-40. Insurers and others to afford coverage for active medical treatment in tax-supported institutions.

(a) Whenever any policy of insurance governed by Articles 1 through 64 of this Chapter provides for benefits for charges of hospitals or physicians, the policy shall provide for payments of benefits for charges made for medical care rendered in or by duly licensed State tax-supported institutions, including charges for medical care of cerebral palsy, other orthopedic and crippling disabilities, mental and nervous diseases or disorders, mental retardation, alcoholism and drug or chemical dependency, and respiratory illness, on a basis no less favorable than the basis which would apply had the medical care been rendered in or by any other public or private institution or provider. The term "State tax-supported institutions" shall include community mental health centers and other health clinics which are certified as Medicaid providers.

(b) No policy shall exclude payment for charges of a duly licensed State tax-supported institution because of its being a specialty facility for one particular type of illness nor because it does not have an operating room and related equipment for the performance of surgery, but it is not required that benefits be payable for domiciliary or custodial care, rehabilitation, training, schooling, or occupational therapy.

(c) The restrictions and regulations of this section shall not apply to any policy which is individually underwritten or provided for a specific individual and the members of his family as a nongroup policy but shall apply to any group policy of insurance governed by Articles 1 through 64 of this Chapter. (1975, c. 345, s. 1; 1981, c. 816, ss. 1, 2.)

§ 58-51-45. Policies to be issued to any person possessing the sickle cell trait or hemoglobin C trait.

No insurance company licensed in this State pursuant to the provisions of Articles 1 through 64 of this Chapter shall refuse to issue or deliver any policy (regardless of whether any of such policies shall be defined as individual, family, group, blanket, franchise, industrial or otherwise) which is currently being issued for delivery in this State, and which affords benefits or coverage for any medical treatment or service authorized or permitted to be furnished by a hospital, clinic, family health plan, neighborhood health plan, health maintenance organization, physician, physician's assistant, nurse practitioner or any medical service facility or personnel by reason of the fact that the person to be insured possesses sickle cell trait or hemoglobin C trait, nor shall any such policy issued and delivered in this State carry a higher premium rate or charge by reason of the fact that the person to be insured possesses said trait. (1975, c. 599, s. 1.)

§ 58-51-50. Coverage for chemical dependency treatment.

(a)   As used in this section, the term "chemical dependency" means the pathological use or abuse of alcohol or other drugs in a manner or to a degree that produces an impairment in personal, social or occupational functioning and which may, but need not, include a pattern of tolerance and withdrawal.

(b)   Every insurer that writes a policy or contract of group or blanket health insurance or group or blanket accident and health insurance that is issued, renewed, or amended on or after January 1, 1985, shall offer to its insureds benefits for the necessary care and treatment of chemical dependency that are not less favorable than benefits for physical illness generally. Except as provided in subsection (c) of this section, benefits for treatment of chemical dependency shall be subject to the same durational limits, dollar limits, deductibles, and coinsurance factors as are benefits for physical illness generally.

(c)   Every group policy or group contract of insurance that provides benefits for chemical dependency treatment and that provides total annual benefits for all illnesses in excess of eight thousand dollars ($8,000) is subject to the following conditions:

(1) The policy or contract shall provide, for each 12-month period, a minimum benefit of eight thousand dollars ($8,000) for the necessary care and treatment of chemical dependency.

(2) The policy or contract shall provide a minimum benefit of sixteen thousand dollars ($16,000) for the necessary care and treatment of chemical dependency for the life of the policy or contract.

(d) Provisions for benefits for necessary care and treatment of chemical dependency in group policies or group contracts of insurance shall provide benefit payments for the following providers of necessary care and treatment of chemical dependency:

(1) The following units of a general hospital licensed under Article 5 of General Statutes Chapter 131E:

a. Chemical dependency units in facilities licensed after October 1, 1984;

b. Medical units;

c. Psychiatric units; and

(2) The following facilities or programs licensed after July 1, 1984, under Article 2 of General Statutes Chapter 122C:

a. Chemical dependency units in psychiatric hospitals;

b. Chemical dependency hospitals;

c. Residential chemical dependency treatment facilities;

d. Social setting detoxification facilities or programs;

e. Medical detoxification or programs; and

(3) Duly licensed physicians and duly licensed practicing psychologists and certified professionals working under the direct supervision of such physicians or psychologists in facilities described in (1) and (2) above and in day/night

programs or outpatient treatment facilities licensed after July 1, 1984, under Article 2 of General Statutes Chapter 122C.

Provided, however, that nothing in this subsection shall prohibit any policy or contract of insurance from requiring the most cost effective treatment setting to be utilized by the person undergoing necessary care and treatment for chemical dependency.

(e) Coverage for chemical dependency treatment as described in this section shall not be applicable to any group policy holder or group contract holder who rejects the coverage in writing.

(f) Notwithstanding any other provisions of this section, a group health benefit plan that covers both medical and surgical benefits and chemical dependency treatment benefits shall, with respect to the chemical dependency treatment benefits, comply with all applicable standards of Subtitle B of Title V of Public Law 110-343, known as the Paul Wellstone and Pete Domenici Mental Health Parity and Addiction Equity Act of 2008.

(g) Subsection (f) of this section applies only to a group health benefit plan covering a large employer as defined in G.S. 58-68-25(a)(10). (1983 (Reg. Sess., 1984), c. 1110, s. 7; 1985, c. 589, s. 43(a), (b); 1989, c. 175, s. 1; 1991, c. 720, s. 64; 2009-382, s. 20.)

§ 58-51-55. No discrimination against mentally ill or chemically dependent individuals.

(a) Definitions. - As used in this section, the term:

(1) "Mental illness" has the same meaning as defined in G.S. 122C-3(21), with a mental disorder defined in the Diagnostic and Statistical Manual of Mental Disorders, DSM-IV, or a subsequent edition published by the American Psychiatric Association, except those mental disorders coded in the DSM-IV or subsequent editions as substance-related disorders (291.0 through 292.9 and 303.0 through 305.9), those coded as sexual dysfunctions not due to organic disease (302.70 through 302.79), and those coded as "V" codes.

(2) "Chemical dependency" has the same meaning as defined in G.S. 58-51-50, with a mental disorder defined in the Diagnostic and Statistical Manual of

Mental Disorders, DSM-IV, or subsequent editions published by the American Psychiatric Association.

(b)   Coverage of Physical Illness. - No insurance company licensed in this State under this Chapter shall, solely because an individual to be insured has or had a mental illness or chemical dependency:

(1)   Refuse to issue or deliver to that individual any policy that affords benefits or coverages for any medical treatment or service for physical illness or injury;

(2)   Have a higher premium rate or charge for physical illness or injury coverages or benefits for that individual; or

(3)   Reduce physical illness or injury coverages or benefits for that individual.

(b1)   [Expired October 1, 2001.]

(c)   Chemical Dependency Coverage Not Required. - Nothing in this section requires an insurer to offer coverage for chemical dependency, except as provided in G.S. 58-51-50.

(d)   Applicability. - This section applies only to group health insurance contracts, other than excepted benefits as defined in G.S. 58-68-25. For purposes of this section, "group health insurance contracts" include MEWAs, as defined in G.S. 58-49-30(a).

(e)   Nothing in this section requires an insurer to cover treatment or studies leading to or in connection with sex changes or modifications and related care. (1989, c. 369, s. 3; 1991, c. 720, s. 81; 1997-259, s. 21; 1999-132, s. 4.2; 2007-268, s. 1.)

§ 58-51-57. Coverage for mammograms and cervical cancer screening.

(a)   Every policy or contract of accident or health insurance, and every preferred provider benefit plan under G.S. 58-50-56, that is issued, renewed, or amended on or after January 1, 1992, shall provide coverage for examinations and laboratory tests for the screening for the early detection of cervical cancer and for low-dose screening mammography. The same deductibles, coinsurance, and other limitations as apply to similar services covered under the policy, contract, or plan shall apply to coverage for examinations and laboratory tests for the screening for the early detection of cervical cancer and low-dose screening mammography.

(a1) As used in this section, "examinations and laboratory tests for the screening for the early detection of cervical cancer" means conventional PAP smear screening, liquid-based cytology, and human papilloma virus (HPV) detection methods for women with equivocal findings on cervical cytologic analysis that are subject to the approval of and have been approved by the United States Food and Drug Administration.

(b) As used in this section, "low-dose screening mammography" means a radiologic procedure for the early detection of breast cancer provided to an asymptomatic woman using equipment dedicated specifically for mammography, including a physician's interpretation of the results of the procedure.

(c) Coverage for low-dose screening mammography shall be provided as follows:

(1) One or more mammograms a year, as recommended by a physician, for any woman who is at risk for breast cancer. For purposes of this subdivision, a woman is at risk for breast cancer if any one or more of the following is true:

a. The woman has a personal history of breast cancer;

b. The woman has a personal history of biopsy-proven benign breast disease;

c. The woman's mother, sister, or daughter has or has had breast cancer; or

d. The woman has not given birth prior to the age of 30;

(2) One baseline mammogram for any woman 35 through 39 years of age, inclusive;

(3) A mammogram every other year for any woman 40 through 49 years of age, inclusive, or more frequently upon recommendation of a physician; and

(4) A mammogram every year for any woman 50 years of age or older.

(d) Reimbursement for a mammogram authorized under this section shall be made only if the facility in which the mammogram was performed meets mammography accreditation standards established by the North Carolina Medical Care Commission.

(e) Coverage for the screening for the early detection of cervical cancer shall be in accordance with the most recently published American Cancer Society guidelines or guidelines adopted by the North Carolina Advisory Committee on Cancer Coordination and Control. Coverage shall include the examination, the laboratory fee, and the physician's interpretation of the laboratory results. Reimbursements for laboratory fees shall be made only if the laboratory meets accreditation standards adopted by the North Carolina Medical Care Commission. (1991, c. 490, s. 1; 1997-519, s. 3.3; 2003-186, s. 2.)

§ 58-51-58. Coverage for prostate-specific antigen (PSA) tests.

(a) Every policy or contract of accident and health insurance, and every preferred provider benefit plan under G.S. 58-50-56, that is issued, renewed, or amended on or after January 1, 1994, shall provide coverage for prostate-specific antigen (PSA) tests or equivalent tests for the presence of prostate cancer. The same deductibles, coinsurance, and other limitations as apply to similar services covered under the policy, contract, or plan shall apply to coverage for prostate-specific antigen (PSA) tests or equivalent tests for the presence of prostate cancer.

(b) As used in this section, "prostate-specific antigen (PSA) tests or equivalent tests for the presence of prostate cancer" means serological tests for determining the presence of prostate cytoplasmic protein (PSA) and the generation of antibodies to it, as a novel marker for prostatic disease.

(c) Coverage for prostate-specific antigen (PSA) tests or equivalent tests for the presence of prostate cancer shall be provided when recommended by a physician. (1993, c. 269, s. 1; 1997-519, s. 3.4.)

§ 58-51-59. Coverage of certain prescribed drugs for cancer treatment.

(a) No policy or contract of accident or health insurance, and no preferred provider benefit plan under G.S. 58-50-56, that is issued, renewed, or amended on or after January 1, 1994, and that provides coverage for prescribed drugs approved by the federal Food and Drug Administration for the treatment of certain types of cancer shall exclude coverage of any drug on the basis that the drug has been prescribed for the treatment of a type of cancer for which the drug has not been approved by the federal Food and Drug Administration. The drug, however, must be approved by the federal Food and Drug Administration and must have been proven effective and accepted for the treatment of the specific type of cancer for which the drug has been prescribed in any one of the following established reference compendia:

(1) The National Comprehensive Cancer Network Drugs & Biologics Compendium;

(2) The ThomsonMicromedex DrugDex;

(3) The Elsevier Gold Standard's Clinical Pharmacology; or

(4) Any other authoritative compendia as recognized periodically by the United States Secretary of Health and Human Services.

(b) Notwithstanding subsection (a) of this section, coverage shall not be required for any experimental or investigational drugs or any drug that the federal Food and Drug Administration has determined to be contraindicated for treatment of the specific type of cancer for which the drug has been prescribed.

(c) This section shall apply only to cancer drugs and nothing in this section shall be construed, expressly or by implication, to create, impair, alter, limit, notify, enlarge, abrogate, or prohibit reimbursement for drugs used in the treatment of any other disease or condition. (1993, c. 506, s. 4.1; 1997-519, s. 3.5; 2009-170, s. 1.)

§ 58-51-60. Meaning of term "preexisting conditions" in certain policies.

At the time of issuing any new policy of individual or family hospitalization insurance or individual accident and health insurance to insureds over age 65, the term "preexisting conditions," or its equivalent in said policy shall include only conditions specifically eliminated by rider. (1955, c. 850, s. 5.)

§ 58-51-61. Coverage for certain treatment for diabetes.

(a) Every policy or contract of accident or health insurance, and every preferred provider benefit plan under G.S. 58-50-56, that is issued, renewed, or amended on or after October 1, 1997, shall provide coverage for medically appropriate and necessary services, including diabetes outpatient self-management training and educational services, and equipment, supplies, medications, and laboratory procedures used to treat diabetes. Diabetes outpatient self-management training and educational services shall be provided by a physician or a health care professional designated by the physician. The insurer shall determine who shall provide and be reimbursed for the diabetes outpatient self-management training and educational services. The same deductibles, coinsurance, and other limitations as apply to similar services covered under the policy, contract, or plan shall apply to the diabetes coverage required under this section.

(b) For the purposes of this section, "physician" is a person licensed to practice in this State under Article 1 or Article 7 of Chapter 90 of the General Statutes. (1997-225, s. 1; 1997-519, s. 3.11.)

§ 58-51-62. Coverage for reconstructive breast surgery following mastectomy.

(a) Every policy or contract of accident and health insurance, and every preferred provider benefit plan under G.S. 58-50-56 that provides coverage for mastectomy shall provide coverage for reconstructive breast surgery following a mastectomy. The coverage shall include coverage for all stages and revisions of reconstructive breast surgery performed on a nondiseased breast to establish symmetry if reconstructive surgery on a diseased breast is performed, as well as coverage for prostheses and physical complications in all stages of mastectomy, including lymphademas. The same deductibles, coinsurance, and other limitations as apply to similar services covered under the policy, contract, or plan shall apply to coverage for reconstructive breast surgery. Reconstruction of the nipple/areolar complex following a mastectomy is covered without regard to the lapse of time between the mastectomy and the reconstruction, subject to the approval of the treating physician.

(b) As used in this section, the following terms have the meanings indicated:

(1) "Mastectomy" means the surgical removal of all or part of a breast as a result of breast cancer or breast disease.

(2) "Reconstructive breast surgery" means surgery performed as a result of a mastectomy to reestablish symmetry between the two breasts, and includes reconstruction of the mastectomy site, creation of a new breast mound, and creation of a new nipple/areolar complex. "Reconstructive breast surgery" also includes augmentation mammoplasty, reduction mammoplasty, and mastopexy of the nondiseased breast.

(c) A policy, contract, or plan subject to this section shall not:

(1) Deny coverage described in subsection (a) of this section on the basis that the coverage is for cosmetic surgery;

(2) Deny to a woman eligibility or continued eligibility to enroll or to renew coverage under the terms of the contract, policy, or plan, solely for the purpose of avoiding the requirements of this section;

(3) Provide monetary payments or rebates to a woman to encourage her to accept less than the minimum protections available under this section;

(4) Penalize or otherwise reduce or limit the reimbursement of an attending provider because the provider provided care to an individual participant or beneficiary in accordance with this section; or

(5) Provide incentives, monetary or otherwise, to an attending provider to induce the provider to provide care to an individual participant or beneficiary in a manner inconsistent with this section.

(d) Written notice of the availability of the coverage provided by this section shall be delivered to every policyholder under an individual policy, contract, or plan and to every certificate holder under a group policy, contract, or plan upon initial coverage under the policy, contract, or plan and annually thereafter. The notice required by this subsection may be included as a part of any yearly informational packet sent to the policyholder or certificate holder. (1997-312, s. 1; 1997-456, s. 40(a); 1997-519, s. 3.9; 1999-351, s. 3.1; 2001-334, s. 13.1.)

§ 58-51-63. Coverage for abortions not allowed in plans offered through Exchange.

(a) Pursuant to the authority granted to states under 42 U.S.C. § 18023(a), no qualified health plan offered through an Exchange created under Subchapter III of Chapter 157 of Title 42 of the U.S. Code and operating within this State shall include coverage for abortion services.

(b) The coverage limitation in subsection (a) of this section shall not apply to an abortion performed when the pregnancy is the result of an act of rape or incest or the life of the mother is endangered by a physical disorder, physical illness, or physical injury, including a life-endangering physical condition caused by or arising from the pregnancy itself. (2013-366, s. 2(a).)

§ 58-51-65. Industrial sick benefit insurance defined.

Industrial sick benefit insurance is hereby defined as that form of insurance for which premiums are payable weekly and which provides for the payment of a weekly indemnity on account of sickness or accident in addition to a benefit in case of death. Such death benefit shall not exceed one hundred and fifty dollars ($150.00). There shall be a provision for the payment of weekly premium, eighty percent (80%) of which shall be allocated for the purchase of sick and accident coverages and twenty percent (20%) thereof for the purchase of death benefits. (1945, c. 385.)

§ 58-51-70. Industrial sick benefit insurance; provisions.

Policies issued under the industrial sick benefit plan shall contain the substance of provisions contained in G.S. 58-51-15 and in addition shall contain the following:

(1) A provision for grace for the payment of the additional premium or assessment or proportion thereof for such death benefits of not less than four weeks during which period the death benefit shall continue in force;

(2) A provision for incontestability of the death benefit coverage after not more than two years except for

a. Nonpayment of premiums, and

b. Misstatement of age;

(3) A provision that the death benefit is noncancellable by the company except for nonpayment of premium.

The Commissioner may approve any form of certificate to be issued under the industrial sick benefit plan which omits or modifies any of the provisions hereinbefore required, if he deems such omission or modification suitable for the character of such insurance and not unjust to the persons insured thereunder. (1945, c. 385; 1953, c. 1095, s. 4; 1979, c. 755, s. 14.)

§ 58-51-75. Blanket accident and health insurance defined.

(a) Any policy or contract of insurance against death or injury resulting from accident or from accidental means which insures a group of persons conforming to the requirements of one of the following subdivisions (1) to (7), inclusive, shall be deemed a blanket accident policy. Any policy or contract which insures a group of persons conforming to the requirements of one of the following subdivisions (3), (5), (6) or (7) against total or partial disability, excluding such disability from accident or from accidental means, shall be deemed a blanket health insurance policy. Any policy or contract of insurance which combines the coverage of blanket accident insurance and of blanket health insurance on such a group of persons shall be deemed a blanket accident and health insurance policy:

(1) Under a policy or contract issued to any common carrier or to any operator, owner, or lessee of a means of transportation, who or which shall be deemed the policyholder, covering a group defined as all persons or all persons of a class who may become passengers on the common carrier or the means of transportation.

(2) Under a policy or contract issued to an employer, or the trustee of a fund established by the employer, who shall be deemed the policyholder, covering any group of employees defined by reference to exceptional hazards incident to such employment, insuring such employee against death or bodily injury resulting while, or from, being exposed to such exceptional hazard.

(3) Under a policy or contract issued to a college, school or other institution of learning or to the head or principal thereof, who or which shall be deemed the policyholder.

(4) Under a policy or contract issued in the name of any volunteer fire department, emergency medical service, rescue first aid, civil defense, or any other such volunteer organization, which shall be deemed the policyholder, covering any group of members or other participants defined by reference to specified hazards incident to any activities or operations sponsored or supervised by such policyholder.

(5) Under a policy or contract issued to and in the name of an incorporated or unincorporated association of persons having a common interest or calling, which association shall be deemed the policyholder, having not less than 25 members, and formed for purposes other than obtaining insurance, covering all of the members of such association.

(6) Under a policy or contract issued to the head of a household, who shall be deemed the policyholder, whereunder the benefits thereof shall provide for the payment by the insurer of amounts for expenses incurred by the policyholder on account of hospitalization or medical or surgical aid for the policyholder, his or her spouse, his or her child or children, or other persons chiefly dependent on him or her for support and maintenance.

(7) Under a policy or contract issued to or in the name of any municipal or county recreation commission or department, sports team, league, tournament, or sponsor thereof, which shall be deemed the policyholder, covering participants, members, coaches, counselors, employees, officials, or supervisors defined by reference to specified hazards incident to activities or operations sponsored or supervised by such policyholder or on the premises of such policyholder.

(8) Under a policy or contract issued to any incorporated or unincorporated religious, charitable, recreational, educational, athletic, or civic organization or

branch thereof, which shall be deemed the policyholder, covering any group of members, participants, or volunteers defined by reference to specified hazards incident to activities or operations sponsored or supervised by such policyholder or on the premises of such policyholder.

(9) Under a policy or contract issued to any overnight, day, religious, equestrian, adventure, wilderness, athletic, or other camp, or the sponsor thereof, which shall be deemed the policyholder, covering any group of campers, participants, counselors, employees, volunteers, or supervisors defined by reference to specified hazards incident to activities or operations sponsored or supervised by such policyholder or on the premises of such policyholder.

(10) Under a policy or contract issued to any bank, credit union, or other financial institution, which shall be deemed the policyholder, to insure any group of account holders or members of the policyholder and as defined by reference in the policy or contract, in which premiums for such insurance are paid by the policyholder, as authorized by the account holder or member from account holder or member funds on deposit with the policyholder, collected from the account holders or members by way of account billing or member billing, or by the policyholder and account holders jointly.

(11) Any other risk or class of risks which, in the discretion of the Commissioner, may be properly eligible for blanket accident, health, or accident and health insurance. The discretion of the Commissioner may be exercised on an individual risk basis or class of risks or both after the Commissioner has made the following findings:

a. The issuance of the blanket policy is not contrary to the best interest of the public.

b. The issuance of the blanket policy would result in economies of acquisition or administration.

c. The benefits are reasonable in relation to the premiums charged.

(b) All benefits under any blanket accident, blanket health or blanket accident and health insurance policy shall be payable to the person insured, or to his designated beneficiary or beneficiaries, or to his estate, or to a person or persons chiefly dependent upon the person insured for support and maintenance, except that if the person insured be a minor, such benefits may be made payable to his parent, guardian, or other person actually supporting the minor.

(c) Nothing contained in this section shall be deemed to affect the legal liability of policyholders for the death of or injury to, any such member of such group. (1945, c. 385; 1947, c. 721; 1953, c. 1095, s. 5; 1961, c. 603; 2013-199, s. 19.)

§ 58-51-80. Group accident and health insurance defined.

(a) Any policy or contract of insurance against death or injury resulting from accident or from accidental means which covers more than one person except blanket accident policies as defined in G.S. 58-51-75, shall be deemed a group accident insurance policy. Any policy or contract which insures against disablement, disease or sickness of the insured (excluding disablement which results from accident or from accidental means) and which covers more than one person, except blanket health insurance policies as defined in G.S. 58-51-75, shall be deemed a group health insurance policy or contract. Any policy or contract of insurance which combines the coverage of group accident insurance and of group health insurance shall be deemed a group accident and health insurance policy. No policy or contract of group accident, group health or group accident and health insurance, and no certificates thereunder, shall be delivered or issued for delivery in this State unless it conforms to the requirements of subsection (b).

(b) No policy or contract of group accident, group health or group accident and health insurance shall be delivered or issued for delivery in this State unless the group of persons thereby insured conforms to the requirements of the following subdivisions:

(1) Under a policy issued to an employer, principal, or to the trustee of a fund established by an employer or two or more employers in the same industry or kind of business, or by a principal or two or more principals in the same industry or kind of business, which employer, principal, or trustee shall be deemed the policyholder, covering, except as hereinafter provided, only employees, or agents, of any class or classes thereof determined by conditions pertaining to employment, or agency, for amounts of insurance based upon some plan which will preclude individual selection. The premium may be paid by the employer, by the employer and the employees jointly, or by the employee;

and where the relationship of principal and agent exists, the premium may be paid by the principal, by the principal and agents, jointly, or by the agents. If the premium is paid by the employer and the employees jointly, or by the principal and agents jointly, or by the employees, or by the agents, the group shall be structured on an actuarially sound basis.

(1a) Under a policy issued to an association or to a trust or to the trustee or trustees of a fund established, created, or maintained for the benefit of members of one or more associations. The association or associations shall have at the outset a minimum of 500 persons and shall have been organized and maintained in good faith for purposes other than that of obtaining insurance; shall have been in active existence for at least five years; and shall have a constitution and bylaws that provide that (i) the association or associations hold regular meetings not less than annually to further purposes of the members; (ii) except for credit unions, the association or associations collect dues or solicit contributions from members; and (iii) the members, other than associate members, have voting privileges and representation on the governing board and committees. The policy is subject to the following requirements:

a. The policy may insure members of the association or associations, employees of the association or associations, or employees of members, or one or more of the preceding or all of any class or classes for the benefit of persons other than the employee's employer.

b. The premium for the policy shall be paid from funds contributed by the association or associations, or by employer members, or by both, or from funds contributed by the covered persons or from both the covered persons and the association, associations, or employer members. The premium rates for each association policy shall be developed, and applied to the certificates thereunder, on an actuarially sound basis.

c. Repealed by Session Laws 1997-259, s. 8.

(1b) Under a policy issued to a creditor as defined in G.S. 58-57-5 who shall be deemed the policyholder, to insure debtors as defined in G.S. 58-57-5 of the creditor to provide indemnity for payments becoming due on a specific loan or other credit transaction as defined in G.S. 58-51-100, with or without insurance against death by accident, subject to the following requirements:

a. The debtors eligible for insurance under the policy shall be all of the debtors of the creditor whose indebtedness is repayable in installments, or all of any class or classes thereof determined by conditions pertaining to the indebtedness or to the purchase giving rise to the indebtedness. The policy may provide that the term "debtors" shall include the debtors of one or more subsidiary corporations, and the debtors of one or more affiliated corporations, proprietors or partnerships if the business of the policyholder and of such affiliated corporations, proprietors or partnerships is under common control through stock ownership, contract or otherwise.

b. The premium for the policy shall be paid from the creditor's funds, from charges collected from the insured debtors, or from both. A policy on which part or all of the premium is to be derived from the collection from the insured debtors or identifiable charges not required of uninsured debtors shall not include, in the class or classes of debtors eligible for insurance, debtors under obligations outstanding at its date of issue without evidence of individual insurability unless the group is structured on an actuarially sound basis. A policy on which no part of the premium is to be derived from the collection of such identifiable charges must insure all eligible debtors, or all except any as to whom evidence of individual insurability is not satisfactory to the insurer.

c. The policy may be issued only if the group of eligible debtors is then receiving new entrants at the rate of at least 100 persons yearly, or may reasonably be expected to receive at least 100 new entrants during the first policy year, and only if the policy reserves to the insurer the right to require evidence of individual insurability if less than seventy-five percent (75%) of the new entrants become insured.

d. Premiums for this coverage shall be actuarially equivalent to the rates authorized under Article 57 of Chapter 58 of the General Statutes for credit accident and health insurance.

(2), (3) Repealed by Session Laws 1997-259, s. 8.

(c) The term "employees" as used in this section shall be deemed to include, for the purposes of insurance hereunder, employees of a single employer, the officers, managers, and employees of the employer and of subsidiary or affiliated corporations of a corporation employer, and the individual proprietors, partners, and employees of individuals and firms of which the business is controlled by the insured employer through stock ownership, contract or otherwise. With the exception of disability income insurance, employees shall be added to the group coverage no later than 90 days after their first day of employment. Employment shall be considered continuous and not be considered broken except for unexcused absences from work for reasons other than illness or injury. The term "employee" is defined as a nonseasonal person who works on a full-time basis, with a normal work week of 30 or more hours and who is otherwise eligible for coverage, but does not include a person who works on a part-time, temporary, or substitute basis. The term "employer" as used herein may be deemed to include the State of North Carolina, any county, municipality or corporation, or the proper officers, as such, of any unincorporated municipality or any department or subdivision of the State, county, such corporation, or municipality determined by conditions pertaining to the employment. When determining employee eligibility for a large employer, as defined in G.S. 58-68-25(10), an individual proprietor, owner, or operator shall be defined as an "employee" for the purpose of obtaining coverage under the employee group health plan and shall not be held to a minimum workweek requirement as imposed on other eligible employees.

(d) The term "agents" as used in this section shall be deemed to include, for the purposes of insurance hereunder, agents of a single principal who are under contract to devote all, or substantially all, of their time in rendering personal services for such principal, for a commission or other fixed or ascertainable compensation.

(e) The benefits payable under any policy or contract of group accident, group health and group accident and health insurance shall be payable to the employees, or agents, or to some beneficiary or beneficiaries designated by the employee or agent, other than the employer or principal, but if there is no designated beneficiary as to all or any part of the insurance at the death of the employee or agent, then the amount of insurance payable for which there is no designated beneficiary shall be payable to the estate of the employee or agent, except that the insurer may in such case, at its option, pay such insurance to any one or more of the following surviving relatives of the employee or agent: wife, husband, mother, father, child, or children, brothers or sisters; and except that payment of benefits for expenses incurred on account of hospitalization or medical or surgical aid, as provided in subsection (f), may be made by the insurer to the hospital or other person or persons furnishing such aid. Payment so made shall discharge the insurer's obligation with respect to the amount of insurance so paid.

(f) Any policy or contract of group accident, group health or group accident and health insurance may include provisions for the payment by the insurer of benefits to the employee or agent of the insured group, on account of hospitalization or medical or surgical aid for himself, his spouse, his child or children, or other persons chiefly dependent upon him for support and maintenance.

(g) Any policy or contract of group accident, group health or group accident and health insurance may provide for readjustment of the rate of premium based on the experience thereunder at the end of the first year, or at any time during any subsequent year based upon at least 12 months of experience: Provided that any such readjustment after the first year shall not be made any more frequently than once every six months. Any rate adjustment must be preceded by a 45-day notice to the contract holder before the effective date of any rate increase or any policy benefit revision. A notice of nonrenewal shall be given to the contract holder 45 days prior to termination. Any refund under any plan for readjustment of the rate of premium based on the experience under group policies and any dividend paid under the policies may be used to reduce the employer's or principal's contribution to group insurance for the employees of the employer, or the agents of the principal, and the excess over the contribution by the employer, or principal, shall be applied by the employer, or principal, for the sole benefit of the employees or agents.

(h) Nothing contained in this section applies to any contract issued by any corporation defined in Article 65 of this Chapter. (1945, c. 385; 1947, c. 721; 1951, c. 282; 1953, c. 1095, ss. 6, 7; 1987, c. 752, s. 19; 1989, c. 485, s. 41; c. 775, ss. 1, 2; 1991, c. 644, s. 11; c. 720, s. 88; 1991 (Reg. Sess., 1992), c. 837, s. 4; 1993, c. 408, ss. 3, 3.1; c. 409, s. 14; 1995, c. 507, ss. 23A.1(c), 23A.1(d); 1997-259, ss. 8, 9; 2000-132, s. 1; 2003-221, s. 12; 2005-223, ss. 1(a), 2(c).)

§ 58-51-81. Group accident and health insurance for public school students.

(a) Notwithstanding G.S. 58-51-80, a policy of group accident, health, or accident and health insurance may be delivered or issued to a local board of education or to any of its schools, as policyholder, covering only students for amounts of insurance based upon some plan that will preclude individual selection. The premium may be paid by the board, jointly by the board and the students or any other persons on behalf of the students, or by the students and any other persons on behalf of the students. In addition to the authority granted in G.S. 115C-47(6), any board may establish fees for the payment of premiums by or on behalf of the covered students.

(b) Entities subject to Articles 65 and 67 of this Chapter may provide their products in the same manner described in subsection (a) of this section. (1993 (Reg. Sess., 1994), c. 716, s. 1.)

§ 58-51-85. Group or blanket accident and health insurance; approval of forms and filing of rates.

No policy of group or blanket accident, health or accident and health insurance shall be delivered or issued for delivery in this State unless the form of the policy contracts including the master policy contract, the individual certificates thereunder, the applications for the contract, and a schedule of the premium rates pertaining to such form or forms, have been filed with and the forms approved by the Commissioner. (1945, c. 385; 1991, c. 720, s. 34.)

§ 58-51-90. Definition of franchise accident and health insurance.

Accident and health insurance on a franchise plan is hereby declared to be that form of accident and health insurance issued to five or more employees of any corporation, copartnership or individual employer or any governmental corporation, agency or department thereof, or 10 or more members of any trade or professional association or of a labor union or of any other association where such association or union has a constitution or bylaws and is formed in good faith for purposes other than that of obtaining insurance, where such persons, with or without their dependents, are issued the same form of an individual policy varying only as to amounts and kinds of coverage applied for by such persons, under an arrangement whereby the premiums on such policies may be paid to the insurer periodically by the employer, with or without payroll deductions, or by the association for its members, or by some designated person acting on behalf of such employer or association. The provisions of this section shall not be construed so as to repeal G.S. 58-51-75 and 58-51-80 or any parts thereof. (1947, c. 721; 1961, c. 646.)

§ 58-51-95. Approval by Commissioner of forms, classification and rates; hearing; exceptions.

(a) No policy of insurance against loss or expense from the sickness, or from the bodily injury or death by accident of the insured shall be issued or delivered to any person in this State nor shall any application, rider or endorsement be used in connection therewith until a copy of the form thereof and of the classification of risks and the premium rates, or, in the case of cooperatives or assessment companies the estimated cost pertaining thereto, have been filed with the Commissioner.

(b) No such policy shall be issued, nor shall any application, rider or endorsement be used in connection therewith, until the expiration of 90 days after it has been so filed unless the Commissioner shall sooner give his written approval thereto.

(c) The Commissioner may within 90 days after the filing of any such form, disapprove such form

(1) If the benefits provided therein are unreasonable in relation to the premium charged, or

(2) If it contains a provision or provisions which are unjust, unfair, inequitable, misleading, deceptive or encourage misrepresentation of such policy.

(d) If the Commissioner shall notify the insurer which has filed any such form that it does not comply with the provisions of this section or sections, it shall be unlawful thereafter for such insurer to issue such form or use it in connection with any policy. In such notice the Commissioner shall specify the reasons for his disapproval and state that a hearing will be granted within 20 days after request in writing by the insurer.

(e) The Commissioner may at any time, after a hearing of which not less than 20 days' written notice shall have been given to the insurer, withdraw his approval of any such form on any of the grounds stated in this section. It shall be unlawful for the insurer to issue such form or use it in connection with any policy after the effective date of such withdrawal of approval. The notice of any hearing called under this paragraph shall specify the matters to be considered at such hearing and any decision affirming disapproval or directing withdrawal of approval under this section shall be in writing and shall specify the reasons therefor: Provided, that the provisions of this section shall not apply to workers' compensation insurance, accidental death or disability benefits issued supplementary to life insurance or annuity contracts, medical expense benefits under liability policies or to group accident and health insurance.

(f) An insurer may revise rates chargeable on policies subject to this section, other than noncancellable policies, with the approval of the Commissioner if the Commissioner finds that the revised rates are not excessive, not inadequate, and not unfairly discriminatory; and exhibit a reasonable relationship to the benefits provided by the policies. The approved rates shall be guaranteed by the insurer, as to the policyholders affected by the rates, for a period of not less than 12 months; or as an alternative to the insurer giving the guarantee, the approved rates may be applicable to all policyholders at one time if the insurer chooses to apply for that relief with respect to those policies no more frequently than once in any 12-month period. The rates shall be applicable to all policies of the same type; provided that no rate revision may become effective for any policy unless the insurer has given the policyholder written notice of the rate revision 45 days before the effective date of the revision. The policyholder must then pay the revised rate in order to continue the policy in force. The Commissioner may adopt reasonable rules, after notice and hearing, to require the submission of supporting data and such information as the Commissioner considers necessary to determine whether the rate revisions meet these standards. In adopting the rules under this subsection, the Commissioner may require identification of the types of rating methodologies used by filers and may also address issue age or attained age rating, or both; policy reserves used in rating; and other recognized actuarial principles of the NAIC, the American Academy of Actuaries, and the Society of Actuaries.

(g) For policies subject to this section, an individual health insurer shall not increase an individual's renewal premium for continued health insurance coverage under the terms of the individual's health insurance policy based on any health status-related factors in relation to the individual or a dependent of the individual, including:

(1) Health status.

(2) Medical condition (including physical and mental illnesses).

(3) Claims experience.

(4) Duration from issue.

(5) Receipt of health care.

(6)   Medical history.

(7)   Genetic information.

(h)   Every policy that is subject to this section and that provides individual accident and health insurance benefits to a resident of this State shall return to policyholders benefits that are reasonable in relation to the premium charged. The Commissioner may adopt rules or utilize existing rules to establish minimum standards for loss ratios of policies on the basis of incurred claims experience and earned premiums in accordance with accepted actuarial principles and practices to assure that the benefits are reasonable in relation to the premium charged. Every insurer providing policies in this State subject to this section shall not less than annually file for approval its rates, rating schedules, and supporting documentation to demonstrate compliance with the applicable loss ratio standards of this State as adopted by the Commissioner. All filings of rates and rating schedules shall comply with the standards adopted by the Commissioner. The filing shall include a certification by an individual who is either a Fellow or an Associate of the Society of Actuaries or a Member of the American Academy of Actuaries that the rates are not excessive, not inadequate, and not unfairly discriminatory; and that the rates exhibit a reasonable relationship to the benefits provided by the policy. Nothing in this subsection shall require an insurer to provide certification with respect to a previous rate period, or to require an insurer to reduce properly filed and approved rates before the end of a rate period. This subsection does not apply to any long-term care policy issued in this State on or after February 1, 2003, and noncancellable accident and health insurance.

(i)   For any long-term care policy issued in this State on or after February 1, 2003, an insurer shall on or before March 15 of each year:

(1)   Provide to the Commissioner an actuarial certification listing all of its long-term care policy forms available for sale in this State as of December 31 of the prior year, stating that the current premium rate schedule for each form is sufficient to cover anticipated costs under moderately adverse experience and stating that the premium rate schedule is reasonably expected to be sustainable over the life of the form with no future premium increases anticipated.

(2)   For any policy form for which the statement in subdivision (1) of this subsection cannot be made or is qualified, submit a plan of corrective action to the Commissioner for approval.

(j) For purposes of this section, accident and health insurance means insurance against death or injury resulting from accident or from accidental means and insurance against disablement, disease, or sickness of the insured. This includes Medicare supplemental insurance, long-term care, nursing home, or home health care insurance, or any combination thereof, specified disease or illness insurance, hospital indemnity or other fixed indemnity insurance, short-term limited duration health insurance, dental insurance, vision insurance, and medical, hospital, or surgical expense insurance or any combination thereof. Notwithstanding any other provision to the contrary, subsection (h) of this section does not apply to disability income insurance. (1951, c. 784; 1979, c. 755, s. 15; 1989, c. 485, s. 56; 1991, c. 636, s. 3; c. 720, s. 4; 2001-334, s. 17.3; 2005-223, s. 1(b); 2005-412, ss. 1(a), 1(b).)

§ 58-51-100. Credit accident and health insurance.

Credit accident and health insurance is declared to be insurance against death or personal injury by accident or by any specified kind or kinds of accident, and insurance against sickness, ailment, or bodily injury of a debtor who may be indebted to any person, firm, or corporation extending credit to such debtor. The amount of credit accident and health insurance written shall not exceed the installment payment. (1953, c. 1096, s. 2; 1961, c. 1071.)

§ 58-51-105. Hospitalization insurance defined.

Hospitalization insurance is declared to be any form of accident and health insurance which provides indemnity or payment for expenses incurred due to or in connection with hospitalization of the insured, or his dependents. (1953, c. 1096, s. 3.)

§ 58-51-110. Renewal, discontinuance, or replacement of group health insurance.

(a) This section applies to group accident, group health, or group accident and health policies or certificates that are delivered, issued for delivery, renewed, or used in this State which provide hospital, surgical, or major medical expense insurance, or any combination of these coverages, on an expense incurred or service basis. It specifically includes a certificate issued under a policy that was issued to a trust located out of this State, but which includes participating employers located in this State. Renewal of these policies or certificates is presumed to occur on the anniversary date that the coverage was first effective on the employees of the employer.

(b) Whenever a contract described in subsection (a) of this section is replaced by another group contract within 15 days of termination of coverage of the previous group contract, the liability of the succeeding insurer for insuring persons covered under the previous group contract is:

(1) Each person who is eligible for coverage in accordance with the succeeding insurer's plan of benefits, regardless of any other provisions of the new group contract relating to active employment or hospital confinement or pregnancy, shall be covered by the succeeding insurer's plan of benefits; and

(2) Each person not covered under the succeeding insurer's plan of benefits in accordance with subdivision (b)(1) of this section must nevertheless be covered by the succeeding insurer if that person was validly covered, including benefit extension, under the prior plan on the date of discontinuance and if the person is a member of the class of persons eligible for coverage under the succeeding insurer's plan. (1989, c. 775, s. 3; 1991, c. 720, s. 88; 1991 (Reg. Sess., 1992), c. 837, s. 4; 2001-334, s. 6.)

§ 58-51-115. Coordination of benefits with Medicaid.

(a) As used in this section and in G.S. 58-51-120 and G.S. 58-51-125:

(1) "Health benefit plan" means any accident and health insurance policy or certificate; a nonprofit hospital or medical service corporation contract; a health maintenance organization subscriber contract; a plan provided by a multiple employer welfare arrangement; the State Health Plan for Teachers and State Employees and any optional plans or programs operating under Part 2 of Article 3 of Chapter 135 of the General Statutes; or a plan provided by another benefit arrangement. "Health benefit plan" does not mean a Medicare supplement policy as defined in G.S. 58-54-1(5).

(2) "Health insurer" means any health insurance company subject to Articles 1 through 63 of this Chapter, including a multiple employee welfare arrangement, and any corporation subject to Articles 65 and 67 of this Chapter; a group health plan, as defined in section 607(1) of the Employee Retirement Income Security Act of 1974; and the State Health Plan for Teachers and State Employees and any optional plans or programs operating under Part 2 of Article 3 of Chapter 135 of the General Statutes.

(b) No health insurer shall take into account that an individual is eligible for or is provided medical assistance in this or any other state under 42 U.S.C. § 1396a (section 1902 of the Social Security Act) in insuring that individual or making payments under its health benefit plan for benefits to that individual or on that individual's behalf. (1993 (Reg. Sess., 1994), c. 644, s. 1; 1995, c. 193, s. 43; 1999-293, s. 9; 2007-298, s. 8.6; 2007-323, s. 28.22A(o); 2007-345, s. 12.)

§ 58-51-116. ERISA plans may not require Medicaid to pay first.

An employee benefit plan as defined in ERISA shall not include any provision which, because an individual is provided or is eligible for benefits or service pursuant to a State plan under Title XIX of the Social Security Act (Medicaid), has the effect of limiting or excluding coverage or payment for any health care for that individual under the terms of the employee benefit plan, provided that the individual is one who would otherwise be covered or entitled to benefits or services under the employee benefit plan. (1993, c. 321, s. 238.1; 2001-446, s. 4.3.)

§ 58-51-120. Coverage of children.

(a) No health insurer shall deny enrollment of a child under the health benefit plan of the child's parent on any of the following grounds:

(1) The child was born out of wedlock.

(2) The child is not claimed as a dependent on the parent's federal income tax return.

(3) The child does not reside with the parent or in the insurer's service area.

(b) If a parent is required by a court or administrative order to provide health benefit plan coverage for a child, and the parent is eligible for family health benefit plan coverage through a health insurer, the health insurer:

(1) Must allow the parent to enroll, under the family coverage, a child who is otherwise eligible for the coverage without regard to any enrollment season restrictions.

(2) Must enroll the child under family coverage upon application of the child's other parent or the Department of Health and Human Services in connection with its administration of the Medical Assistance or Child Support Enforcement Program if the parent is enrolled but fails to make application to obtain coverage for the child.

(3) May not disenroll or eliminate coverage of the child unless the health insurer is provided satisfactory written evidence that:

a. The court or administrative order is no longer in effect; or

b. The child is or will be enrolled in comparable health benefit plan coverage through another health insurer, which coverage will take effect not later than the effective date of disenrollment.

(c) If a child has health benefit plan coverage through the health insurer of a noncustodial parent, that health insurer shall do all of the following:

(1) Provide such information to the custodial parent as may be necessary for the child to obtain benefits through that coverage.

(2) Permit the custodial parent (or the health care provider, with the custodial parent's approval) to submit claims for covered services without the approval of the noncustodial parent.

(3) Make payments on claims submitted in accordance with subdivision (2) of this subsection directly to the custodial parent, the provider, or the Department of Health and Human Services.

(d) No health insurer may impose requirements on any State agency that has been assigned the rights of an individual eligible for medical assistance under Medicaid and covered for health benefits from the insurer that are different from requirements applicable to an agent or assignee of any other individual so covered. (1993 (Reg. Sess., 1994), c. 644, s. 1; 1997-443, s. 11A.118(a).)

§ 58-51-125. Adopted child coverage.

(a)   Definitions. - As used in this section:

(1)   "Child" means, in connection with any adoption or placement for adoption of the child, an individual who has not attained 18 years of age as of the date of the adoption or placement for adoption.

(2)   "Placement for adoption" means the assumption and retention by a person of a legal obligation for total or partial support of a child in anticipation of the adoption of the child. The child's placement with a person terminates upon the termination of such legal obligations.

(b)   Coverage Effective Upon Placement for Adoption. - If a health benefit plan provides coverage for dependent children of persons covered by the plan, the plan shall provide benefits to dependent children placed with covered persons for adoption under the same terms and conditions that apply to the natural, dependent children of covered persons, irrespective of whether the adoption has become final.

(c)   Restrictions Based on Preexisting Conditions at Time of Placement for Adoption Prohibited. - A health benefit plan may not restrict coverage under the plan of any dependent child adopted by a covered person, or placed with a covered person for adoption, solely on the basis of any preexisting condition of the child at the time that the child would otherwise become eligible for coverage under the plan, if the adoption or placement for adoption occurs while the covered person is eligible for coverage under the plan. (1993 (Reg. Sess., 1994), c. 644, s. 1.)

§ 58-51-130. Standards for disability income insurance policies.

(a)   Definitions. - As used in this section:

(1) "Disability income insurance policy" or "policy" means a policy of accident and health insurance that provides payments when the insured is unable to work because of illness, disease, or injury.

(2) "Policy" includes the certificates referred to in subsection (b) of this section.

(b) Applicability. - This section applies to all policies used in this State, including certificates issued under group policies that are used in this State. This section also applies to a certificate issued under a policy issued and delivered to a trust or to an association outside of this State and covering persons residing in this State.

(c) Disclosure Standards. - Every disability income insurance policy shall include provisions, where applicable, addressing:

(1) Terms of renewability.

(2) Initial and subsequent conditions of eligibility.

(3) Nonduplication of coverage.

(4) Preexisting conditions.

(5) Probationary periods.

(6) Elimination periods.

(7) Requirements for replacement.

(8) Recurrent conditions.

(9) Definitions of terms.

(d) Preexisting Conditions. - If an insurer does not seek a prospective insured's medical history in the application or enrollment process, the insurer shall not deny a claim for disabilities that commence more than 24 months after the effective date of the insured person's coverage on the grounds the disability is caused by a preexisting condition. A policy shall not define a preexisting condition more restrictively than "a condition for which medical advice, diagnosis, care, or treatment was received or recommended within the 24-month period immediately preceding the effective date of coverage of the insured person."

(e)   Exceptions. - Nothing in this section prohibits an insurer from:

(1)   Using an application or enrollment form designed to elicit the medical history of a prospective insured.

(2)   Underwriting based on answers on the form according to the insurer's established standards.

(3)   Contesting the answers in accordance with G.S. 58-51-15(a)(2)a.

(f)   Required Provisions. - Each policy shall include:

(1)   A description of the principal benefits and coverage provided in the policy.

(2)   A statement of the exceptions, reductions, and limitations contained in the policy.

(3)   A statement of the renewal provisions, including any reservation by the insurer of a right to change premiums.

(g)   Other Applicable Provisions. - G.S. 58-51-95(f) applies to individual policies and G.S. 58-51-80(g) applies to group policies.

(h)   Other Income Sources. - If a policy contains a provision that provides for integration of benefits with other income sources, it shall include a definition of what is considered other income sources and a complete description of how benefits will be reduced by other income sources, if at all. No disability income policy shall provide that the amount of any disability benefit paid to the insured shall be reduced by reason of any cost-of-living increase, designated as such under the federal Social Security Act, if the cost-of-living increase occurs during the period for which benefits are payable. (1999-351, s. 2.)

Article 52.

Joint Action to Insure Elderly.

§ 58-52-1. Definitions.

Wherever used in this Article, the following terms shall have the respective meanings hereinafter set forth or indicated, unless the context otherwise requires:

(1)   "Association" means a voluntary unincorporated association formed for the sole purpose of enabling joint and cooperative action to provide accident and health insurance in accordance with this Article in this or any other State having legislation enabling the issuance of insurance of the type provided in this Article.

(2)   "Insurer" means any insurance company which is authorized under Articles 1 through 64 of this Chapter to transact accident and health insurance business in this State. (1963, c. 1125.)

§ 58-52-5. Joint action to insure persons 65 years of age or over and their spouses permitted; associations of insurers; individual and group policies.

Notwithstanding any other provisions of Articles 1 through 64 of this Chapter or any other law which may be inconsistent herewith, any insurer may join with one or more other insurers to plan, develop, underwrite, offer, sell and provide to or for any resident person of this State, or of another state if permitted by the laws of such other state, who is 65 years of age or over and to the spouse of such person, insurance against financial loss from accident or sickness, or both. Such insurance may also cover an employer's nonresident employees and nonresident retired employees 65 years of age or older and their spouses, provided such employees are regularly employed within this State or were so employed at the time of their retirement. Such insurance may be offered, issued and administered through an association of two or more insurers which association is formed for the purpose of offering, selling, issuing and administering such insurance, and may be in the form of a policy insuring a resident who is 65 years of age or older, and the spouse of such resident, if any, or in the form of a group policy insuring residents 65 years of age or older and the spouses of such residents, or in both forms. On such insurance each insurer shall be severally liable for a percentage of the risks determined under the articles of association of the association. The insurer members of such association may agree with respect to premium rates, policy provisions, commission rates and other matters within the scope of this Article. (1963, c. 1125; 1965, c. 677; 1991, c. 720, s. 72.)

§ 58-52-10. Regional plans authorized.

If "over 65" accident and health insurance plans exist or hereafter come into existence in other states pursuant to legislative authority similar to that herein given, North Carolina insurers may jointly participate with insurers of such other states in forming a regional plan to carry out the purposes of this Article. Any association formed for the operation of a regional plan shall be exempt from the provisions of G.S. 58-3-85 and may engage in business in North Carolina through its insurer members only, without being separately licensed. (1963, c. 1125.)

§ 58-52-15. Forms and rate manuals subject to § 58-51-1; disapproval of rates.

The forms of the policies, applications, certificates or other evidence of insurance coverage and the rate manual showing rates, rules and classification of risks applicable thereto shall be subject to the applicable provisions of G.S. 58-51-1. The Commissioner may disapprove the premium rates for such insurance, or any class thereof, if he finds that such rates are by reasonable assumptions excessive in relation to the benefits provided. In determining whether such rates by reasonable assumptions are excessive in relation to the benefits provided, the Commissioner shall give due consideration to past and prospective claim experience on such insurance, or other comparable insurance, within and outside this State, and to fluctuations in such claim experience, to a reasonable risk charge, to contribution to surplus and contingency funds, to past and prospective expenses, both within and outside this State, and to all other relevant factors within and outside this State, including any differing operating methods of the insurers joining in the issue of such insurance. In the event of any such disapproval, the decision of the Commissioner shall be subject to review under G.S. 58-2-75. In exercising the powers conferred by this section, the Commissioner shall not be bound by any other requirements of Articles 1 through 64 of this Chapter with respect to standard provisions required to be included in the forms of the policies, applications, certificates or other evidence of insurance coverage filed with the Commissioner. (1963, c. 1125.)

§ 58-52-20. Organization of associations of insurers; powers; annual statements; mutual insurers may participate.

An association formed for the purposes of this Article shall adopt articles of association for the organization, administration and regulation of its affairs, which articles of association and any amendments thereto shall be filed within 30 days of adoption of same with the Commissioner. Such association may establish requirements for membership of insurers, hold title to property, incur expenses for advertising, soliciting and administering such insurance, including payment of salary or compensation to persons employed by it, enter into contracts, limit the liability of and among its members, and shall be subject to the provisions of G.S. 1-69.1.

Such association shall file annually with the Commissioner, on such date and in such form as the Commissioner may prescribe, a statement with respect to its operations.

For the purpose of implementing joint action of insurers in furnishing accident and health insurance coverage to persons 65 years of age and older and their spouses, in accordance with the intent of this Article as expressed herein, insurers operating on a mutual plan, or on any other membership basis, may participate in such a plan, and the persons insured through the plan shall not be entitled to membership in any such insurer nor shall they be entitled to any dividend rights, voting rights, or any other rights peculiar to mutual insurance policyholders and participants in membership insurance plans. (1963, c. 1125; 1991, c. 720, s. 4.)

§ 58-52-25. No additional licensing required.

Accident and health insurance authorized by this Article and offered by or through an association formed for the purpose of this Article may be solicited and offered directly by such association, any insurer member of such association, and by or through any person authorized by the Department to sell accident and health insurance in this State, without any additional license being required. (1963, c. 1125; 1991, c. 720, s. 60.)

Article 53.

Group Health Insurance Continuation and Conversion Privileges.

Part 1. Continuation.

§ 58-53-1. Definitions.

As used in this Article, the following terms have the meanings specified:

(1) "Group policy" means a group accident and health insurance policy issued by an insurance company and a group contract issued by a service corporation or health maintenance organization or similar corporation or organization.

(2) "Individual policy" or "converted policy" means an individual health insurance policy issued by an insurance company or an individual contract issued by a service corporation or health maintenance organization or similar corporation or organization.

(3) "Insurance" and "insured" refer to coverage under a group policy, individual policy or converted policy on a premium-paying basis, and do not include coverage provided by reason of a disability extension.

(4) "Insurer" means the entity issuing a group policy or an individual or converted policy.

(5) "Medicare" means Title XVIII of the United States Social Security Act as added by the Social Security Amendments of 1965 or as later amended or superseded.

(5a) "Member" or "employee" includes an insured spouse or dependent of a member or of an employee.

(6) "Premium" includes any premium or other consideration payable for coverage under a group or individual policy.

(7) "Reasonable and customary" means the most frequently used level of charge made for the supplies or for a specific service in the geographic subarea in which such supplies or services are received, of like kind or by physicians, or other practitioners, with similar qualifications. (1981, c. 706, s. 1; 1983, c. 142, s. 1; 1997-259, s. 10.)

§ 58-53-5. Continuation of group hospital, surgical, and major medical coverage after termination of employment or membership.

A group policy delivered or issued for delivery in this State that insures employees or members for hospital, surgical or major medical insurance on an expense incurred or service basis under this Chapter, other than for specific diseases or for accidental injuries only, shall provide that employees or members whose coverage under the group policy would otherwise terminate because of termination of active employment or membership, or termination of membership in the eligible class or classes under the policy, shall be entitled to continue their hospital, surgical, and medical insurance under that group policy, for themselves and their eligible spouses and dependents with respect to whom they were insured on the date of termination, subject to all of the group policy's terms and conditions and to the conditions specified in this Part. Provided, the terms and conditions set forth in this Part are intended as minimum requirements and shall not be construed to impose additional or different requirements upon those group hospital, surgical, or major medical plans that provide continuation benefits equal to or better than those required in this Part. (1981, c. 706, s. 1; 1997-259, s. 11.)

§ 58-53-10. Eligibility.

Continuation shall only be available to an employee or member who has been continuously insured under the group policy, or for similar benefits under any other group policy that it replaced, during the period of three consecutive months immediately before the date of termination. The employee or member may elect continuation for a period of not fewer than 60 days after the date of termination or loss of eligibility. The employee or member shall make the first contribution upon the election to continue coverage, and the coverage shall be retroactive to the date of termination or loss of eligibility. (1981, c. 706, s. 1; 2001-334, s. 7.1.)

§ 58-53-15. Exception.

Continuation shall not be available for any person who is or could be covered by any other arrangement of hospital, surgical, or medical coverage for individuals in a group, whether insured or uninsured, within 31 days immediately following the date of termination; or whose insurance terminated because he failed to pay any required contribution for the insurance. (1981, c. 706, s. 1.)

§ 58-53-20. Benefits not included.

Continuation is not required to include dental, vision care, or prescription drug benefits, or any other benefits provided under the group policy in addition to its hospital, surgical, or major medical benefits. (1981, c. 706, s. 1.)

§ 58-53-25. Notification to employee.

In addition to the notification requirement set forth in G.S. 58-53-40, notification may be included on insurance identification cards or may be given by the employer, orally or in writing as a part of the exit process from the employment. (1981, c. 706, s. 1.)

§ 58-53-30. Payment of premiums.

An employee or member electing continuation must pay to the group policyholder or his employer, in advance, the amount of contribution required by the policyholder or employer, but not more than one hundred two percent (102%) of the full group rate for the insurance applicable under the group policy on the due date of each payment. The employee or member may not be required to pay the amount of the contribution less often than monthly. In order to be eligible for continuation of coverage, the employee or member must make a written election of continuation, on a form furnished by the group policyholder or by the insurer. (1981, c. 706, s. 1; 1999-273, s. 1; 2001-334, s. 7.2.)

§ 58-53-35. Termination of continuation.

(a)	Continuation of insurance under the group policy for any person shall terminate on the earliest of the following dates:

(1)	The date 18 months after the date the employee's or member's insurance under the policy would otherwise have terminated because of termination of employment or members;

(2)	The date ending the period for which the employee or member last makes his required contribution, if he discontinues his contributions;

(3)	The date the employee or member becomes or is eligible to become covered for similar benefits under any arrangement of coverage for individuals in a group, whether insured or uninsured;

(4)	The date on which the group policy is terminated or, in the case of a multiple employer plan, the date his employer terminates participation under the group master policy. When this occurs the employee or member shall have the privilege described in G.S. 58-53-45 if the date of termination precedes that on which his actual continuation of insurance under that policy would have terminated. The insurer that insured the group before the date of termination shall make a converted policy available to the employee or member.

(b)	Notwithstanding subdivision (a)(4) of this section, if the employer replaces the group policy with another group policy, the employee is entitled to continue under the successor group policy for any unexpired period of continuation to which the employee is entitled. (1981, c. 706, s. 1; 1983, c. 142, s. 2; 1993, c. 529, s. 3.8; 1997-259, s. 12.)

§ 58-53-40. Notification.

A notification of the continuation privilege shall be included in each individual certification of coverage. (1981, c. 706, s. 1.)

§ 58-53-41. Extension of election period and effect on coverage.

(a) Definitions. - As used in this section, the following terms have the meanings specified:

(1) "Act" means the federal American Recovery and Reinvestment Act of 2009, P.L. 111-5, effective February 17, 2009.

(2) "Assistance eligible individual" has the same meaning as found in section 3001 of the Act.

(b) An employee or member who does not have an election of continuation coverage, as described in this Part, in effect on June 8, 2009, but who would be an assistance eligible individual under Title III of the Act if that election were in effect, may elect continuation coverage pursuant to the Part. The election shall be made no later than 60 days after the date the administrator of the group policy subject to this Part (or other entity involved) provides the notice required by section 3001(a)(7) of the Act. The administrator of the group policy subject to this Part (or other entity involved) shall provide such individuals with additional notice of the right to elect coverage pursuant to this section within 60 days after June 8, 2009.

(c) Continuation of coverage elected pursuant to subsection (b) of this section shall commence with the first period of coverage beginning on or after June 8, 2009, and shall not extend beyond the period of continuation coverage that would have been required under G.S. 58-53-35 if the coverage had instead been elected pursuant to G.S. 58-53-10.

(d) With respect to any individual electing continuation coverage pursuant to this section, the period beginning on the date of the qualifying event and ending on the date of the first period of coverage on or after June 8, 2009, shall be disregarded for purposes of determining the 63-day period referred to in G.S. 58-68-30(c)(2)a. and G.S. 58-51-17(a)(2)a. (2009-62, s. 1.)

Part 2. Conversion.

§ 58-53-45. Right to obtain individual policy upon termination of group hospital, surgical or major medical coverage.

A group policy delivered or issued for delivery in this State that insures employees or members for hospital, surgical, or medical insurance on an expense incurred or service basis under Articles 1 through 67 of this Chapter other than for specific diseases or for accidental injuries only, shall provide that an employee or member whose insurance under the group policy has been terminated shall be entitled to have a converted policy issued to him by the insurer under whose group policy he was last insured, without evidence of insurability, subject to the terms and conditions specified in this Part. Provided, the terms and conditions set forth in this Part are intended as minimum requirements and shall not be construed to impose additional or different requirements upon those group hospital, surgical, or major medical plans already in force, or hereafter placed into effect, that provide conversion benefits equal to or better than those required in this Part. (1981, c. 706, s. 1.)

§ 58-53-50. Restrictions.

A converted policy shall not be available to an employee or member if termination of his insurance under the group policy occurred because:

(1) Of termination of employment or membership and either he was not entitled to continuation of group coverage under Part 1 of this Article or failed to elect such continuation;

(2) He failed to make timely payment of any required contribution for the cost of continuation of insurance;

(3) He had not been continuously covered under the group policy or for similar benefits under any other group policy that it replaced during the period of three consecutive months immediately prior to termination of active employment ending with such termination;

(4) The group policy terminated or an employer's participation terminated, and the insurance is replaced by similar coverage under another group policy within 31 days of date of termination; or

(5) He failed to continue his insurance for the entire maximum period of 18 months following termination of active employment as provided for in Part 1 of this Article, unless that failure to continue was because of change of insurer by the employer and the change of insurer was consummated during the one year continuation period. In that event the employee or member shall be entitled to be issued a converted policy by the insurer that provided the group policy to the employer before the change of insurer. (1981, c. 706, s. 1; 1983, c. 142, s. 3; 1993 (Reg. Sess., 1994), c. 569, s. 9; 1997-259, s. 13.)

§ 58-53-55. Time limit.

In order to be eligible for conversion, written application and the first premium payment for the converted policy must be made to the insurer not later than 31 days after the date of termination of insurance provided under Part 1 of this Article. The effective date of the converted policy shall be the day following the later of:

(1) The termination of insurance under the group policy when it is not replaced by one providing similar coverage within 31 days of the termination date of the immediately prior group plan; or

(2) The termination of the period of continued coverage under the group policy or policies. (1981, c. 706, s. 1; 1993 (Reg. Sess., 1994), c. 569, s. 10; 1997-259, s. 14.)

§ 58-53-60. Premium.

(a) The premium for the converted policy or group conversion trust certificate shall be determined in accordance with the insurer's table of premium rates applicable to the age and class of risk to be covered under that policy and to the type and amount of insurance provided.

(b) All insurers licensed to do business in this State, who issue conversion policies or group conversion trust certificates under this Part, have the right to increase that element of the premium that applies to hospital room and board benefit increases provided for in G.S. 58-53-95(5) by an amount proportionate to the increase promulgated by the Commissioner. Such premium increases shall be filed with the Commissioner.

(c) All premium rates and adjustments to premium rates for converted policies or group conversion trust certificates shall be reasonable and must be filed with and approved by the Commissioner prior to use. A premium rate shall be deemed to be reasonable if the insurer demonstrates that the premium charged is expected to produce an incurred loss ratio to earned premiums of not less than sixty percent (60%) for all policies or group conversion trust certificates providing similar benefits offered and issued by the insurer. If an insurer experiences an incurred loss ratio of greater than eighty percent (80%) for all such policies, it shall be deemed reasonable for that insurer to increase premium rates to a level that will produce a prospective incurred loss ratio of no greater than eighty percent (80%), and the insurer shall file such new rates with the Commissioner not more often than once a year. (1981, c. 706, s. 1; 1983, c. 669; 1995, c. 517, s. 30.)

§ 58-53-65. Coverage.

The converted policy shall cover the employee or member and his eligible dependents who were covered by the group policy on the date of termination of insurance. At the option of the insurer, a separate converted policy may be issued to cover any such eligible dependent. (1981, c. 706, s. 1.)

§ 58-53-70. Exclusions.

An insurer shall not be required to issue a converted policy covering any person if such person is or can be covered by Medicare. Furthermore, an insurer shall not be required to issue a converted policy covering any person if:

(1) a. Such person is covered for similar benefits by another hospital, surgical, medical or major medical expense insurance policy, or hospital or medical service subscriber contract or medical practice or other prepayment plan, or by any other plan or program;

b. Such person is or could be covered for similar benefits, whether or not covered for such benefits, under any arrangement of coverage for individuals in a group, whether insured or uninsured; or

c. Similar benefits are provided for or available to such person, whether or not covered for such benefits, by reason of any State or federal law; and

(2) The benefits under sources of the kind referred to in subdivision (1)a of this section for such person, or benefits provided or available under sources of the kind referred to in subdivisions (1)b and (1)c of this section for such person, together with the converted policy's benefits would result in overinsurance according to the insurer's standards for overinsurance; or

(3) An enrollee's enrollment in a health maintenance organization has been terminated for cause in accord with the terms of the enrollee's evidence of coverage or the health maintenance organization's contract with the group. (1981, c. 706, s. 1; 1991, c. 195, s. 2.)

§ 58-53-75. Information.

A converted policy may provide that an insurer may at any time request information of an insured policyholder with respect to any person covered thereunder as to whether he is covered for the similar benefits described in G.S. 58-53-70(1)a or is or could be covered for the similar benefits described in G.S. 58-53-70(1)b and 58-53-70(1)c. The converted policy may provide that as of any premium due date an insurer may refuse to renew the policy or the coverage of any insured person for the following reasons only:

(1) Either those similar benefits for which such person is or could be covered, together with the converted policy's benefits, would result in overinsurance according to the insurer's standards for overinsurance, or the policyholder of the converted policy fails to provide the requested information;

(2) Fraud or material misrepresentation in applying for any benefits under the converted policy;

(3) Eligibility of any insured person for coverage under Medicare, or under any other State or federal law providing benefits substantially similar to those provided by the converted policy; or

(4) Termination of an enrollee's enrollment in a health maintenance organization for cause in accord with the terms of the enrollee's evidence of coverage or the health maintenance organization's contract with the group. (1981, c. 706, s. 1; 1991, c. 195, s. 3.)

§ 58-53-80. Excess benefits.

An insurer shall not be required to issue a converted policy providing benefits in excess of the equivalent value of hospital, surgical, or major medical insurance under the group policy from which conversion is made. (1981, c. 706, s. 1.)

§ 58-53-85. Preexisting conditions.

The converted policy shall not exclude, as a preexisting condition, any condition covered by the group policy. However, the converted policy may provide for a reduction of its hospital, surgical or medical benefits by the amount of any such benefits payable under the group policy after the individual's insurance terminates thereunder. The converted policy may also provide that during the first policy year the benefits payable under the converted policy, together with the benefits payable under the group policy, shall not exceed those that would have been payable had the individual's insurance under the group policy remained in force and effect. (1981, c. 706, s. 1.)

§ 58-53-90. Basic coverage plans.

(a) Subject to the provisions of this Article, if the group insurance policy from which conversion is made insures the employee or member for basic hospital and surgical expense insurance, the employee or member shall be entitled to obtain a converted policy providing, at his option, coverage on an expense incurred basis under any of the following plans:

(1) Plan A:

a. Hospital room and board daily expense benefits in a maximum dollar amount approximating the average semiprivate rate charged in the major metropolitan area of this State, for a maximum duration of 70 days;

b. Miscellaneous hospital expense benefits up to a maximum amount of 10 times the hospital room and board daily expense benefits; and

c. Surgical expense benefits according to a surgical procedures schedule consistent with those customarily offered by the insurer under group or individual health insurance policies and providing a maximum benefit of eight hundred dollars ($800.00).

(2) Plan B:

Identical to Plan A, except that (i) the maximum hospital room and board daily expense benefit is seventy-five percent (75%) of the corresponding Plan A maximum and (ii) the surgical schedule maximum is six hundred dollars ($600.00).

(3) Plan C:

Identical to Plan A, except that (i) the maximum hospital room and board daily expense benefit is fifty percent (50%) of the corresponding Plan A maximum and (ii) the surgical schedule maximum is four hundred dollars ($400.00).

(b) The maximum dollar amount for the maximum hospital room and board daily expense benefit of Plan A shall be determined by the Commissioner and may be redetermined by him from time to time as to converted policies issued subsequent to such redetermination. Such redetermination shall not be made more often than once in three years. The Plan A maximum, and the corresponding maximums in Plans B and C, shall be rounded to the nearest multiple ten dollars ($10.00), provided that rounding may be to the next higher or lower multiple of ten dollars ($10.00) if otherwise exactly midway between. (1981, c. 706, s. 1.)

§ 58-53-95. Major medical plans.

Subject to the provisions of this Article, if the group policy from which conversion is made insures the employee or member for major medical expense insurance, the employee or member shall be entitled to obtain a converted policy providing catastrophic or major medical coverage under a plan meeting the following requirements:

(1) A maximum benefit at least equal to either, at the option of the insurer,

a. A maximum payment per covered person for all covered medical expenses incurred during that person's lifetime, equal to the lesser of the maximum benefit provided under the group policy or one hundred thousand dollars ($100,000); or

b. A maximum payment for each unrelated injury or sickness, equal to the lesser of the maximum benefit provided under the group policy or one hundred thousand dollars ($100,000).

(2) Payment of benefits at the rate of eighty percent (80%) of covered medical expenses that are in excess of the deductible, until twenty percent (20%) of such expenses in a benefit period reaches one thousand dollars ($1,000), after which benefits will be paid at the rate of one hundred percent (100%) during the remainder of such benefit period. Payment of benefits for outpatient treatment of mental illness, if provided in the converted policy, may be at a lesser rate but not less than fifty percent (50%).

(3) A deductible for each benefit period which, at the option of the insurer, shall be (i) the sum of the benefits deductible and one hundred dollars ($100.00), or (ii) the corresponding deductible in the group policy. The term "benefits deductible," as used in this Part, means the value of any benefits provided on an expense incurred basis that are provided with respect to covered medical expenses by any other group or individual hospital, surgical, or medical insurance policy or medical practice or other prepayment plan, or any other plan, or program whether insured or uninsured, or by reason of any State or federal law and if, pursuant to G.S. 58-53-100, the converted policy provides both basic hospital or surgical coverage and major medical coverage, the value of such basic benefits.

If the maximum benefit is determined by subdivision (1)a of this section, the insurer may require that the deductible be satisfied during a period of not less than three months if the deductible is one hundred dollars ($100.00) or less, and not less than six months if the deductible exceeds one hundred dollars ($100.00).

(4) The benefit period shall be each calendar year when the maximum benefit is determined by subdivision (1)a of this section or 24 months when the maximum benefit is determined by subdivision (1)b of this section.

(5) The term "covered medical expenses," as used in this Part, shall include, in the case of hospital room and board charges, at a minimum the lesser of the dollar amount in G.S. 58-53-90(a)(1) and the average semiprivate room and board rate for the hospital in which the individual is confined, and at a minimum twice such amount for charges in an intensive care unit. Any surgical procedures schedule shall be consistent with those customarily offered by the insurer under group or individual health insurance policies and must provide at least a one thousand two hundred dollar ($1,200) maximum. (1981, c. 706, s. 1.)

§ 58-53-100. Alternative plans.

At the option of the insurer, such plans of benefits set forth in G.S. 58-53-90 and 58-53-95 may be provided under one policy. Instead of providing the plans of benefits set forth in G.S. 58-53-90 and 58-53-95, the insurer may elect to provide a policy of comprehensive medical expense benefits without first dollar coverage. Said policy shall conform to the requirements of G.S. 58-53-95; provided, however, that an insurer electing to provide such a policy shall make available the following deductible options: one hundred dollars ($100.00), five hundred dollars ($500.00), and one thousand dollars ($1,000). Alternatively, such a policy may provide for deductible options equal to the greater of the benefits deductible and the amount specified in the preceding sentence. (1981, c. 706, s. 1.)

§ 58-53-105. Insurer option.

The insurer may, at its option, offer alternative plans for group health conversion in addition to those required by this Part. Furthermore, if any insurer customarily offers individual policies on a service basis, that insurer may, in lieu of converted policies on an expense incurred basis, make available converted policies on a service basis which, in the opinion of the Commissioner satisfy the intent of this Part. (1981, c. 706, s. 1.)

§ 58-53-110. Other conversion provisions.

(a)   If coverage would in any event have been continued under the group policy on an employee following his retirement prior to the time he is or could be covered by Medicare and provided he would have been eligible for continuation under the group policy as specified in G.S. 58-53-10, the employee or member may elect, in lieu of such continuation of group insurance, to have the same conversion rights as would apply had that insurance terminated at retirement.

(b)   The converted policy may provide for reduction or termination of coverage of any person upon his eligibility for coverage under Medicare or under any other State or federal law providing for benefits similar to those provided by the converted policy.

(c)   Subject to the conditions set forth in this subsection, the conversion privilege shall also be available (i) to the surviving spouse, if any, at the death of the employee or member, with respect to the spouse and any eligible children whose coverage under the group policy terminates by reason of such death, or if the group policy provides for continuation of dependents' coverage following the employee's or member's death, at the end of such continuation, or (ii) to the spouse of the employee or member upon termination of coverage of the spouse because the spouse becomes ineligible because of divorce, separation, or otherwise, while the employee or member remains insured under the group policy, with respect to the spouse and such children whose coverage under the group policy terminates at the same time, or (iii) to a child solely with respect to himself upon termination of his coverage by reason of ceasing to be an eligible family member under the group policy, if a conversion privilege is not otherwise provided above with respect to such termination.

(d)   The insurer may elect to provide group insurance coverage in lieu of the issuance of a converted individual policy, notwithstanding the maximum period of group continuation specified in G.S. 58-53-35(1).

(e)   A notification of the conversion privilege shall be included in each certificate of coverage.

(f) A converted policy which is delivered outside this State may be on a form which could be delivered in such other jurisdiction as a converted policy had the group policy been issued in that jurisdiction. (1981, c. 706, s. 1; 1983, c. 668, s. 1.)

§ 58-53-115. Article inapplicable to certain plans.

The provisions of this article shall not apply to hospital, surgical or major medical plans offered by employers on a self-insured basis. (1981, c. 706, s. 2.)

Article 54.

Medicare Supplement Insurance Minimum Standards.

§ 58-54-1. Definitions.

Unless the context clearly indicates otherwise, the following words, as used in this Article, have the following meanings:

(1) "Applicant" means (i) in the case of an individual Medicare supplement policy or subscriber contract, the person who seeks to contract for insurance benefits; and (ii) in the case of a group Medicare supplement policy or subscriber contract, the proposed certificate holder.

(2) "Certificate" means any certificate issued under a group Medicare supplement policy, which certificate has been delivered or issued for delivery in this State.

(3) "Insurer" includes entities subject to Articles 65 through 67 of this Chapter.

(4) "Medicare" means the "Health Insurance for the Aged Act", Title XVIII of the Social Security Amendments of 1965, as then constituted or later amended.

(5) "Policy" means a Medicare supplement policy, which is a group or individual policy of accident and health insurance under Articles 1 through 64 of this Chapter, a subscriber contract under Articles 65 and 66 of this Chapter, or an evidence of coverage under Article 67 of this Chapter, other than a policy issued pursuant to a contract under section 1876 or section 1833 of the federal

Social Security Act (42 U.S.C. § 1395 et seq.), or an issued policy under a demonstration project authorized pursuant to amendments to the federal Social Security Act, that is advertised, marketed, or designed primarily as a supplement to reimbursements under Medicare for the hospital, medical, or surgical expenses of persons eligible for Medicare. (1989, c. 729, s. 1; 1991 (Reg. Sess., 1992), c. 815, s. 1; 1993, c. 553, s. 19.)

§ 58-54-5. Applicability and scope.

(a)   Except as otherwise specifically provided, this Article applies to:

(1)   All policies delivered or issued for delivery in this State on or after August 7, 1989; and

(2)   All certificates issued under group policies that have been delivered or issued for delivery in this State on or after August 7, 1989.

(b)   This Article does not apply to an insurance contract of one or more employers or labor organizations, or of the trustees of a fund established by one or more employers or labor organizations, or combination thereof, for employees or former employees or a combination thereof, or for members or former members, or a combination thereof, of the labor organizations.

(c)   This Article does not prohibit or apply to insurance contracts or health care benefit plans, including group conversion policies, that are provided to Medicare eligible persons and that are not marketed or held out to be Medicare supplement policies or benefit plans. (1989, c. 729, s. 1.)

§ 58-54-10. Standards for policy provisions.

(a) No policy in force in this State shall contain benefits that duplicate benefits provided by Medicare.

(b)   The Commissioner shall adopt rules to establish specific standards for provisions of policies. Such standards shall be in addition to and in accordance with applicable State law. No requirement of State law relating to minimum required policy benefits, other than the minimum standards contained in this

Article, applies to policies. The standards may include without limitation to: terms of renewability; initial and subsequent conditions of eligibility; nonduplication of coverage; probationary periods; benefit limitations, exceptions, and reductions; elimination periods; requirements for replacement; recurrent conditions; and definitions of terms.

(c) The Commissioner may adopt rules that specify prohibited policy provisions not otherwise specifically authorized by State law that, in the opinion of the Commissioner, are unjust, unfair, or unfairly discriminatory to any person insured or proposed for coverage under a policy.

(d) Notwithstanding any other provision of State law, a policy may not deny a claim for losses incurred more than six months from the effective date of coverage for a preexisting condition. A policy may not define a preexisting condition more restrictively than a condition for which medical advice was given or treatment was recommended by or received from a physician within six months before the effective date of coverage.

(e) Repealed by Session Laws 1991 (Regular Session, 1992), c. 815, s. 3. (1989, c. 729, s. 1; 1991, c. 490, s. 6; 1991 (Reg. Sess., 1992), c. 815, s. 3.)

§ 58-54-15. Minimum standards for benefits, marketing practices, compensation arrangements, reporting practices, and claims payments.

The Commissioner shall adopt rules to establish minimum standards for benefits, marketing practices, compensation arrangements, reporting practices, and claims payments under policies. (1989, c. 729, s. 1; 1989 (Reg. Sess., 1990), c. 941, s. 8; 1993, c. 504, s. 38.)

§ 58-54-20. Loss ratio standards and filing requirements.

(a) Every insurer providing group Medicare supplement insurance benefits to a resident of this State pursuant to G.S. 58-54-5 shall file a copy of the master policy and any certificate used in this State in accordance with the filing requirements and procedures applicable to group policies issued in this State.

(b) Policies shall return to policyholders benefits that are reasonable in relation to the premium charged. The Commissioner shall adopt rules to establish minimum standards for loss ratios of policies on the basis of incurred claims experience, or incurred health care expenses where coverage is provided by a health maintenance organization on a service rather than reimbursement basis, and earned premiums in accordance with accepted actuarial principles and practices. Every insurer providing policies or certificates in this State shall annually file its rates, rating schedules, and supporting documentation to demonstrate that it is in compliance with the applicable loss ratio standards of this State. All filings of rates and rating schedules shall demonstrate that the actual and expected losses in relation to premiums comply with the requirements of this Article.

(c) No insurer shall provide compensation to its agents or other producers that is greater than the renewal compensation that would have been paid on an existing policy if the existing policy is replaced by another policy with the same insurer where the new policy benefits are substantially similar to the benefits under the old policy and the old policy was issued by the same insurer or insurer group. (1989, c. 729, s. 1; 1991 (Reg. Sess., 1992), c. 815, s. 4.)

§ 58-54-25. Disclosure standards.

(a) In order to provide for full and fair disclosure in the sale of policies, no policy or certificate shall be delivered in this State unless an outline of coverage is delivered to the applicant at the time application is made.

(b) The Commissioner shall prescribe the format and content of the outline of coverage required by subsection (a) of this section. For purposes of this section, "format" means style, arrangement, and overall appearance, including such items as the size, color, and prominence of type and arrangement of text and captions. Such outline of coverage shall include:

(1) A description of the principal benefits and coverage provided in the policy;

(2) A statement of the exceptions, reductions, and limitations contained in the policy;

(3) A statement of the renewal provisions, including any reservation by the insurer of a right to change premiums; and

(4) A statement that the outline of coverage is a summary of the policy issued or applied for and that the policy should be consulted to determine governing contractual provisions.

(c) The Commissioner may prescribe by rule a standard form and the contents of an informational brochure for persons eligible for Medicare, which is intended to improve the buyer's ability to select the most appropriate coverage and improve the buyer's understanding of Medicare. Except in the case of direct response insurance policies, the Commissioner may require by rule that the information brochure be provided to any prospective insured eligible for Medicare concurrently with delivery of the outline of coverage. With respect to direct response insurance policies, the Commissioner may require by rule that the prescribed brochure be provided upon request to any prospective insured eligible for Medicare, but in no event later than the time of policy delivery.

(d) The Commissioner may adopt rules for captions or notice requirements, determined to be in the public interest and designed to inform prospective insureds that particular insurance coverages are not Medicare supplement coverages, for all accident and health insurance policies sold to persons eligible for Medicare, other than: Medicare supplement policies; disability income policies; basic, catastrophic, or major medical expense policies; or single premium, nonrenewable policies.

(e) The Commissioner may further adopt rules to govern the full and fair disclosure of the information in connection with the replacement of accident and health insurance policies, subscriber contracts, or certificates by persons eligible for Medicare.

(f) No insurer shall use attained age as a structure or methodology for its Medicare supplement insurance rates unless the structure or methodology is fully disclosed to the applicant at the time of application or to the insured at the time of delivery if the purchase is by mail order. All types of solicitation materials shall clearly indicate that the premiums are based on attained age, which means that those premiums will increase each year. The Commissioner shall prescribe by rule the format and content of the attained age rating disclosure notice. The notice shall include:

(1) A statement that attained age rating means that rates increase as the insured ages or by the age group in which the insured is.

(2) An illustration based on actual attained age that states the dollar amount of premium increase for the insured over a period of not less than 10 policy years and that displays the life expectancy of the insured at the beginning of the period.

(3) A statement that premiums for other Medicare supplement policies that are on issue age bases do not increase as the insured ages.

(4) A statement that other Medicare supplement policies that are on issue age bases should be compared to policies on attained age bases. (1989, c. 729, s. 1; 1991 (Reg. Sess., 1992), c. 815, s. 2; 1998-211, s. 12.)

§ 58-54-30. Notice of free examination.

Policies or certificates shall have a notice prominently printed on the first page of the policy or certificate or attached thereon stating in substance that the applicant has the right to return the policy or certificate within 30 days of its delivery and to have the premium refunded if, after examination of the policy or certificate, the applicant is not satisfied for any reason. Any refund made pursuant to this section shall be paid directly to the applicant by the insurer in a timely manner. (1989, c. 729, s. 1.)

§ 58-54-35. Filing requirements for advertising.

Every insurer providing Medicare supplement insurance or benefits in this State shall provide a copy of any Medicare supplement advertisement intended for use in this State whether through written, radio, or television medium to the Commissioner for review or approval by the Commissioner. (1989, c. 729, s. 1.)

§ 58-54-40. Penalties.

In addition to any other applicable penalties for violations of Articles 1 through 64 or 65 and 66 or 67 of this Chapter, the Commissioner may require any person that has violated or is violating any provision of this Article or any rule adopted under this Article to either (i) cease marketing any policy or certificate in this State that is related directly or indirectly to a violation or (ii) take such actions as are necessary to comply with this Article or such rules. (1989, c. 729, s. 1.)

§ 58-54-45. By reason of disability.

(a) In addition to any rule adopted under this Article that is directly or indirectly related to open enrollment, an insurer shall at least make standardized Medicare Supplement Plan A available to persons eligible for Medicare by reason of disability before age 65 and also standardized Plan C or F if marketing either Plan to persons eligible for Medicare due to age. This action shall be taken without regard to medical condition, claims experience, or health status. To be eligible, a person must submit an application during the six-month period beginning with the first month the person first enrolls in Medicare Part B. For those persons that are retroactively enrolled in Medicare Part B due to a retroactive eligibility decision made by the Social Security Administration, the application must be submitted within a six-month period beginning with the month in which the person receives notification of the retroactive eligibility decision.

(b) Persons eligible for Medicare by reason of disability before age 65 who are enrolled in a managed care plan and whose coverage under the managed care plan is terminated through cancellation, nonrenewal, or disenrollment have the guaranteed right to purchase Medicare Supplement Plans A and C from any insurer within 63 days after the date of termination or disenrollment.

(c) An insurer may develop premium rates specific to the disabled population. No insurer shall discriminate in the pricing of the Medicare supplement plans referred to in this section because of the health status, claims experience, receipt of health care, or medical condition of an applicant where an application for the plan is submitted during an open enrollment or is submitted within 63 days after the managed care plan is terminated. The rates and any applicable rating factors for the Medicare supplement plans referred to in this section shall be filed with and approved by the Commissioner. (1998-211, s. 13; 2001-334, ss. 10.1, 10.2; 2005-223, s. 6; 2009-382, s. 11.)

§ 58-54-50. Rules for compliance with federal law and regulations.

The Commissioner may adopt temporary rules necessary to conform Medicare supplement policies and certificates to the requirements of federal law and regulations, including:

(1) Requiring refunds or credits if the policies or certificates do not meet loss ratio requirements.

(2) Establishing a uniform methodology for calculating and reporting loss ratios.

(3) Assuring public access to policies, premiums, and loss ratio information of issuers of Medicare supplement insurance.

(4) Establishing standards for Medicare Select policies and certificates.

(5) Any other changes required by Congress or the U.S. Department of Health and Human Services, or any successor agency. (1998-211, s. 13; 2001-334, s. 11.1.)

Article 55.

Long-Term Care Insurance.

Part 1. General Provisions.

§ 58-55-1. Short title.

This Article may be cited as the "Long-Term Care Insurance Act". (1987, c. 331.)

§ 58-55-5. Dual options.

(a) No policy that conditions the eligibility of benefits on prior hospitalization may be delivered or issued for delivery in this State unless the insurer or other entity offering that policy also offers a policy that does not condition eligibility of benefits on such a requirement.

(b) Policies that were delivered, issued for delivery, or renewed on and after October 1, 1989, that did not condition the eligibility of benefits on prior hospitalizations shall be amended, upon the insured's written request, to condition eligibility of benefits on prior hospitalization, provided that the insured receives the appropriate reduction in premium. (1991, c. 644, s. 24.)

§ 58-55-10. Purposes.

The purposes of this Article are to promote the public interest, to promote the availability of long-term care insurance policies, to protect applicants for long-term care insurance from unfair or deceptive sales or enrollment practices, to establish standards for long-term care insurance, to facilitate public understanding and comparison of long-term care insurance policies, and to facilitate flexibility and innovation in the development of long-term care insurance coverage. (1987, c. 331.)

§ 58-55-15. Scope.

This Article applies to long-term care insurance policies in this State. This Article does not supersede the obligations of any person subject to its provisions to comply with other applicable laws and rules if those laws and rules do not conflict with this Article. The laws and rules established to govern Medicare supplement insurance policies shall not apply to long-term care insurance. A policy that is not advertised, marketed, or offered as long-term care insurance or nursing home insurance is not subject to this Article. (1987, c. 331; 1991, c. 720, s. 84.)

§ 58-55-20. Definitions.

As used in this Article:

(1) "Applicant" means:

a. In the case of an individual long-term care insurance policy, the person who seeks to contract for benefits; and

b. In the case of a group long-term care insurance policy, the proposed certificate holder.

(2) "Certificate" means any certificate issued under a group long-term care insurance policy, which policy has been delivered or issued for delivery in this State.

(3) "Group long-term care insurance" means a long-term care insurance policy that is delivered or issued for delivery in this State and issued to:

a. One or more employers or labor organizations, or to a trust or to the trustees of a fund established by one or more employers or labor organizations, or both, for employees or former employees or both, or for members or former members or both, of the employers or labor organizations; or

b. Any professional, trade, or occupational association for its members or former or retired members, or all, if such association:

(i) Comprises individuals all of whom are or were actively engaged in the same profession, trade, or occupation; and

(ii) Has been maintained in good faith for purposes other than obtaining insurance; or

c. An association or to a trust or to the trustee or trustees of a fund established, created, or maintained for the benefit of members of one or more associations. Prior to advertising, marketing, or offering such policy within this State, the association or associations, or the insurer of the association or associations, shall file evidence with the Commissioner that the association or associations have at the outset a minimum of 100 persons and have been organized and maintained in good faith for purposes other than that of obtaining insurance; have been in active existence for at least one year; and have a constitution and bylaws which provide that (i) the association or associations hold regular meetings not less than annually to further purposes of the members, (ii) except for credit unions, the association or associations collect dues or solicit contributions from members, and (iii) the members have voting privileges and representation on the governing board and committees. Ninety days after such filing the association or associations will be deemed to have satisfied such organizational requirements, unless the Commissioner makes a finding that the association or associations do not satisfy those organizational requirements.

d. A group other than as described in subdivisions (3)a., (3)b., and (3)c. of this section, subject to a finding by the Commissioner that:

(i) The issuance of the group policy is not contrary to the best interest of the public;

(ii) The issuance of the group policy would result in economies of acquisition or administration; and

(iii) The benefits are reasonable in relation to the premiums charged.

(4) "Long-term care insurance" means any policy or certificate advertised, marketed, offered, or designed to provide coverage for not less than 12 consecutive months for each covered person on an expense incurred, indemnity, prepaid, or other basis, for one or more necessary or medically necessary diagnostic, preventive, therapeutic, rehabilitative, maintenance, or personal care services, provided in a setting other than an acute care unit of a hospital. "Long-term care insurance" includes:

a. Group and individual annuities and life insurance policies or riders that supplement or directly provide long-term care insurance.

b. A policy or rider that provides for payment of benefits based upon cognitive impairment or the loss of functional capacity.

c. Qualified long-term care insurance contracts.

d. Group and individual policies whether issued by insurers, fraternal benefit societies, nonprofit health, hospital, and medical service corporations, prepaid health plans, health maintenance organizations, or any similar organization. "Long-term care insurance" does not include any policy that is offered primarily to provide basic Medicare supplement coverage, basic hospital expense coverage, basic medical-surgical expense coverage, hospital confinement indemnity coverage, major medical expense coverage, disability income protection coverage, accident only coverage, specified disease or specified accident coverage, or limited benefit health coverage.

With regard to life insurance, "long-term care insurance" does not include life insurance policies that accelerate the death benefit specifically for one or more of the qualifying events of terminal illness, medical conditions requiring extraordinary medical intervention or permanent institutional confinement, and that provide the option of a lump-sum payment for those benefits and where neither the benefits nor the eligibility for the benefits is conditioned upon the receipt of long-term care.

(5) "Policy" means any policy, contract, certificate, subscriber agreement, rider, or endorsement delivered or issued for delivery in this State by an insurer, fraternal benefit society, nonprofit health, hospital or medical service corporation, prepaid health plan, health maintenance organization, or any similar organization. (1987, c. 331, s. 1; c. 864, s. 68; 2007-298, s. 4; 2007-484, s. 43.5.)

§ 58-55-25. Limits of group long-term care insurance.

No group long-term care insurance coverage may be offered to a resident of this State under a group policy issued in another state to a group described in G.S. 58-55-20(3)d, unless the Commissioner or the insurance regulator of the other state having statutory and regulatory long-term care insurance requirements substantially similar to those adopted in this State has made a determination that such requirements have been met. (1987, c. 331; 1991, c. 720, s. 44.)

§ 58-55-30. Disclosure and performance standards for long-term care insurance.

(a) The Commissioner may adopt rules that include standards for full and fair disclosure setting forth the manner, content, and required disclosures for the sale of long-term care insurance policies, terms of renewability, initial and subsequent conditions of eligibility, nonduplication of coverage provisions, coverage of dependents, pre-existing conditions, termination of insurance, probationary periods, limitations, exceptions, reductions, elimination periods, requirements for replacement, recurrent conditions, and definitions of terms.

(b) No long-term care insurance policy may:

(1) Be cancelled, nonrenewed, or otherwise terminated on the grounds of the age or the deterioration of the mental or physical health of the insured individual or certificate holder; or

(2) Contain a provision establishing a new waiting period in the event existing coverage is converted to or replaced by a new or other form within the same company, except with respect to an increase in benefits voluntarily selected by the insured individual or group policyholder; or

(3) Provide coverage for skilled nursing care only or provide significantly more coverage for skilled care in a facility than coverage for lower levels of care.

(c) Pre-existing condition:

(1) No long-term care insurance policy, other than that issued to a group defined in G.S. 58-55-20(3)a, shall use a definition of "pre-existing condition" that is more restrictive than the following: "pre-existing condition" means a condition for which medical advice or treatment was recommended by, or received from a provider of health care services, within six months preceding the effective date of coverage of an insured person.

(2) No long-term care insurance policy, other than that issued to a group defined in G.S. 58-55-20(3)a, shall exclude coverage for a loss or confinement that is the result of a pre-existing condition unless such loss or confinement begins within six months following the effective date of coverage of an insured person.

(d) Except as provided in G.S. 58-55-5, no long-term care insurance policy may be delivered or issued for delivery in this State if it:

(1) Conditions eligibility for any benefits on a prior hospitalization requirement; or

(2) Conditions eligibility for benefits provided in an institutional care setting on the receipt of a higher level of institutional care.

(d1) Except as provided in G.S. 58-55-5, any long-term care insurance policy containing any limitations or conditions for eligibility other than those prohibited by law shall describe in a separate paragraph of the policy, to be entitled "Limitations or Conditions on Eligibility for Benefits", the limitations or conditions, including any required number of days of confinement.

(d2) A long-term care insurance policy that contains a benefit advertised, marketed, or offered as home health care or a home care benefit may not condition receipt of benefits on a prior institutionalization requirement.

(d3) A long-term care insurance policy that conditions eligibility for noninstitutional benefits on the prior receipt of institutional care shall not require a prior institutional stay of more than 30 days for which benefits are paid.

(e) The Commissioner may adopt rules establishing loss ratio standards for long-term care insurance policies, provided that a specific reference to long-term care insurance policies is contained in the rules.

(f) An individual long-term care insurance policyholder has the right to return the policy within 30 days of its delivery and to have the premium refunded if, after examination of the policy, the policyholder is not satisfied for any reason. Individual long-term care insurance policies shall have a notice prominently printed on the first page of the policy or attached thereto stating in substance that unless the policyholder has received benefits under the policy, the policyholder has the right to return the policy within 30 days of its delivery and to have the premium refunded if, after examination of the policy, the policyholder is not satisfied for any reason.

(g) A person insured under a long-term care insurance policy issued pursuant to a direct response has the right to return the policy within 30 days of its delivery and to have the premium refunded if, after examination, the insured person is not satisfied for any reason. Long-term care insurance policies issued pursuant to a direct response solicitation shall have a notice prominently printed on the first page or attached thereto stating in substance that unless the insured person has received benefits under the policy, the insured person shall have the right to return the policy within 30 days of its delivery and to have the premium refunded if after examination the insured person is not satisfied for any reason.

(h) An outline of coverage shall be delivered to an applicant for an individual long-term care insurance policy at the time of application for an individual policy. In the case of direct response solicitations, the insurer shall deliver the outline of coverage upon the applicant's request; but regardless of request shall make such delivery no later than at the time of policy delivery. Such outline of coverage shall include:

(1) A description of the principal benefits and coverage provided in the policy;

(2) A statement of the principal exclusions, reductions, and limitations contained in the policy;

(3) A statement of the renewal provisions, including any reservation in the policy of a right to change premiums; and

(4) A statement that the outline of coverage is a summary of the policy issued or applied for, and that the policy should be consulted to determine governing contractual provisions.

(i) A certificate issued pursuant to a group long-term care insurance policy, which policy is delivered or issued for delivery in this State, shall include:

(1) A description of the principal benefits and coverage provided in the policy;

(2) A statement of the principal exclusions, reductions, and limitations contained in the policy; and

(3) A statement that the group master policy determines governing contractual provisions.

(j) No policy or certificate may be advertised, marketed, or offered as long-term care or nursing home insurance unless it complies with the provisions of this Article.

(k) The Commissioner shall adopt rules to establish minimum standards for marketing practices and compensation arrangements for long-term care insurance. (1987, c. 331; 1989, c. 207, ss. 1-4; 1989 (Reg. Sess., 1990), c. 941, s. 9; 1991, c. 720, ss. 45, 86; 1993, c. 504, s. 39, c. 553, s. 20.)

§ 58-55-31. Additional requirements.

(a) No policy shall be used in this State unless it provides for an offer of nonforfeiture, which shall not be less than an offer of reduced paid-up insurance benefits, extended term insurance benefits, or a shortened benefit period. No policy shall pay a cash surrender value unless the dividends or refunds are applied as a reduction of future premiums or an increase in future benefits.

(b) The Commissioner shall adopt rules to provide for annual reports by insurers of the number of claims denied, number of rescissions, and the percentage of sales involving the replacement of policies.

(c) No policy shall be used in this State unless the insurer has developed a financial or personal asset suitability test to determine whether or not issuing long-term care insurance to an applicant is appropriate. For purposes of this section:

(1) All insurers except those issuing life insurance that accelerates the death benefit for long-term care shall use the financial or suitability form and format standards as developed and adopted by the NAIC. A personal long-term care worksheet and disclosure notice of issues an applicant should know before buying long-term care insurance shall be completed and provided before an application is taken.

(2) Each applicant that does not meet the recommended financial or personal asset suitability test criteria shall receive a letter of notification and shall be given an option to waive the results of the financial suitability test and proceed with the purchase of the policy.

(d) The Commissioner shall adopt standards to handle consumer complaints about noncompliance with State requirements. (1997-259, s. 15.)

§ 58-55-35. Facilities, services, and conditions defined.

(a) Whenever long-term care insurance provides coverage for the facilities, services, or physical or mental conditions listed below, unless otherwise defined in the policy and certificate, and approved by the Commissioner, such facilities, services, or conditions are defined as follows:

(1) "Adult care home" shall be defined in accordance with the terms of G.S. 131D-2.1(3).

(1a) "Adult day care program" shall be defined in accordance with the provisions of G.S. 131D-6(b).

(2) "Chore" services include the performance of tasks incidental to activities of daily living that do not require the services of a trained homemaker or other specialist. Such services are provided to enable individuals to remain in their own homes and may include such services as: assistance in meeting basic care needs such as meal preparation; shopping for food and other necessities; running necessary errands; providing transportation to essential service facilities; care and cleaning of the house, grounds, clothing, and linens.

(3) "Combination home" shall be defined in accordance with the terms of G.S. 131E-101(1a).

(4) Repealed by Session Laws 1995, c. 535, s. 3.

(5) "Family care home" shall be defined in accordance with the terms of G.S. 131D-2.1(9).

(6) Renumbered.

(7) Repealed by Session Laws 1995, c. 535, s. 3.

(8) "Home health services" shall be defined in accordance with the terms of G.S. 131E-136(3).

(9) "Homemaker services" means supportive services provided by qualified para-professionals who are trained, equipped, assigned, and supervised by professionals within the agency to help maintain, strengthen, and safeguard the care of the elderly in their own homes. These standards must, at a minimum, meet standards established by the North Carolina Division of Social Services and may include: Providing assistance in management of household budgets; planning nutritious meals; purchasing and preparing foods; housekeeping duties; consumer education; and basic personal and health care.

(10) "Hospice" shall be defined in accordance with the terms of G.S. 131E-176(13a).

(11) "Intermediate care facility for the mentally retarded" shall be defined in accordance with the terms of G.S. 131E-176(14a).

(12) "Nursing home" shall be defined in accordance with the terms of G.S. 131E-101(6).

(13) "Respite care, institutional" means provision of temporary support to the primary caregiver of the aged, disabled, or handicapped individual by taking over the tasks of that person for a limited period of time. The insured receives care for the respite period in an institutional setting, such as a nursing home, family care home, rest home, or other appropriate setting.

(14) "Respite care, non-institutional" means provision of temporary support to the primary caregiver of the aged, disabled, or handicapped individual by taking over the tasks of that person for a limited period of time in the home of the insured or other appropriate community location.

(15) "Skilled Nursing Facility" shall be defined in accordance with the terms of G.S. 135-40.1(18).

(16) "Supervised living facility for developmentally disabled adults" means a residential facility, as defined in G.S. 122C-3(14), which has two to nine developmentally disabled adult residents.

(b) Whenever long-term care insurance provides coverage for organic brain disorder syndrome, progressive dementing illness, or primary degenerative dementia, such phrases shall be interpreted to include Alzheimer's Disease. Clinical diagnosis of "organic brain disorder syndrome", "progressive dementing illness", and "primary degenerative dementia" must be accepted as evidence that such conditions exist in an insured when a pathological diagnosis cannot be made; provided that such medical evidence substantially documents the diagnosis of the condition and the insured received treatment for such condition.

(c) All long-term care insurance policies must be filed with and approved by the Commissioner before they can be used in this State and are subject to the provisions of Article 38 of this Chapter. (1987, c. 331, s. 1; 1989, c. 207, ss. 5, 6; 1991, c. 721, s. 85; 1995, c. 535, s. 3; 2001-209, s. 4; 2008-187, s. 38(a); 2009-462, s. 4(a).)

§ 58-55-50. Rules for compliance with federal law and regulations.

The Commissioner may adopt temporary rules necessary to conform long-term care policies and certificates to the requirements of federal law and regulations, including any changes required by Congress or the U.S. Department of Health and Human Services, or any successor agencies. (2001-334, s. 11.2.)

Part 2. Long-Term Care Partnership.

§ 58-55-55. Definitions.

The following definitions apply in this section:

(1)   Asset. - Resources and income.

(2)   Department. - The Department of Health and Human Services.

(3)   Division. - The Division of Medical Assistance.

(4)   Estate recovery. - The placing of a statutory claim on the estate of a deceased Medicaid recipient, as provided by G.S. 108A-70.5.

(5)   Medicaid. - The federal medical assistance program established under Title XIX of the Social Security Act.

(6)   Qualified long-term care partnership policy or qualified policy. - A long-term care insurance policy approved for use in North Carolina and that meets all the requirements of the federal Deficit Reduction Act of 2005, P.L. 109-171.

(7)   Resource. - Cash or its equivalent and real or personal property that is available to an applicant or recipient.

(8)   Resource disregard. - The amount of resources of an applicant for long-term care Medicaid that is equal to the amount of benefits paid to the applicant under a qualified long-term care partnership policy.

(9)   Resource protection. - An amount equal to the resource disregard given to a Medicaid recipient during the long-term care Medicaid eligibility determination process. (2010-68, s. 4.)

§ 58-55-60. Qualified long-term care partnership policy.

A qualified long-term care partnership policy is a long-term care insurance policy or a certificate issued under a group long-term care insurance policy that satisfies all of the following requirements:

(1) The policy meets the requirements for a qualified long-term care insurance contract, as defined in section 7702B of the Internal Revenue Code of 1986 (26 U.S.C. § 7702B(b)).

(2) The effective date of the coverage is on or after January 1, 2011, or 60 days after approval of the Medicaid State Plan amendment, whichever is later.

(3) The policy covers an insured who was a resident of North Carolina or another reciprocal partnership state when coverage first became effective under the policy.

(4) The policy meets the federal consumer protection requirements of section 1917(b) of the Social Security Act as amended by section 6021(a) of the Deficit Reduction Act of 2005, P.L. 109-171 of the Social Security Act (42 U.S.C. § 1396p(b)(5)(A)).

(5) The policy is issued with and retains inflation protection coverage which meets the inflation standards based on the insured's then attained age as defined in sub-subdivisions a., b., and c. below:

a. Policies or certificates issued to an individual who is under 61 years old must provide compound annual inflation protection.

b. Policies or certificates issued to an individual who is 61 to 76 years old must provide some level of inflation protection. This may include simple interest or compound inflation protection.

c. For purchasers 76 years old or older, inflation protection may be offered but is not required.

Notwithstanding the above, purchasers of qualified long-term care insurance policies may adjust their inflation protection as they age. However, their policies shall continue to be qualified long-term care insurance policies as long as the inflation protection in the qualified policies continues to meet the minimum requirements for the insured's attained age.

(6)   The policy states that it is intended to be a qualified long-term care insurance policy as defined in section 7702B(b) of the Internal Revenue Code of 1986.

(7)   A qualified policy issued, executed, and delivered in North Carolina shall be accompanied by a Partnership Disclosure Notice explaining the benefits associated with a qualified policy and indicating that at the time issued, the policy is a qualified long-term care insurance partnership policy in North Carolina. The Partnership Disclosure Notice shall also include a statement indicating that by purchasing this partnership policy, the insured does not automatically qualify for Medicaid. Notices providing additional information may be used in conjunction with the Partnership Disclosure Notice described in this section if filed and approved by the Commissioner. The Notice shall state the following in at least 12-point font:

"Partnership Policy Status: Your long-term care insurance policy is intended to qualify as a Partnership Policy under the North Carolina Long-Term Care Partnership Program as of your policy's effective date. For Medicaid applicants applying for help with the cost of long-term care, this means that an amount of your resources equal to the dollar amount of long-term care insurance benefits paid to you or on your behalf under this policy may be disregarded for purposes of determining your eligibility for long-term care Medicaid and from any subsequent recovery by the State from your estate for payment of Medicaid paid services. The amount that may be disregarded at eligibility will be equal to the amount of the long-term care partnership benefits paid out prior to the time you apply for long-term care Medicaid. As a result, you may qualify for coverage of the cost of your long-term care needs under Medicaid without first being required to substantially exhaust your personal resource s. The amount that may be protected from recovery by the State from your estate will be equal to the amount disregarded for purposes of eligibility for long-term care Medicaid. If you are already a recipient of long-term care Medicaid, this policy will not allow a resource disregard or estate recovery resource protection. The purchase of a Partnership Policy does not automatically qualify you for Medicaid.

Please note that this policy may lose long-term care partnership program status if you move to a different state that does not recognize North Carolina's Long-Term Care Partnership Program or you modify this policy after issuance. This policy may also lose long-term care partnership program status due to changes in federal or state laws.

If you have questions regarding long-term care insurance and the North Carolina Long-Term Care Partnership Program, you may contact the Seniors' Health Insurance Information Program of the Department of Insurance at 1-800-443-9354."

In the case of a group insurance contract, this Partnership Disclosure Notice shall be provided to the insured upon the issuance of the certificate. The insurer shall include in that Notice that the amount of the insured's resources that may be disregarded at eligibility will be equal to the amount of qualified long-term care partnership policy benefits paid prior to the time the insured applied for long-term care Medicaid. The insurer shall also include in the notice a warning to the insured that the policy may lose long-term care partnership program status if the insured moves to another state that does not recognize North Carolina's Long-Term Care Partnership Program, or if the policy is modified after issuance.

(8) When the insured's remaining lifetime maximum benefit is equal to 90 times the current daily benefit, or three times the current monthly benefit, the insurer shall notify the insured in writing advising the insured to go to the local department of social services to apply for Medicaid if the insured had not already done so. (2010-68, s. 4.)

§ 58-55-65. Compliance with federal regulations.

(a) The Commissioner may adopt rules to conform long-term care policies and certificates to the requirements of federal law and regulations, including any changes required by Congress or the U.S. Department of Health and Human Services, or any successor agencies.

(b) The tax-qualified long-term care provisions required of the Health Insurance Portability and Accountability Act of 1996, including subsequent amendments and editions, are hereby incorporated into Article 55 of Chapter 58 of the General Statutes.

(c) The long-term care partnership provisions required of the Deficit Reduction Act of 2005, including subsequent amendments and editions, are hereby incorporated into Article 55 of Chapter 58 of the General Statutes. (2010-68, s. 4.)

§ 58-55-70. Disclosure notices.

(a) Prior to making a change requested by the policyholder to a qualified long-term care partnership policy that would result in the loss to the policy of qualified policy status, the insurer shall provide to the policyholder a written explanation within 30 calendar days of how this action would affect the insured and shall obtain the insured's signature indicating consent to the change.

(b) If a qualified long-term care partnership policy subsequently loses qualified policy status, the insurer shall explain in writing within 30 calendar days to the policyholders the reason for the loss of status.

(c) The disclosures required in this section shall be provided to any insured who exchanges a policy for a qualified long-term care partnership policy. (2010-68, s. 4.)

§ 58-55-75. Exchange of long-term care policies for long-term care partnership policies.

An insurer shall offer, on a onetime basis, in writing, to all existing policyholders that were issued a long-term care policy on or after February 8, 2006, the option to exchange their existing long-term care coverage for coverage that is intended to qualify under North Carolina's Long-Term Care Partnership Program. The insurer shall provide notification of this onetime offer within 180 days from the date on which the company begins to offer partnership coverage in the State. The mandatory offer of an exchange shall only apply to products issued by the insurer that are comparable to the type of policy form, such as group policies and individual policies, and on the policy series that the company has certified as partnership qualified. This exchange may be subject to underwriting and premium adjustment. A policy received in an exchange after the effective date of North Carolina's Long-Term Care Partnership Program is treated as newly issued and is eligible for qualified policy status. For purposes of applying the Medicaid rules relating to qualified long-term care partnership policies, the addition of a rider, endorsement, or change in schedule page for a policy may be treated as giving rise to an exchange. The effective date of the long-term care partnership policy shall be the date the policy was exchanged. (2010-68, s. 4.)

§ 58-55-80. Information sharing.

(a) In order to assist in the performance of the Commissioner's duties under the long-term care partnership program specified in the federal Deficit Reduction Act of 2005, the Commissioner may:

(1) Share information, including identifying information, related to the long-term care partnership program with other state and federal agencies, the National Association of Insurance Commissioners, and any entity contracting with the federal government under the program.

(2) Receive information, including identifying information, related to the long-term care partnership program from other state and federal agencies, the National Association of Insurance Commissioners, and any entity contracting with the federal government under the program, and shall maintain as confidential or privileged any identifying information received with notice or the understanding that it is confidential or privileged under the laws of the jurisdiction that is the source of the document, material, or information. Information received under this subdivision of this subsection is not a "public record" as defined in G.S. 132-1.

(3) Enter into agreements governing sharing and use of information consistent with this section.

(b) No waiver of an existing privilege or claim of confidentiality in the identifying information shall occur as a result of disclosure to the Commissioner under this section or as a result of sharing as authorized in subsection (a) of this section.

(c) A privilege established under the law of any state or jurisdiction that is substantially similar to the privilege established under this section shall be available and enforced in any proceeding in, and in any court of, this State.

(d) As used in this section, "identifying information" has the same meaning as in G.S. 14-113.20(b). (2010-68, s. 4.)

Article 56.

Third Party Administrators.

§ 58-56-1: Repealed by Session Laws 1991, c. 627, s. 2.

§ 58-56-2. Definitions.

The following definitions apply in this Article:

(1) Affiliate. Any person who, directly or indirectly, through one or more intermediaries, controls, is controlled by, or is under common control with a specified entity or person.

(2) Control. Defined in G.S. 58-19-5(2).

(3) Insurance. Any coverage offered or provided by an insurer.

(4) Insurer. A person who undertakes to provide life or health insurance or benefits in this State that are subject to this Chapter. The term "insurer" does not include a bona fide employee benefit plan established by an employer, an employee organization, or both, for which the insurance laws of this State are preempted pursuant to the Employee Retirement Income Security Act of 1974.

(5) Third party administrator. A person who directly or indirectly solicits or effects coverage of, underwrites, collects charges or premiums from, or adjusts or settles claims on residents of this State, or residents of another state from offices in this State, in connection with life or health insurance or annuities, except any of the following:

a. An employer on behalf of its employees or the employees of one or more of its affiliates.

b. A union on behalf of its members.

c. An insurer that is licensed under Articles 1 through 67 of this Chapter or that is acting as an insurer with respect to a policy lawfully issued and delivered by it and pursuant to the laws of a state in which the insurer is licensed to write insurance.

d. An agent or broker who is licensed by the Commissioner to sell life or health insurance and whose activities are limited exclusively to the sale of insurance.

e. A creditor on behalf of its debtors with respect to insurance covering a debt between the creditor and its debtors.

f. A trust and its trustees, agents, and employees acting pursuant to the trust established in conformity with 29 U.S.C. § 186.

g. A trust exempt from taxation under section 501(a) of the Internal Revenue Code and its trustees and employees acting pursuant to the trust, or a custodian and the custodian's agents or employees acting pursuant to a custodian account that meets the requirements of section 401(f) of the Internal Revenue Code.

h. A financial institution subject to supervision or examination by federal or state banking authorities, or a mortgage lender, to the extent the financial institution or mortgage lender collects and remits premiums to licensed insurance agents or authorized insurers in connection with loan payments.

i. An attorney-at-law who adjusts or settles claims in the normal course of business as an attorney-at-law and who does not collect charges or premiums in connection with life or health insurance or annuities.

j. An adjuster licensed by the Commissioner whose activities are limited to adjustment of claims.

k. A person who acts solely as a TPA of one or more bona fide employee benefit plans established by an employer, an employee organization, or both, for which the insurance laws of this State are preempted pursuant to the Employee Income Security Act of 1974. The person shall comply with the requirements of G.S. 58-56-51(f).

l. A managing general agent as defined in G.S. 58-34-2(a)(3), whose activities are limited exclusively to the scope of the activities set forth in the managing general agency contract filed by an insurer with the Commissioner in accordance with G.S. 58-34-2(i).

(6) TPA. A third party administrator.

(7) Underwriting. This term includes the acceptance of employer or individual applications for coverage of individuals in accordance with the written rules of the insurer, the planning and coordination of an insurance program, and the ability to procure bonds and excess insurance. (1991, c. 627, s. 1; 2005-215, s. 16.)

§ 58-56-5: Reserved for future codification purposes.

§ 58-56-6. Written agreement necessary.

(a) No TPA may act as a TPA without a written agreement between the TPA and the insurer. The written agreement shall be retained as part of the official records of both the insurer and the TPA for the duration of the agreement and for five years thereafter. The agreement shall contain all provisions required by this Article, to the extent those requirements apply to the functions performed by the TPA.

(b) The agreement shall include a statement of duties that the TPA is expected to perform on behalf of the insurer and the kinds of insurance the TPA is to be authorized to administer. The agreement shall provide for underwriting or other standards pertaining to the business underwritten by the insurer.

(c) The insurer or TPA may, with written notice, terminate the agreement for cause as provided in the agreement. The insurer may suspend the underwriting authority of the TPA during the pendency of any dispute regarding the cause for termination of the agreement. The insurer must fulfill any lawful obligations with respect to policies affected by the agreement, regardless of any dispute between the insurer and the TPA. (1991, c. 627, s. 1.)

§ 58-56-10: Repealed by Session Laws 1991, c. 627, s. 2.

§ 58-56-11. Payment to TPA.

If an insurer uses the services of a TPA, the payment to the TPA of any premiums or charges for insurance by or on behalf of the insured party is considered payment to the insurer. The payment of return premiums or claim payments forwarded by the insurer to the TPA is not considered payment to the insured party or claimant until the payments are received by the insured party or claimant. This section does not limit any right of the insurer against the TPA resulting from the failure of the TPA to make payments to the insurer, insured parties, or claimants. (1991, c. 627, s. 1.)

§ 58-56-15: Repealed by Session Laws 1991, c. 627, s. 2.

§ 58-56-16. Records to be kept.

(a)   Every TPA shall maintain and make available to the insurer complete books and records of all transactions performed on behalf of the insurer. The books and records shall be maintained in accordance with prudent standards of insurance record keeping and must be maintained for a period of at least five years after the date of their creation.

(b)   The Commissioner shall have access to books and records maintained by a TPA for the purposes of examination, audit, and inspection. The Commissioner shall keep confidential any trade secrets contained in those books and records, including the identity and addresses of policyholders and certificate holders, except that the Commissioner may use the information in any judicial or administrative proceeding instituted against the TPA.

(c)   The insurer shall own the records generated by the TPA pertaining to the insurer, but the TPA shall retain the right to continuing access to books and records to permit the TPA to fulfill all of its contractual obligations to insured parties, claimants, and the insurer.

(d) In the event the insurer and the TPA cancel their agreement, notwithstanding the provisions of subsection (a) of this section, the TPA may, by written agreement with the insurer, transfer all records to a new TPA rather than retain them for five years. In this case, the new TPA shall acknowledge, in writing, that it is responsible for retaining the records of the prior TPA as required in subsection (a) of this section. (1991, c. 627, s. 1.)

§ 58-56-20: Repealed by Session Laws 1991, c. 627, s. 2.

§ 58-56-21. Approval of advertising.

A TPA may use only the advertising pertaining to the business underwritten by an insurer that has been approved in writing by the insurer in advance of its use. (1991, c. 627, s. 1.)

§ 58-56-25: Repealed by Session Laws 1991, c. 627, s. 2.

§ 58-56-26. Responsibilities of the insurer.

(a) If an insurer uses the services of a TPA, the insurer is responsible for determining the benefits, premium rates, underwriting criteria, and claims payment procedures applicable to the coverage and for securing reinsurance, if any. The rules pertaining to these matters must be provided, in writing, by the insurer to the TPA. The responsibilities of the TPA as to any of these matters shall be set forth in the agreement between the TPA and the insurer.

(b) It is the sole responsibility of the insurer to provide for competent administration of its programs.

(c) In cases where a TPA administers benefits for more than 100 certificate holders on behalf of an insurer, the insurer shall, at least semiannually, conduct a review of the operations of the TPA. At least one semiannual review shall be an on-site audit of the operations of the TPA. On July 1, 2010, and annually thereafter, every insurer shall file with the Commissioner a certification of completion of the audits as required by this subsection and performed during the previous calendar year, in the format, content, and manner as specified by the Commissioner. The insurer shall maintain in its corporate records documentation of the audits conducted to support its certification of audits for a period of five years or, if a domestic insurer, until the completion of the next quinquennial examination.

(d) The Commissioner may adopt rules necessary to implement, administer, and enforce the provisions of this section. (1991, c. 627, s. 1; 2009-382, ss. 12, 13.)

§ 58-56-30: Repealed by Session Laws 1991, c. 627, s. 2.

§ 58-56-31. Premium collection and payment of claims.

(a) All insurance charges or premiums collected by a TPA on behalf of or for an insurer, and the return of premiums received from that insurer, shall be held by the TPA in a fiduciary capacity. These funds shall be immediately remitted to the person entitled to them or shall be deposited promptly in a fiduciary account established and maintained by the TPA in a federally or State insured financial institution. The agreement between the TPA and the insurer shall require the TPA to periodically render an accounting to the insurer detailing all transactions performed by the TPA pertaining to the business underwritten by the insurer.

(b) If charges or premiums deposited in a fiduciary account have been collected on behalf of or for one or more insurers, the TPA shall keep records clearly recording the deposits in and withdrawals from the account on behalf of each insurer. The TPA shall keep copies of all the records and, upon request of an insurer, shall furnish the insurer with copies of the records pertaining to the deposits and withdrawals.

(c) The TPA shall not pay any claim by withdrawals from a fiduciary account in which premiums or charges are deposited. Withdrawals from this account shall be made only as provided in the agreement between the TPA and the insurer. The agreement shall address, but not be limited to, the following:

(1)   Remittance to an insurer entitled to remittance.

(2)   Deposit in an account maintained in the name of the insurer.

(3)   Transfer to and deposit in a claims-paying account, with claims to be paid as provided in subsection (d) of this section.

(4)   Payment to a group policyholder for remittance to the insurer entitled to the remittance.

(5)   Payment to the TPA of its commissions, fees, or charges.

(6)   Remittance of a return premium to the person entitled to the return premium.

(d)   All claims paid by the TPA from funds collected on behalf of or for an insurer shall be paid only on drafts or checks of and as authorized by the insurer. (1991, c. 627, s. 1.)

§ 58-56-35: Repealed by Session Laws 1991, c. 627, s. 2.

§ 58-56-36. Compensation to the TPA.

A TPA shall not enter into any agreement or understanding with an insurer that makes the amount of the TPA's commissions, fees, or charges contingent upon savings effected in the adjustment, settlement, and payment of losses covered by the insurer's obligations. This section does not prohibit a TPA from receiving performance-based compensation for providing hospital or other auditing services and does not prevent the compensation of a TPA from being based on premiums or charges collected or the number of claims paid or processed. (1991, c. 627, s. 1.)

§ 58-56-40: Repealed by Session Laws 1991, c. 627, s. 2.

§ 58-56-41. Notice to covered individuals; disclosure of charges and fees.

(a)   When the services of a TPA are used, the TPA shall provide a written notice approved by the insurer to covered individuals advising them of the identity of, and relationship among, the TPA, the policyholder, and the insurer.

(b)   When a TPA collects funds, the reason for collection of each item must be identified to the insured party and each item must be shown separately from any premium. Additional charges may not be made for services to the extent the services have been paid for by the insurer.

(c)   The TPA shall disclose to the insurer all charges, fees and commissions received from all services in connection with the provision of administrative services for the insurer, including any fees or commissions paid by insurers providing reinsurance. (1991, c. 627, s. 1.)

§ 58-56-45: Repealed by Session Laws 1991, c. 627, s. 2.

§ 58-56-46. Delivery of materials to covered individuals.

Any policies, certificates, booklets, termination notices, and other written communications delivered by the insurer to the TPA for delivery to insured parties or covered individuals shall be delivered by the TPA promptly after receipt of instructions from the insurer to deliver them. (1991, c. 627, s. 1.)

§ 58-56-50: Repealed by Session Laws 1991, c. 627, s. 2.

§ 58-56-51. License required.

(a)   No person shall act as, offer to act as, or hold himself or herself out as a TPA in this State without a valid TPA license issued by the Commissioner.

Licenses shall be renewed annually. Failure to submit a complete renewal application shall result in the expiration of the license of the TPA as a matter of law; provided, however, the Commissioner may grant the TPA an extension of time for good cause.

(b)   Each application for the issuance or renewal of a license shall be made upon a form prescribed by the Commissioner and shall be accompanied by a nonrefundable filing fee of three hundred dollars ($300.00) and evidence of maintenance of a fidelity bond, errors and omissions liability insurance, or other security, of a type and in an amount to be determined by rules of the Commissioner. Applications for issuance of licenses shall include or be accompanied by the following information and documents:

(1)   All organizational documents of the TPA, including any articles of incorporation, articles of association, partnership agreement, trade name certificate, or trust agreement, any other applicable documents, and all amendments to these documents.

(2)   The bylaws, rules, regulations, or similar documents regulating the internal affairs of the TPA.

(3)   The names, addresses, official positions, and professional qualifications of the individuals who are responsible for the conduct of affairs of the TPA, including all (i) members of the board of directors, board of trustees, executive committee, or other governing board or committee, (ii) the principal officers in the case of a corporation or the partners or members in the case of a partnership or association, (iii) all shareholders holding directly or indirectly ten percent (10%) or more of the voting securities of the TPA, and (iv) any other person who exercises control or influence over the affairs of the TPA.

(4)   Annual financial statements or reports for the two most recent years that prove that the applicant is solvent and any other information the Commissioner may require in order to review the current financial condition of the applicant.

(5)   A general description of the business operations, including information on staffing levels and activities proposed in this State and nationwide. The description must provide details setting forth the TPA's capability for providing a sufficient number of experienced and qualified personnel in the areas of claims processing, record keeping, and underwriting.

(6) If the applicant will be managing the solicitation of new or renewal business, evidence that it employs or has contracted with an agent licensed by this State for soliciting and taking applications. Any applicant that intends to directly solicit insurance contracts or to otherwise act as an insurance agent must provide proof of having a license as an insurance agent in this State.

(7) Any other pertinent information required by rules of the Commissioner.

The information required by subdivisions (1) through (7) of this subsection, including any trade secrets, shall be kept confidential; provided that the Commissioner may use that information in any judicial or administrative proceeding instituted against the TPA. Applications for renewals of licenses shall include or be accompanied by any changes in the information required by subdivisions (1) through (7) of this subsection.

(c) Each applicant shall make available for inspection by the Commissioner copies of all contracts with insurers or other persons using the services of the TPA.

(d) The Commissioner may refuse to issue a license if the Commissioner determines that the TPA, or any individual responsible for the conduct of affairs of the TPA as defined in subdivision (b)(3) of this section, is not competent, trustworthy, financially responsible in accordance with subsection (b) of this section, or of good personal and business reputation, or has had an insurance or a TPA license denied, suspended, or revoked for cause by any state.

(e) A TPA is not required to be licensed as a TPA in this state if all of the following conditions are met:

(1) The TPA's principal place of business is in another state.

(2) The TPA is not soliciting business as a TPA in this State.

(3) In the case of any group policy or plan of insurance serviced by the TPA, no more than either five percent (5%) or 100 certificate holders, whichever is fewer, reside in this State.

(f) A person is not required to be licensed as a TPA in this State if the person provides services exclusively to one or more bona fide employee benefit plans each of which is established by an employer, an employee organization, or both, and for which the insurance laws of this State are preempted pursuant to the Employee Retirement Income Security Act of 1974. Persons who are not required to be licensed shall register with the Commissioner annually, verifying their status as described in this subsection. Failure to submit an annual verification shall result in the expiration of the registration of the TPA as a matter of law; provided, however, the Commissioner may grant the TPA an extension of time for good cause.

(g)   A TPA shall notify the Commissioner of any material change in its ownership, control, or other fact or circumstance affecting its qualification for a license in this State, within 10 business days after the change.

(h)   No bonding shall be required by the Commissioner of any TPA whose business is restricted solely to benefit plans that are either fully insured by an authorized insurer or that are bona fide employee benefit plans established by an employer, any employee organization, or both, for which the insurance laws of this State are preempted pursuant to the Employee Retirement Income Security Act of 1974. (1991, c. 627, s. 1; 2007-298, ss. 7.4, 7.5; 2007-484, s. 43.5; 2009-451, s. 21.16(a).)

§ 58-56-52. Prohibitions.

(a)   No insurance company shall act as a third party administrator with respect to residents of this State, or residents of another state from offices in this State, in connection with life or health insurance or annuities unless that insurance company is authorized to do the business of insurance in this State and otherwise complies with the applicable laws of this State.

(b)   No insurance company shall enter into an agreement with an unauthorized insurance company to provide administrative services for residents of this State, or residents of another state from offices in this State, in connection with life or health insurance or annuities that would subject the unauthorized insurer to this section. (2005-209, s. 1.)

§ 58-56-55: Repealed by Session Laws 1991, c. 627, s. 2.

§ 58-56-56. Waiver of application for license.

Upon request from a TPA, the Commissioner may waive the application requirements of G.S. 58-56-51(b) if the TPA has a valid license as a TPA issued in a state that has standards for TPAs that are at least as stringent as those contained in this Article. (1991, c. 627, s. 1.)

§ 58-56-60: Repealed by Session Laws 1991, c. 627, s. 2.

§ 58-56-61. Reserved for future codification purposes.

§ 58-56-65. Committee on Third Party Administrators.

The Commissioner is authorized to appoint a Committee on Third Party Administrators in conformance with the provisions of G.S. 58-2-30. (1987, c. 676.)

§ 58-56-66. Grounds for suspension or revocation of license.

(a)   The Commissioner shall, after notice and opportunity for hearing, suspend or revoke the license of a TPA if the Commissioner finds that either of the following apply to the TPA:

(1)   The TPA is using methods or practices in the conduct of its business that render its further transaction of business in this State hazardous or injurious to insured persons or the public.

(2)   The TPA has failed to pay any judgment rendered against it in this State within 60 days after the judgment has become final.

(b)   The Commissioner may, after notice and opportunity for hearing, suspend or revoke the license of a TPA if the Commissioner finds that any of the following apply to the TPA:

(1) The TPA has violated a rule or an order of the Commissioner or any provision of this Chapter.

(2) The TPA has refused to be examined or to produce its accounts, records, and files for examination, or any of its officers has refused to give information with respect to its affairs or has refused to perform any other legal obligation as to that examination, when required by the Commissioner.

(3) The TPA has, without just cause, refused to pay proper claims or perform services arising under its contracts or has, without just cause, caused covered individuals to accept less than the amount due them or caused covered individuals to employ attorneys or bring suit against the TPA to secure full payment or settlement of the claims.

(4) The TPA is an affiliate of or under the same general management, interlocking directorate, or ownership as another TPA or insurer that unlawfully transacts business in this State without having a license.

(5) The TPA at any time fails to meet any qualification for which issuance of the license could have been refused had the failure then existed and been known to the Commissioner at the time of the application.

(6) The TPA has been convicted of, or has entered a plea of guilty or nolo contendere to, a felony without regard to whether judgment was withheld.

(7) The TPA is under suspension or revocation in another state.

(c) The Commissioner may without advance notice or hearing immediately suspend the license of any TPA if the Commissioner finds that any of the following apply to the TPA:

(1) The TPA is insolvent or financially impaired. "Financially impaired" means that the TPA is unable or potentially unable to fulfill its contractual obligations.

(2) A proceeding for receivership, conservatorship, rehabilitation, or other delinquency proceeding regarding the TPA has been commenced in any state.

(3) The financial condition or business practices of the TPA otherwise pose an imminent threat to the public health, safety, or welfare of the residents of this State. (1991, c. 627, s. 1.)

Article 57.

Regulation of Credit Insurance.

§ 58-57-1. Application of Article.

All credit life insurance, all credit accident and health insurance, all credit property insurance, all credit insurance on credit card balances, all family leave credit insurance, and all credit unemployment insurance written in connection with direct loans, consumer credit installment sale contracts of whatever term permitted by G.S. 25A-33, leases, or other credit transactions shall be subject to the provisions of this Article, except credit insurance written in connection with direct loans of more than 15 years' duration. The provisions of this Article shall be controlling as to such insurance and no other provisions of Articles 1 through 64 of this Chapter shall be applicable unless otherwise specifically provided; nor shall such insurance be subject to the provisions of this Article where the issuance of such insurance is an isolated transaction on the part of the insurer not related to an agreement or a plan for insuring debtors of the creditor. (1975, c. 660, s. 1; 1987, c. 826, ss. 1, 12; 1993, c. 226, s. 1; 1999-351, s. 5.2.)

§ 58-57-5. Definitions.

As used in this Article, unless the context requires otherwise, the following words or terms shall have the meanings herein ascribed to them, respectively:

(1) Repealed by Session Laws 1991, c. 720, s. 6.

(2) "Credit accident and health insurance" means insurance on a debtor to provide indemnity for payments becoming due on a specific loan or other credit transaction as defined in G.S. 58-51-100, with or without insurance against death by accident.

(2a) "Credit insurance agent" means an agent of an insurance company licensed in this State who is authorized to solicit, negotiate or effect credit life insurance, credit accident and health insurance, credit unemployment insurance, credit property insurance, or any of them, but only to the extent as is authorized and limited in this Article.

(3) "Credit life insurance" means insurance on the life of a debtor pursuant to or in connection with a specific loan or other credit transaction as defined in G.S. 58-58-10.

(4) Recodified as G.S. § 58-57-5(2a) (See Note.)

(4a) "Credit transaction" means any transaction by the terms of which the repayment of money loaned or loan commitment made, or payment for goods, services, or properties sold or leased, is to be made at a future date or dates.

(4b) "Credit unemployment insurance" means insurance on a debtor in connection with a specified loan or other credit transaction to provide payment to a creditor of the debtor for the installment payments or other periodic payment becoming due while the debtor is involuntarily unemployed as defined in the policy.

(5) "Creditor" means any lender of money or vendor or lessor of goods, services, property, rights or privileges, including any person that directly or indirectly provides credit in connection with any such sale or lease, for which payment is arranged through a credit-related transaction; or any successor to the right, title or interest of any such lender, vendor, lessor, or person extending credit, and an affiliate, associate, or subsidiary of any of them, or any director, officer, or employee of any of them or any other person in any way associated with any of them.

(5a) "Critical period conversion ratio" means the ratio of the benefit value of the critical period divided by the benefit value of the full term.

(5b) "Critical period coverage" means insurance coverage for which benefits are limited to a stated number of payments or the payments end with the expiration of the policy, whichever is less.

(6) "Debtor" means a borrower of money or a purchaser or lessee of goods, services, property, rights or privileges for which payment is arranged through a credit transaction.

(6a) "Family leave credit insurance" means insurance on a debtor in connection with a specified loan or other credit transaction to provide payment to a creditor of the debtor for the installment payments or other periodic payments becoming due when the debtor suffers a loss of income because of a voluntary, employer-approved leave of absence for qualifying events specified in G.S. 58-57-115(d).

(7) "Indebtedness" means the total amount payable for the term of the loan by debtor to creditor in connection with a loan or other credit transaction, including principal, interest, allowable charges, and any premiums authorized hereunder.

(7a) "Joint accident and health coverage" means credit accident and health insurance covering two or more debtors; provided that only one monthly benefit, as defined in G.S. 58-57-15(b), shall be payable each month on a specific indebtedness regardless of the number of debtors insured.

(8) "Joint life coverage" means credit life insurance covering two or more lives, the entire amount of insurance being payable upon the death of the first insured debtor to die.

(9) "Lease" means a contract whereby the lessee of a "motor vehicle," as defined in G.S. 20-4.01(23), contracts to pay as compensation for use a sum substantially equivalent to or in excess of the aggregate value of the property, but not exceeding the term of years in G.S. 58-57-1.

(10) "Open-end credit" means credit extended by a creditor under an agreement in which:

a. The creditor reasonably contemplates repeated transactions;

b. The creditor imposes a finance charge from time to time on an outstanding unpaid balance; and

c. The amount of credit that may be extended to the debtor during the term of the agreement (up to any limit set by the creditor) is generally made available to the extent that any outstanding balance is repaid.

"Open-end credit" includes credit card balances.

(11) "Truncated coverage" means a credit insurance benefit with a term of insurance coverage that is less than the term of the credit transaction. (1975, c. 660, s. 1; 1987, c. 826, ss. 2, 3; 1991, c. 720, s. 6; 1993, c. 226, s. 2; 1995, c. 193, s. 45; c. 208, s. 1; 1999-351, s. 5.3; 2005-181, s. 1; 2007-298, s. 6.1; 2007-484, s. 43.5.)

§ 58-57-10. Forms of insurance which are authorized.

Credit life insurance and credit accident and health insurance shall be issued only in the following forms:

(1) Individual policies of life insurance issued to debtors on the term plan;

(2) Individual policies of accident and health insurance issued to debtors on a term plan or disability benefit provisions in individual policies of credit life insurance;

(3) Group policies of life insurance issued to creditors providing insurance upon the lives of debtors on the term plan;

(4) Group policies of accident and health insurance issued to creditors on a term plan insuring debtors or disability benefit provisions in group credit life insurance policies to provide such coverage. (1975, c. 660, s. 1.)

§ 58-57-15. Amount.

(a) Credit Life Insurance. -

(1) The amount of credit life insurance shall not exceed the amount of unpaid indebtedness as it exists from time to time, less any unearned interest or finance charges; provided, however, that if the amount of credit insurance is based on a predetermined schedule, the amount of credit insurance shall not exceed the scheduled amount of unpaid indebtedness, less any unearned

interest or finance charges, plus an amount equal to three monthly installments or the equivalent thereof.

(2) Notwithstanding the provisions of the above subdivision, insurance on seasonal credit line commitments (such as may be found in agricultural credit transactions) not exceeding one year in duration may be written up to the amount of the loan commitment on a nondecreasing or level term plan.

(3) Notwithstanding this or any other section, insurance on education credit transaction commitments may be written for the amount of such commitment.

(b) Credit Accident and Health and Credit Unemployment Insurance. - The total amount of indemnity payable by credit accident and health or credit unemployment insurance in the event of disability or unemployment, as defined in the policy, shall not exceed the indebtedness; and the amount of each monthly benefit shall not exceed the indebtedness divided by the number of months in the term of the loan. A daily benefit equal in amount to one thirtieth of the scheduled monthly payment is permissible. For open-end credit transactions, the total amount of indemnity payable shall not exceed the amount of unpaid indebtedness at the time disability or unemployment begins, including interest and insurance charges that would accrue on that indebtedness using the creditor's minimum payment schedule. The periodic indemnity may exceed the creditor's minimum payment amount. (1975, c. 660, s. 1; 1981, c. 759, s. 1; 1993, c. 226, s. 3; c. 553, s. 75.)

§ 58-57-20. Term; termination prior to scheduled maturity.

Except as otherwise provided in this section, the term of any credit life insurance or credit accident and health insurance shall, subject to acceptance by the insurer, commence on the date when the debtor becomes obligated to the creditor, except that, where a group policy provides coverage with respect to existing obligations, the insurance on a debtor with respect to such indebtedness shall commence on the effective date of the policy. For credit insurance offered to the debtor subsequent to the date the debtor becomes obligated to the creditor, the term of the insurance shall, subject to the acceptance by the insurer, commence not more than 30 days following the insurer's receipt of the debtor's request for the insurance. The term of such insurance shall not extend more than 15 days beyond the maturity date of the indebtedness or final installment thereof; but the term of the insurance may be less than the term of the indebtedness to provide truncated coverage in connection with transactions having initial terms of more than 60 months or consistent with any age or other termination provisions contained in the policy. If the indebtedness is discharged due to prepayment, the insurance in force shall be terminated unless otherwise requested by the insured in writing. If the indebtedness is discharged due to renewal or refinancing prior to such maturity date, the insurance in force shall be terminated before any new insurance may be issued in connection with the renewed or refinanced indebtedness. In all cases of termination prior to scheduled maturity, a refund shall be paid or credited as provided in G.S. 58-57-50. (1975, c. 660, s. 1; 1991, c. 720, s. 30; 1993, c. 226, s. 4.)

§ 58-57-25. Insurance to be evidenced by individual policy; notice of proposed insurance or certificate; required and prohibited provisions; when debtor to receive copy.

(a) All individual credit insurance sold shall be evidenced by an individual policy. All group insurance sold where any part of the premium is paid by the debtors or by the creditors from identifiable charges collected from the insured debtors shall be evidenced by a certificate of insurance.

(b) Each individual policy or certificate of credit insurance shall set forth the name and home-office address of the insurer, the identity of the insured debtor by name or otherwise, the premium or amount of payment, if any, by the debtor separately for each type of credit insurance if not disclosed in other documents furnished to the debtor, a description of the coverage including the amount and term thereof, and any exceptions, limitations or restrictions, and shall state that the benefits shall be paid to the creditor to reduce or extinguish the unpaid indebtedness, and wherever the amount of insurance may exceed the unpaid indebtedness, that any such excess shall be payable to a beneficiary other than the creditor named by the debtor, or to his estate. For open-end credit, the premium shall be disclosed as the monthly amount charged for each one hundred dollars ($100.00) or one thousand dollars ($1,000) of outstanding indebtedness.

(c) No individual policy of credit insurance and no group policy of credit insurance shall be delivered or issued for delivery in this State unless each contains in substance all of the following provisions:

(1)   In each policy there shall be a provision that the policy, or the policy and application therefor, if any, or if a copy of the application is endorsed upon or attached to the policy when issued, shall constitute the entire insurance contract between the parties, and that all statements made by the creditor or by the individual debtors shall, in the absence of fraud, be deemed representations and not warranties.

(2)   In each such policy there shall be a provision that the validity of the policy shall not be contested, except for nonpayment of premiums, after it has been in force for two years from its date of issue; and that no statement made by any person insured under the policy relating to his insurability shall be used in contesting the validity of the insurance with respect to which such statement was made after such insurance has been in force on such insured for a period of two years during such person's lifetime, and prior to the date on which the claim thereunder arose. Provided, however, that unless the insured writes his own age on the form and signs a statement that he has done so, there shall be no denial of claims grounded on the debtor's age. Provided further, if the indebtedness is paid by renewal or refinancing prior to the scheduled maturity date, the effective date of the coverage with respect to any policy provision shall be deemed to be the first date on which the debtor became insured under the policy covering the original prior indebtedness that was renewed or refinanced, at least to the extent of the amount and term of the coverage outstanding at the time of renewal and refinancing of the debt.

(3)   In each such policy there shall be a provision that when a claim for the death, disability, or unemployment of the insured arises thereunder, settlement shall be made upon receipt of due proof of such death, disability, or unemployment.

(4)   On the face of each such policy there shall be placed a title which shall briefly and accurately describe the nature and form of the policy.

(5)   Each such policy, including rider and endorsement, shall be identified by a form number in the lower left-hand corner of the first page thereof, and no restriction, condition or provision in or endorsed on such policy shall be valid unless such provision or condition is printed in type as large as 10-point type, one-point leaded.

(6)   In each such policy there shall be a provision that the insured debtor shall have the right to rescind the insurance policy or certificate of insurance

upon giving written notice to the insurer within 30 days from the date the insured debtor received such policy or certificate.

(d) No individual policy of credit insurance and no group policy of credit insurance shall be delivered or issued for delivery in this State if it contains any provision:

(1) Limiting the time within which any action at law or in equity may be commenced to less than three years after the cause of action accrues; or

(2) To the effect that the agent soliciting the insurance is the agent of the person insured under the policy, or making the acts or representations of such agent binding upon the person so insured under the policy.

(e) If said individual policy or certificate of group insurance is not delivered to the debtor at the time the debtor requests credit insurance or mailed to the debtor within 30 days thereafter, a written notification must be furnished to the debtor within the 30-day period, which notification shall set forth the following:

(1) The name and home-office address of the insurer;

(2) The identity of the debtor, by name or otherwise;

(3) The premium or identifiable charge to the debtor, if any, separately for each type of credit insurance;

(4) The amount and term of the coverage provided, if possible, otherwise a clear description of the means of determining the amount and time of expiry;

(5) A brief description of the coverage provided;

(6) A statement that, if the insurance is declined by the insurer or otherwise does not become effective, any premium or identifiable charge will be refunded or credited to the debtor; and

(7) A statement that, upon acceptance by the insurer, the insurance coverage provided shall become effective as specified in G.S. 58-57-20.

Any portion of the information required in said notification may be furnished by other documents, if copies of such documents are attached to said notification. If an insurance policy or certificate of insurance is not delivered to the insured debtor at the time the debtor requests credit insurance, the debtor shall be given the right to rescind the insurance policy or certificate of insurance upon giving written notice to the insurer within 30 days from the date the insured debtor receives such policy or certificate. (1975, c. 660, s. 1; 1981, c. 759, s. 3; 1993, c. 226, s. 5.)

§ 58-57-30. Forms to be filed with Commissioner; approval or disapproval by Commissioner.

(a) All forms of policies, certificates of insurance, notices of proposed insurance, endorsements and riders intended for use in this State shall be filed with the Commissioner.

(b) The Commissioner shall, within 90 days after the filing of any such policies, certificates of insurance, notices of proposed insurance, endorsements and riders, disapprove any such form if it contains provisions which are contrary to, or not in accordance with, any provision of this Article, Article 38 of this Chapter, or of any rule or regulation promulgated thereunder. Unless disapproved in writing within such 90 days, a form shall be deemed approved.

(c) If the Commissioner notifies the insurer that the form is disapproved, it is unlawful thereafter for such insurer to issue or use such form for a period of 60 days, or until the Commissioner has issued a final order after hearing, whichever is earlier. In such notice, the Commissioner shall specify the reason for his disapproval and state that a hearing will be granted within 20 days after request in writing by the insurer. No such policy, certificate of insurance, notice of proposed insurance, endorsement or rider shall be issued or used until the expiration of 30 days after it has been so filed, unless the Commissioner shall give his prior written approval thereto.

(d) The Commissioner may, at any time after a hearing held not less than 20 days after written notice to the insurer, withdraw his approval of any such form on any ground set forth in subsection (b) above. The written notice of such hearing shall state the reason for the proposed withdrawal.

(e) No insurer shall issue such forms or use them after the effective date of such withdrawal. (1975, c. 660, s. 1; 1979, c. 755, s. 16.)

§ 58-57-35. General premium rate standard.

(a) Benefits provided by credit life, credit accident and health and credit unemployment insurance written under this Article shall be reasonable in relation to the premium charge. This requirement is conclusively presumed to be satisfied if the premium rates to be charged for credit life and credit accident and health insurance are no greater than those premium rates set forth in G.S. 58-57-40, 58-57-45, and 58-57-105 for benefits as described in those sections. If an insurer files premium rates for all or part of its business that are greater than those premium rates to which this conclusive presumption applies, the greater rates may be disapproved by the Commissioner if the insurer fails to demonstrate that the benefits are reasonable in relation to the premium rates filed for the group or groups of insureds to which the premium rates would apply and which groups shall meet credibility standards established by the Commissioner. In making this determination, the Commissioner shall give due consideration to the past and prospective loss experience of the group or groups of insureds to which the rates would apply, to reasonable costs and expenses attributable to the insurer and creditor making the coverage available and to other relevant factors, including a fair return to the insurer and creditor. These premium rates shall be allowed to be applied only to the group or groups with respect to which the rate filing is made and approved. The premium rates for credit unemployment insurance shall be filed with and approved by the Commissioner. The amount charged to a debtor for any credit life, credit accident and health, or credit unemployment insurance shall not exceed the premiums charged by the insurer, as computed at the time the charge to the debtor is determined.

(b) The premium or cost of credit life, disability, or unemployment insurance, when written by or through any lender or other creditor, its affiliate, associate or subsidiary shall not be deemed as interest or charges or consideration or an amount in excess of permitted charges in connection with the loan or credit transaction and any gain or advantage to any lender or other creditor, its affiliate, associate or subsidiary, arising out of the premium or commission or dividend from the sale or provision of such insurance shall not be deemed a violation of any other law, general or special, civil or criminal, of this State, or of any rule, regulation or order issued by any regulatory authority of this State.

(c) If premiums are to be determined according to the age of the insured debtor or by age brackets, an insurer may determine premium rates on a basis actuarially equivalent with the rates provided in G.S. 58-57-35, but such rates shall be filed with and approved by the Commissioner.

(d) Premium rates for benefits provided during a critical period shall be adjusted by a critical period conversion ratio that reduces the rates giving recognition to the shorter benefit period provided. (1975, c. 660, s. 1; 1993, c. 226, s. 6; 2007-298, s. 6.2; 2007-484, s. 43.5.)

§ 58-57-40. Credit life insurance rate standards.

(a) The premium rate standards set forth below are applicable to plans of credit life insurance with or without requirements for evidence of insurability:

(1) Which contain no exclusions or no exclusions other than suicide; and

(2) Which contain no age restrictions, or only age restrictions not making ineligible for the coverage

a. Debtors under 65 at the time the indebtedness is incurred; or

b. Debtors who will not have attained age 66 on the maturity date of the indebtedness.

(b) Rates for use with forms which are more restrictive in any material respect shall reflect such variations in the form or lower rates to the extent that a significant difference in claim cost can reasonably be anticipated unless the insurer demonstrates that such lower rate is not appropriate.

(c) If premiums are payable in one sum in advance, for decreasing term life insurance on indebtedness repayable in substantially equal monthly installments, a premium rate not exceeding sixty-five cents (65¢) per one hundred dollars ($100.00) of initial insured indebtedness per year is authorized. Effective January 1, 1995, a premium rate not exceeding sixty cents (60¢) per one hundred dollars ($100.00) of indebtedness per year is authorized. Effective January 1, 1996, a premium rate not exceeding fifty-five cents (55¢) per one hundred dollars ($100.00) of indebtedness per year is authorized. Effective January 1, 1997, a premium rate not exceeding fifty cents (50¢) per one hundred dollars ($100.00) of indebtedness per year is authorized.

(d) The premium rate of joint life coverage shall not exceed one and two-thirds (1 2/3) the permitted single life rate.

(e) For level term life insurance, a premium rate of one dollar and twenty-five cents ($1.25) per one hundred dollars ($100.00) per year is authorized. Effective January 1, 1995, a premium rate of one dollar and twenty cents ($1.20) per one hundred dollars ($100.00) per year is authorized. Effective January 1, 1996, a premium rate of one dollar and fifteen cents ($1.15) per one hundred dollars ($100.00) per year is authorized. Effective January 1, 1997, a premium rate of one dollar and ten cents ($1.10) per one hundred dollars ($100.00) per year is authorized.

(f) For policies for which monthly premiums are charged on a basis of the then-outstanding balances, a monthly premium per one thousand dollars ($1,000) of outstanding balances is authorized, based on the following formula:

$$Op_n = \frac{20 \, SP_n}{n + 1}$$

where SP_n = Single premium rate per one hundred dollars ($100.00) of initial insured indebtedness repayable in n equal monthly installments.

Op_n = Monthly outstanding balance premium rate per one thousand dollars ($1,000).

n = Original repayment period, in months.

(f1) Notwithstanding the premium rates otherwise set forth in this section for credit life insurance, the premium rates for such insurance written in connection with direct loans with contractual commitments of more than 10 years' duration shall be filed with and approved by the Commissioner. Such premium rates shall exhibit a reasonable relationship to the benefits provided.

(g) For credit life insurance on a basis other than the foregoing, premiums charged shall be actuarially equivalent.

(h) In addition to the premium rate authorized, a charge may also be made for a nonrefundable origination fee per credit life insurance transaction as set forth below:

Insured Indebtedness	Fee Permitted
less than $250.00	none
$250.00 or more but less than $500.00	$1.00
$500.00 or more	$3.00

No third or subsequent origination fee may be charged in connection with a third or subsequent refinancing within any twelve-month period. (1975, c. 660, s. 1; 1987, c. 826, ss. 4, 5, 13; 1991, c. 720, s. 91; 1993, c. 226, s. 7.)

§ 58-57-45. Credit accident and health insurance rate standards.

(a) The rate standards set forth below shall be applicable for contracts which contain a provision excluding or denying claim for disability resulting from preexisting illness, disease or physical condition, for which the debtor received medical advice, consultation, or treatment within the six-month period immediately preceding the effective date of the debtor's coverage and if said disability occurs within the six-month period immediately following such date, but contain no other provision which excludes or restricts liability in the event of disability caused in a certain specified manner, except that they may contain provisions excluding or restricting coverage in the event of normal pregnancy; intentionally self-inflicted injuries; sickness resulting from intoxication, addiction to alcohol or narcotics, or from the use thereof unless administered on the advice of a physician; flight in nonscheduled aircraft; war; military service; and may contain the same age restrictions as those mentioned for credit life insurance in G.S. 58-57-40. Provided, if the indebtedness is paid by renewal or refinancing prior to the scheduled maturity date, the effective date of the coverage with respect to any policy provision shall be deemed to be the first date on which the debtor became insured under the policy covering the original prior indebtedness that was renewed or refinanced, at least to the extent of the amount and term of the coverage outstanding at the time of renewal and refinancing of the debt.

(b) A policy of credit accident and health insurance shall include a definition of "disability" providing that during the first 12 months of disability the insured shall be unable to perform the duties of his occupation at the time the disability occurred (or his previous occupation if the person is unemployed or retired at the time the disability occurs), and thereafter the duties of any occupation for which the insured is reasonably fitted by education, training, or experience.

(c) Any policy to which the rates below apply may require the debtor to be gainfully employed on the effective date of the insurance. Provided, however, that unless the insured writes the name of his employer on the application and signs a statement that he is employed, there shall be no denial of claims grounded on the insured's failure to be employed on the effective date of the insurance.

(d) If premiums are payable in one sum in advance for the entire duration of the indebtedness, for insurance with a preexisting exclusion as defined above, the following premiums are authorized:

Single Premium Rates per $100.00 of Initial Insured Indebtedness

No. of Months Benefits in which Indebtedness is Repayable	Nonretroactive Benefits		Retroactive	
	14-Day	30-Day	7-Day	14-Day
12	1.40	.95	2.60	2.10
24	1.90	1.40	3.50	2.85
36	2.40	1.90	4.35	3.65

48	2.85	2.40	5.25	4.40
2.85				
60	3.35	2.85	6.10	5.20
3.35				
72	3.85	3.35		5.95
3.85				
84	4.30	3.85		6.70
4.30				
96	4.80	4.30		7.50
4.80				
108	5.25	4.80		8.25
5.25				
120	5.75	5.25		9.00
5.75				

For terms other than the above, premiums shall be prorated.

(e)   For policies for which monthly premiums are charged on a basis of the then-outstanding balances, a monthly premium per one thousand dollars ($1,000) of outstanding balances is authorized, based on the following formula:

$$Op_n = \frac{20 \, SP_n}{n + 1}$$

where SP_n = Single premium rate per one hundred dollars ($100.00) of initial indebtedness repayable in n equal monthly installments.

Op_n = Monthly outstanding balance premium rate per one thousand dollars ($1,000).

n = Original repayment period, in months.

(e1) Notwithstanding the premium rates otherwise set forth in this section for credit accident and health insurance, the premium rates for such insurance written in connection with direct loans with contractual commitments of more than 10 years' duration shall be filed with and approved by the Commissioner. Such premium rates shall exhibit a reasonable relationship to the benefits provided.

(f) Premium rate standards for other benefit plans and for indebtedness repayable in installments other than as indicated above shall be actuarially consistent with the above rate standards.

(g) In addition to the premium rate authorized, a charge may also be made for a nonrefundable origination fee per credit accident and health insurance transaction as set forth below:

Insured Indebtedness	Fee Permitted
less than $250.00	none
$250.00 or more but less than $500.00	$1.00
$500.00 or more	$3.00

No third or subsequent origination fee may be charged in connection with a third or subsequent refinancing within any twelve-month period.

(h) The premium rates for joint accident and health coverage shall not exceed one and two-thirds (1 2/3) times the permitted single accident and health rate. (1975, c. 660, s. 1; 1981, c. 759, ss. 2, 4-6, 9; 1987, c. 826, ss. 6, 7, 14; 1993, c. 226, s. 8.)

§ 58-57-50. Premium refunds or credits.

(a) Each individual policy or group certificate shall provide that in the event of termination of the insurance prior to the scheduled maturity date of indebtedness, any refund of an amount paid by the debtor for insurance shall be paid or credited promptly to the person entitled thereto.

(b) The refund of premiums for decreasing term credit life insurance shall be the actuarial method of calculating refunds which produces a refund equal to the original premium multiplied by the ratio of the sum of the remaining insured balances divided by the sum of the original insured balances as of the due date nearest the date of prepayment in full. The refund of premiums for single interest credit property insurance and single interest physical damage insurance shall be equal to the amount computed by the sum of digits formula known as the "Rule of 78." The refund of premiums for level term credit life insurance and dual interest credit property insurance and dual interest physical damage insurance shall be equal to the pro rata unearned gross premiums.

(c) The refund of premiums in the case of credit accident and health insurance shall be equal to one-half the amount computed by the sum-of-digits formula commonly known as the "Rule of 78" plus one-half the amount of the pro rata unearned gross premium.

In lieu thereof the refund may be computed by the "Pure Premium" method. The refund is computed from the schedule of credit accident and health premiums and is equal to the premium from that schedule which would be charged for such insurance in the amount of the total remaining benefits for the remaining term of the indebtedness outstanding on the date of termination.

(d) No refund need be made if the amount thereof is less than one dollar ($1.00).

(e) If a creditor requires a debtor to make any payment for credit life insurance or credit accident and health insurance and an individual policy or group certificate of insurance is not issued, the creditor shall immediately give written notice to such debtor and shall promptly make an appropriate credit to the account. (1975, c. 660, s. 1; 1981, c. 759, s. 8; 1989, c. 485, s. 7; 2005-181, s. 2.)

§ 58-57-55. Issuance of policies.

All policies of credit life insurance and credit accident and health insurance shall be issued only by an insurer authorized to do business in this State and shall be issued only through holders of licenses or authorizations issued by the Commissioner. With the exception of credit insurance issued in accordance with

G.S. 58-57-105, all policies of credit life insurance and credit accident and health insurance shall be delivered or issued for delivery in this State. The enrollment of debtors under a group policy issued to a creditor and authorized under this Article shall not constitute the issuance of a policy of insurance. (1975, c. 660, s. 1; 2005-181, s. 3.)

§ 58-57-60. Claims.

(a) All claims shall be promptly reported to the insurer or its designated claim representative, and the insurer shall maintain adequate claim files. All claims shall be settled as soon as possible and in accordance with the terms of the insurance contract.

(b) All claims shall be paid either by draft drawn upon the insurer or by check of the insurer or by electronic funds transfer or be paid by such other specified method upon the direction of the beneficiary who is entitled thereto pursuant to the policy provisions.

(c) No plan or arrangement shall be used whereby any person, firm or corporation other than the insurer or its designated claim representative shall be authorized to settle or adjust claims. The creditor shall not be designated as claim representative for the insurer in adjusting claims; provided, that a group policyholder may, by arrangement with the group insurer, draw drafts, electronic funds transfers, or checks in payment of claims due to the group policyholder subject to audit and review by the insurer.

(d) A claim acknowledgment shall be sent to the claimant within 30 days after receiving written or electronic notice of the claim. Acknowledgment shall include one of the following:

(1) A statement made to the insured or the claimant advising that the claim is being investigated.

(2) Payment of the claim.

(3) A bona fide written offer of settlement.

(4) A written denial of the claim. (1975, c. 660, s. 1; 1993, c. 226, s. 10; 2005-181, s. 4.)

§ 58-57-65. Existing insurance; choice of insurer.

Credit life insurance and credit accident and health insurance may not be required of any borrower by any creditor. When credit property insurance is required for any indebtedness, the debtor shall be notified in writing of the option of furnishing the required amount of insurance through existing policies owned or controlled by him or of procuring and furnishing the required coverage through any insurer authorized to transact an insurance business within this State. (1975, c. 660, s. 1; 1987, c. 826, s. 8.)

§ 58-57-70: Repealed by Session Laws 2005-181, s. 7, effective January 1, 2006, and applicable to policies or certificates issued or renewed on or after that date.

§ 58-57-71. Enforcement and penalties.

(a) The Commissioner may, after notice and opportunity for a hearing, impose civil penalties or petition for restitution under G.S. 58-2-70, revoke, suspend, or restrict the license of any insurer if:

(1) The insurer fails or refuses to comply with any law, order, or rule applicable to the insurer.

(2) The insurer's financial condition is unsound, or its assets above its liabilities, exclusive of capital, are less than the amount of its capital or required minimum surplus.

(3) The insurer has published or made to the Department or to the public any false statement or report.

(4) The insurer or any of the insurer's officers, directors, employees, or other representatives refuse to submit to any examination authorized by law or refuse to perform any legal obligation in relation to an examination.

(5) The insurer is found to make a practice of unduly engaging in litigation or of delaying the investigation of claims or the adjustment or payment of valid claims.

(b) Any suspension, revocation, or refusal to renew an insurer's license under this section may also be made applicable to the license or registration of any individual regulated under this Chapter who is a party to any of the causes for licensing sanctions listed in subsection (a) of this section.

(c) The Commissioner may impose a civil penalty under G.S. 58-2-70 if an insurer fails to acknowledge a claim within 30 days after receiving written or electronic notice of the claim, but only if the notice contains sufficient information for the insurer to identify the specific coverage involved. Acknowledgment of the claim shall be one of the following:

(1) A statement made to the claimant or to the claimant's legal representative advising that the claim is being investigated.

(2) Payment of the claim.

(3) A bona fide written offer of settlement.

(4) A written denial of the claim. With respect to a claim under an accident, health, or disability policy, if the acknowledgment sent to the claimant indicates that the claim remains under investigation, within 45 days after receipt by the insurer of the initial claim, the insurer shall send a claim status report to the insured and every 45 days thereafter until the claim is paid or denied. The report shall give details sufficient for the insured to understand why processing of the claim has not been completed and whether the insurer needs additional information to process the claim. If the claim acknowledgment includes information about why processing of the claim has not been completed and indicates whether additional information is needed, it may satisfy the requirement for the initial claim status report.

(d) If a foreign insurance company's license is suspended or revoked, the Commissioner shall cause written notification of the suspension or revocation to be given to all of the company's agents in this State. Until the Commissioner restores the company's license, the company shall not write any new business in this State.

(e) The Commissioner may, after considering the standards under G.S. 58-30-60(b), restrict an insurer's license by prohibiting or limiting the kind or amount of insurance written by that insurer. For a foreign insurer, this restriction relates to the insurer's business conducted in this State. The Commissioner shall remove any restriction under this subsection once the Commissioner determines that the operations of the insurer are no longer hazardous to the public or the insurer's policyholders or creditors. (2005-181, s. 6.)

§ 58-57-75. Judicial review.

Any party to the proceeding affected by an order of the Commissioner shall be entitled to judicial review by following the procedure set forth in G.S. 58-2-75 through 58-2-90. (1975, c. 660, s. 1.)

§ 58-57-80: Repealed by Session Laws 2005-181, s. 7, effective January 1, 2006, and applicable to policies or certificates issued or renewed on or after that date.

§ 58-57-85: Repealed by Session Laws 2001-223, s. 3.6.

§ 58-57-90. Credit property insurance; personal household property coverage.

(a) As used in this Article, the term "single interest credit property" insurance means insurance of the personal household property of the debtor against loss, with the creditor as sole beneficiary; and the term "dual credit property" insurance means insurance of personal household property of the debtor, with the creditor as primary beneficiary and the debtor as beneficiary of proceeds not paid to the creditor. For the purpose of this Article, "personal household property" means household furniture, furnishings and appliances designed for household use and not used by the debtor in a business trade or profession.

(b) Premium rates charged shall not exceed eighty-seven cents (87¢) per year per one hundred dollars ($100.00) of insured value for single interest credit property insurance and shall not exceed one dollar and thirty-one cents ($1.31) per year per one hundred dollars ($100.00) of insured value for dual interest credit property insurance. The insured value shall not exceed the lesser of the value of the property or the amount of the initial indebtedness.

In addition to the premium rate authorized, a charge may also be made for a nonrefundable origination fee per credit property insurance transaction as set forth below:

Insured Value	Fee Permitted
less than $250.00	none
$250.00 or more but less than $500.00	$1.00
$500.00 or more	$3.00

No third or subsequent origination fee may be charged in connection with the third or subsequent refinancing within any twelve-month period.

The Department shall collect data on credit property insurance written in North Carolina, including but not limited to: the amount of coverage written, direct premiums, earned premiums, dividends and retrospective rate credits paid, direct losses paid, direct losses incurred, commissions paid, loss ratios and policy provisions. (1981, c. 759, s. 7; 1987, c. 826, s. 9; 1993, c. 226, s. 11; 1993 (Reg. Sess., 1994), c. 720, s. 2.)

§ 58-57-95. Rebate of premiums on credit life and credit accident and health insurance; retention of funds by agent.

It shall be unlawful for any insurance carrier, or officer, agent or representative of an insurance company writing credit life and credit accident and health insurance, as defined in G.S. 58-58-10 and G.S. 58-51-100, or combination credit life, accident and health, hospitalization and disability insurance in connection with loans, to permit any agent or representative of such company to retain any portion of funds received for the payment of losses incurred, or to be incurred, under such policies of insurance issued by such company, or to pay, allow, permit, give or offer to pay, allow, permit or give, directly or indirectly, as an inducement to insurance, or after insurance has been effected, any rebate, discount, abatement, credit or reduction of the premium, to any loan agency, insurance agency or broker, or to any creditor of the debtor on whose account the insurance was issued, or to any person, firm or corporation which received a commission or fee in connection with the issuance of such insurance: Provided, that this section shall not prohibit the payment of commissions to a licensed insurance agent or agency or limited representative on the sale of a policy of credit life and credit accident and health insurance, or combination credit life, accident and health, hospitalization and disability insurance in connection with loans. (1955, c. 1341, s. 1; 1987, c. 629, s. 8.)

§ 58-57-100. Credit property insurance; automobile physical damage insurance.

(a) Single interest or dual interest physical damage insurance may be written on nonfleet private passenger motor vehicles, as defined in G.S. 58-40-10, that are used as collateral for loans made under Article 15 of Chapter 53 of the General Statutes. Automobile physical damage insurance as described in this section is a form of credit property insurance, as referred to in G.S. 53-189. It is subject to the following conditions:

(1) Such insurance may be written only on a motor vehicle that is in compliance with the inspection requirements of Part 2 of Article 3A of Chapter 20 of the General Statutes.

(2) If a motor vehicle is already insured and the lender is named loss payee and that insurance continues in force, then no other physical damage insurance may be written.

(3) Notification must be given orally and in writing to the borrower that he has the option to provide his own insurance coverage at any point during the term of the loan.

(4) The creditor must have either a first or second lien on the motor vehicle to be insured.

(5) The amount of insurance coverage may not exceed the lesser of (i) the principal amount of the loan plus allowable charges, excluding interest, plus two scheduled installment payments or (ii) the actual fair market value of the collateral at the time the insurance is written.

(6) When a creditor accepts other collateral in addition to a motor vehicle as herein defined, the combined insurance on all collateral may not exceed the initial indebtedness of the loan.

(b) Policy forms, rates, rating plans, and classifications for single or dual interest nonfleet private passenger motor vehicle physical damage insurance shall be filed with the Commissioner in accordance with Articles 40 and 41 of this Chapter. Every insurer writing such insurance shall, on or before April 1 of each year, file a supplemental financial statement in such form and detail that the Commissioner prescribes that will enable the Commissioner to review and analyze the filings made under this subsection. (1989, c. 485, s. 13; 1989 (Reg. Sess., 1990), c. 1021, s. 2; 1993 (Reg. Sess., 1994), c. 720, s. 1; 2009-382, s. 34.)

§ 58-57-105. Credit insurance on credit card balances.

(a) Credit card facilities may be used for the solicitation, negotiation, or payment of premiums for credit insurance on the unpaid balance of any credit card account pursuant to G.S. 58-3-145. Solicitation or negotiation for credit insurance on credit card account balances may not be made by unsolicited telephone calls or facsimile transmissions.

(b) If credit life insurance premiums are charged through a credit card facility or if credit life insurance premiums are payable on the then outstanding balances on revolving charge account contracts defined in G.S. 25A-11, a premium not exceeding seventy-four cents (74¢) per one thousand dollars ($1,000) of insured indebtedness per month is authorized. The premium rate for joint credit life insurance may not exceed one and two-thirds (1 2/3) the permitted single credit life insurance premium rate. (1993, c. 226, s. 9; c. 504, s. 46; 1999-365, s. 2.)

§ 58-57-107: Recodified as § 58-3-147, Session Laws 1993, c. 504, s. 40.

§ 58-57-110. Credit unemployment insurance rate standards; policy provisions.

(a)   Each year the Commissioner shall prescribe a minimum incurred loss ratio standard requirement to develop a premium rate reasonable in relation to the benefits provided by credit unemployment insurance coverage. The following requirements must be met:

(1)   Coverage is provided or offered, with or without underwriting, to all debtors regardless of age who are working for salary, wages, or other employment income for at least 30 hours per week and have done so for 12 consecutive months.

(2)   Coverage sets forth a definition of involuntary unemployment as a loss of employment income that may include, but is not limited to, loss caused by layoff, general strike, termination of employment, or lockout.

(3)   Coverage does not contain any exclusion except: debts with irregular monthly payments; voluntary forfeiture of salary, wages, or other employment income; resignation; retirement; sickness, disease, or normal pregnancy; or loss of income due to termination as a result of willful misconduct that is a violation of some established, definite rule of conduct, a forbidden act, or willful dereliction of duty, or criminal misconduct.

(4)   Eligibility for benefits may be based upon registration with the State unemployment office but shall not be limited by any provision requiring registration within a specified time. An insurer may require the insured to provide a copy of the official State unemployment office decision letter regarding the claim for State unemployment benefits in order to qualify for benefits. The official State unemployment office decision letter may only be used to deny a claim for benefits under the credit unemployment coverage if the letter cites a reason listed in G.S. 58-57-110(a)(3).

(b) The Commissioner may approve other policy provisions and coverages consistent with the purposes of unemployment coverage.

(c) Joint coverage rates for credit unemployment insurance shall be one and two-thirds (1 2/3) times the approved single rate of coverage. (1993, c. 226, s. 9; 2005-181, s. 5.)

§ 58-57-115. Family leave credit insurance standards; policy provisions.

(a) Definitions. - As used in this section:

(1) "Foster child" means a minor (i) over whom a guardian has been appointed by the clerk of superior court of any county in North Carolina; or (ii) the primary or sole custody of whom has been assigned by order of a court of competent jurisdiction.

(2) "Immediate family member" means a spouse, child (natural, adopted, or foster), or parent of the insured person.

(3) "Placement in the foster home" means physically residing with the insured person appointed as the guardian or custodian of a foster child or children as long as the insured person has assumed the legal obligation for total or partial support of the foster child or children with the intent that the foster child or children reside with the insured person on more than a temporary or short-term basis.

(b) Coverage. - Insurers may provide coverage for loss of income because of a voluntary, employer-approved leave of absence granted upon the occurrence of any of the qualifying events in subsection (d) of this section. The insured person shall not be required to meet any federal requirements in order to qualify for benefits provided by this coverage. Benefits shall be paid to the creditor to reduce the insured person's indebtedness.

(c) Eligibility. - Coverage may be provided or offered to any debtor who has not yet reached his or her 71st birthday and has been working for wages for at least 30 hours per week for the past five consecutive weeks.

(d) Qualifying Events. - Benefits shall be paid only for the following qualifying events:

(1) An accident involving sickness of, or incapacitation of, an immediate family member that requires the insured person to attend to the family member's needs.

(2) Birth of a child or children of the insured person.

(3) Adoption of a child or children of the insured person.

(4) Placement in the foster home of a foster child or children.

(5) The insured person's principal residence is in a federally declared disaster area.

(6) The insured person is called to active military duty.

(7) The insured person is called to petit or grand jury duty.

(e) Exclusions. - Coverage shall not contain any exclusions except:

(1) Retirement of the insured person from employment.

(2) Voluntary resignation of the insured person from employment.

(3) Seasonal unemployment of the insured person.

(4) Involuntary unemployment of the insured person.

(5) Disability of the insured person.

(6) Employment termination because of willful or criminal misconduct of the insured person.

(f) Notice. - The insurer shall send a notice to the insured person at the insured person's home address to inform the insured person that benefits have been paid, including the dates and the amount of payment. The notice shall be sent to the insured person within 60 days after the last day of the benefit period.

(g) Minimum Amounts. - The minimum monthly benefit amount shall be level for the entire benefit period. The minimum monthly benefit amount shall equal or exceed the minimum monthly payment required by the creditor, plus the premium charge for the coverage attributable to the benefit period.

(h) Miscellaneous Provisions. - Any waiting period for benefits shall not exceed 30 days. The insured shall provide satisfactory evidence of employer approval of qualified leave. Lump-sum benefits may be paid. Refunds of unearned single premiums shall be equal to the pro rata unearned gross premium.

(i) Rates. - Premium rates shall be actuarially demonstrated to generate a sixty percent (60%) incurred loss ratio. Joint coverage rates shall be one and two-thirds (1 2/3) times the approved single rate. Rates shall be filed for approval before they can be used.

(j) Reports. - By March 31 of each year every insurer writing family leave coverage shall file a statistical report of the past calendar year's actuarial experience for that coverage. The report shall demonstrate the actual experience loss ratio for the calendar year and shall include the: number of insureds, total earned premium, total number of incurred claims, total incurred claims, total number of incurred claims for each qualifying event, average monthly benefit per claim for each qualifying event, and premium refunds. (1999-351, s. 5.1.)

Article 58.

Life Insurance and Viatical Settlements.

Part 1. General Provisions.

§ 58-58-1. Definitions; requisites of contract.

All corporations or associations doing business in this State, under any charter or statute of this or any other state, involving the payment of money or other thing of value to families or representatives of policy and certificate holders or members, conditioned upon the continuance or cessation of human life, or involving an insurance, guaranty, contract, or pledge for the payment of endowments or annuities, or who employ agents to solicit such business, are life insurance companies, in all respects subject to the laws herein made and provided for the government of life insurance companies, and shall not make any such insurance, guaranty, contract, or pledge in this State with any citizen, or resident thereof, which does not distinctly state the amount of benefits payable, the manner of payment, the consideration therefor and such other provisions as the Commissioner may require. (1899, c. 54, s. 55; Rev., s. 4773; C.S., s. 6455; 1945, c. 379.)

§ 58-58-5. Industrial life insurance defined.

Industrial life insurance is hereby declared to be that form of life insurance under which the premiums are payable monthly or oftener, provided the face amount of insurance stated in the policy does not exceed one thousand dollars ($1,000) and the words "Industrial Policy" are printed upon the policy as a part of the descriptive matter. (1945, c. 379; 1947, c. 721.)

§ 58-58-10. Credit life insurance defined.

Credit life insurance is declared to be insurance upon the life of a debtor who may be indebted to any person, firm, or corporation extending credit to said debtor. Credit life insurance may include the granting of additional benefits in the event of total and permanent disability of the debtor. (1953, c. 1096, s. 1.)

§ 58-58-15. Any type of survivorship fund in life insurance contract prohibited.

No life insurance company shall hereafter deliver in this State, as a part of or in combination with any insurance, endowment or annuity contract, any agreement or plan, additional to the rights, dividends, and benefits arising out of any such insurance, endowment or annuity contract, which provides for the accumulation of profits over a period of years and for payment of all or any part of such accumulated profits only to members or policyholders of a designated group or class who continue as members or policyholders until the end of a specified period of years. Nor shall any such company deliver in this State any individual life insurance policy which provides that on the death of anyone not specifically named therein, the owner or beneficiary of the policy shall receive the payment or granting of anything of value. (1955, c. 492.)

§ 58-58-20. Tie-in sales with life insurance prohibited.

No life insurance company shall hereafter deliver in this State, as a part of or in combination with any insurance, endowment or annuity contract, any agreement or plan, additional to the rights, dividends, and benefits arising out of any such insurance, endowment, or annuity contract which provides for the sale, solicitation, or delivery of any stock or shares of stock in the company issuing the policy or in any other insurance company or other corporation, or benefit certificate, securities, or any special advisory board contract, or other contracts or resolutions of any kind promising returns and profits, or dividends equivalent to stock dividends as an inducement to or in connection with the sale of the insurance or to the taking of the policy. Nothing herein contained shall be construed as prohibiting any participating insurer from distributing to its policyholders dividends, savings or the unused or unabsorbed portion of premiums and premium deposits. (1957, c. 752.)

§ 58-58-22. Individual policy standard provisions.

No policy of individual life insurance shall be delivered in this State unless it contains in substance the following provisions, or provisions that in the Commissioner's opinion are more favorable to the person insured:

(1)   Grace period. - A provision that the insured is entitled to a grace period of 31 days for the payment of any premium due except the first, during which grace period the death benefit coverage shall continue in force. The policy may provide that if a claim arises under the policy during the grace period, the amount of any premium due or overdue may be deducted from any amount payable under the policy in settlement.

(2)   Incontestability. - A provision that the validity of the policy shall not be contested, except for nonpayment of premium, once it has been in force for two years after its date of issue; and that no statement made by any person insured under the policy about that person's insurability shall be used during the

person's lifetime to contest the validity of the policy after the insurance has been in force for two years.

(3) Misstatement of age or gender. - A provision specifying an equitable adjustment of premiums or benefits, or both, to be made if the age or gender of the person insured has been misstated; the provision to contain a clear statement of the method of adjustment to be used.

(4) Suicide. - A provision that may not limit payment of benefits for a period more than two years after the date of issue of the policy because of suicide and that provides for at least the return of premiums paid on the policy if there is suicide during the two-year period.

(5) Reinstatement. - A provision that, unless the policy has been surrendered for its cash surrender value, or its cash surrender value has been exhausted, the policy will be reinstated at any time within five years after the date of premium default upon written application therefor, the production of evidence of insurability satisfactory to the insurer, the payment of all overdue premiums, and the payment of reinstatement of any other indebtedness to the insurer upon the policy, all with interest at the rate specified. (1995, c. 517, s. 31(a).)

§ 58-58-23. Standard provisions for annuity and pure endowment contracts.

No annuity or pure endowment contract, except a reversionary or survivorship annuity and except a group annuity contract, shall be delivered or issued for delivery in this State unless it contains in substance the following provisions or provisions that in the opinion of the Commissioner are more favorable to the holders of the contracts:

(1) Grace period. - A provision for a grace period of not less than 31 days within which any stipulated payment to the insurer falling due after the first payment may be made. During the grace period, the contract shall continue in full force. If a claim arises under the contract because of death before the expiration of the grace period and before the overdue payment to the insurer is made, the amount of the payments, with interest on any overdue payments, may be deducted from any amount payable under the contract.

(2) Incontestability. - If any statements are required as a condition of issue, there shall be a provision that the contract shall be incontestable during the lifetime of the person or of each of the persons as to whom the statements are required after it has been in force for a period of two years after its date of issue, except for nonpayment of stipulated payments to the insurer.

(3) Misstatements of age or gender. - A provision that if the age or gender of any person upon whose life the contract is made has been misstated, the amount payable or benefits accruing under the contract shall be such as the stipulated payment or payments to the insurer would have been according to the correct age or gender; and if the insurer makes an overpayment because of the misstatement, that amount with interest at the rate specified in the contract may be charged against any current or subsequent payment by the insurer under the contract.

(4) Reinstatement. - A provision that the contract may be reinstated at any time within one year after a default in making stipulated payments to the insurer, unless the cash surrender value has been paid; but all overdue stipulated payments and any indebtedness to the insurer on the contract shall be paid or reinstated with interest at a rate specified in the contract. When applicable, the insurer may also require evidence of insurability satisfactory to the insurer. (1995, c. 517, s. 31(a).)

§ 58-58-25. Policies to be issued to any person possessing the sickle cell trait or hemoglobin C trait.

No insurance company licensed in this State pursuant to the provisions of Articles 1 through 64 of this Chapter shall refuse to issue or deliver any policy of life insurance authorized thereunder solely by reason of the fact that the person to be insured possesses sickle cell trait or hemoglobin C trait; nor shall any such policy issued and delivered in this State carry a higher premium rate or charge by reason of the fact that the person to be insured possesses said traits. The term "sickle cell trait" is defined as the condition wherein the major natural hemoglobin components present in the blood of the individual are hemoglobin A (normal) and hemoglobin S (sickle hemoglobin) as defined by standard chemical and physical analytic techniques, including electrophoresis, and the proportion of hemoglobin A is greater than the proportion of hemoglobin S or one natural parent of the individual is shown to have only normal hemoglobin components (hemoglobin A, hemoglobin A2, hemoglobin F) in the normal proportions by standard chemical and physical analytic tests. The term "hemoglobin C trait" is defined as the condition wherein the major natural hemoglobin components present in the blood of the individual are hemoglobin A (normal) and hemoglobin C as defined by standard chemical and physical analytic techniques, including electrophoresis, and the proportion of hemoglobin A is greater than the proportion of hemoglobin C or one natural parent of the individual is shown to have only normal hemoglobin components (hemoglobin A, hemoglobin A2, hemoglobin F) in the normal proportions by standard chemical and physical analytic tests. (1975, c. 600, s. 1.)

§ 58-58-30. Soliciting agent represents the company.

A person who solicits an application for insurance upon the life of another, in any controversy relating thereto between the insured or his beneficiary and the company issuing a policy upon such application, is the agent of the company and not of the insured. (1907, c. 958, s. 1; C.S., s. 6457.)

§ 58-58-35. Discrimination between insurants forbidden.

A life insurance company doing business in this State shall not make any distinction or discrimination in favor of individuals between insurants of the same class and equal expectation of life in the amount of payment of premiums or rates charged for policies of life or endowment insurance, or in the dividends or other benefits payable thereon, or in any of the terms and conditions of the contracts it makes; nor shall any such company or any agent thereof make any contract of insurance or agreement as to such contract other than as plainly expressed in the policy issued thereon, nor pay or allow as inducement to insurance any rebate of premium payable on the policy, or any special favor or advantage in the dividends or other benefit to accrue thereon, or any valuable consideration or inducement whatever not specified in the policy contract of insurance; nor give, sell, or purchase, or offer to give, sell, or purchase as inducement to insurance or in connection therewith any stocks, bonds, or other securities of any insurance company or other corporation, association, or partnership, or any dividends or profits to accrue therein, or anything of value whatsoever not specified in the policy. (1899, c. 54, s. 57; 1903, c. 438, ss. 5, 10; Rev., s. 4775; 1911, c. 196, s. 7; C.S., s. 6458.)

§ 58-58-40. Misrepresentations of policy forbidden.

No life insurance company doing business in this State, and no officer, director, solicitor, or other agent thereof, shall make, issue, or circulate, or cause to be made, issued, or circulated any estimate, illustration, circular, or statement of any sort misrepresenting the terms of the policy issued by it or the dividends or share of surplus to be received thereon, or shall use any name or title of any policy or class of policies misrepresenting the true nature thereof. Nor shall any such company, agent, or broker make any misrepresentation to any person insured in said company or in any other insurer or governmental agency for the purpose of inducing or tending to induce such person to lapse, forfeit, or surrender his said insurance. (1913, c. 95; C.S., s. 6459; 1947, c. 721.)

§ 58-58-42: Repealed by Session Laws 2001-436, s. 5.

Part 2. Financial Provisions.

§ 58-58-45. Financial Provisions.

The valuation of the reserves on the policies and bonds of every life insurance company incorporated by the laws of this State shall be based upon any recognized standard of valuation and mortality table as the Commissioner should deem best for the security of the business and the safety of the persons insured. The Commissioner shall annually value or cause to be valued the reserves on all policies and annuities of each domestic company and may accept the valuation of such reserves made by the company upon such evidence of its correctness as he may require. Upon this valuation being made by the Commissioner and a certificate thereof furnished by him, each company shall pay to such officer, to defray the expenses thereof, the sum of one cent (1¢) for every thousand dollars ($1,000) of the whole amount insured by its policies so valued. The reserve fund hereinbefore provided for shall not be available for or used for any other purpose than the discharge of policy obligations, but is a trust fund to be held and expended only for the benefit of policyholders. In case of the insolvency of the company, the reserve on outstanding policies may, with the consent of the Commissioner, be used for the reinsurance of its policies to the extent of their pro rata part thereof. (1903, c.

536, s. 4; 1905, c. 410; Rev., s. 4777; 1907, c. 1000, s. 7; C.S., s. 6461; 1945, c. 379.)

§ 58-58-50. Standard Valuation Law.

(a)   This section shall be known as the Standard Valuation Law.

(b)   Each year the Commissioner shall value or cause to be valued the reserve liabilities ("reserves") for all outstanding life insurance policies, annuity contracts, and pure endowment contracts of every life insurance company doing business in this State. In the case of an alien company, the valuation shall be limited to its United States business. The Commissioner may certify the amount of each company's reserves, specifying the mortality or morbidity tables, withdrawal rates, and other assumptions regarding when, and the degree to which, policyholders exercise contract options, such as full or partial withdrawal, rate or rates of interest, and methods, such as net level premium method or other, used in the Commissioner's calculation of the company's reserves. Group methods and approximate averages for fractions of a year or otherwise may be used by the Commissioner in calculating the company's reserves, and the Commissioner may accept the valuation made by the company upon evidence of its correctness that the Commissioner requires. For foreign or alien insurance companies, the Commissioner may accept any valuation made or caused to be made by the insurance regulator of any state or other jurisdiction if (i) that valuation complies with the minimum standard provided in this section and (ii) that regulator accepts as legally sufficient and valid the Commissioner's certificate of valuation when that certificate states that the valuation has been made in a specified manner according to which the aggregate reserves would be at least as great as if they had been computed in the manner prescribed by the law of that state or jurisdiction.

(c)   (1)   Except as otherwise provided in subdivisions (3) and (4) of this subsection, the minimum standard for the valuation of all such policies and contracts issued before the effective date of this section shall be that provided by the laws in effect immediately before that date, except that the minimum standard for the valuation of annuities and pure endowments purchased under group annuity and pure endowment contracts issued before that date shall be that provided by the laws in effect immediately before that date but replacing the interest rates specified in such laws by an interest rate of five percent (5%) per annum, and five and one-half percent (5 ½%) interest for single premium life insurance policies.

(2) Except as otherwise provided in subdivisions (3) and (4) of this subsection, the minimum standards for the valuation of all such policies and contracts issued on or after the effective date of this section shall be the Commissioner's reserve valuation methods defined in subsections (d), (d-1) and (g), five percent (5%) interest for group annuity and pure endowment contracts and three and one-half percent (3 ½%) interest for all other policies and contracts, or, in the case of policies and contracts other than annuity and pure endowment contracts, issued on or after July 1, 1975, four percent (4%) interest for such policies issued prior to April 19, 1979, and four and one-half percent (4 ½%) interest for such policies issued on or after April 19, 1979, and the following tables:

a. For all ordinary policies of life insurance issued on the standard basis, excluding any disability and accidental death benefits in such policies - the Commissioner's 1941 Standard Ordinary Mortality Table for such policies issued prior to the operative date of subdivision (e)(2) of G.S. 58-58-55, the Commissioner's 1958 Standard Ordinary Mortality Table for such policies issued on or after the operative date of subdivision (e)(2) of G.S. 58-58-55 prior to the operative date of subdivision (e)(4) of G.S. 58-58-55, provided that for any category of such policies issued on female risks, all modified net premiums and present values referred to in this section may be calculated according to an age not more than six years younger than the actual age of the insured; and, for such policies issued on or after the operative date of subdivision (e)(4) of G.S. 58-58-55, (i) the Commissioner's 1980 Standard Ordinary Mortality Table, or (ii) at the election of the company for any one or more specified plans of life insurance, the Commissioner's 1980 Standard Ordinary Mortality Table with Ten-Year Select Mortality Factors, or (iii) any ordinary mortality table, adopted after 1980 by the NAIC, that is approved by regulation promulgated by the Commissioner for use in determining the minimum standard of valuation for such policies;

b. For all industrial life insurance policies issued on the standard basis, excluding any disability and accidental death benefits in such policies - the 1941 Standard Industrial Mortality Table for such policies issued prior to the operative date of subdivision (e)(3) of G.S. 58-58-55 and for such policies issued on or after such operative date the Commissioner's 1961 Standard Industrial Mortality Table or any industrial mortality table, adopted after 1980 by the NAIC, that is approved by regulation promulgated by the Commissioner for use in determining the minimum standard of valuation for such policies;

c.   For individual annuity and pure endowment contracts, excluding any disability and accidental death benefits in such policies - the 1937 Standard Annuity Mortality Table or, at the option of the company, the Annuity Mortality Table for 1949, Ultimate, or any modification of either of these tables approved by the Commissioner;

d.   For group annuity and pure endowment contracts, excluding any disability and accidental death benefits in such policies - the Group Annuity Mortality Table for 1951, any modification of such table approved by the Commissioner, or, at the option of the company, any of the tables or modifications of tables specified for individual annuity and pure endowment contracts;

e.   For total and permanent disability benefits in or supplementary to ordinary policies or contracts - for policies or contracts issued on or after January 1, 1966, the tables of Period 2 disablement rates and the 1930 to 1950 termination rates of the 1952 Disability Study of the Society of Actuaries, with due regard to the type of benefit or any tables of disablement rates and termination rates, adopted after 1980 by the NAIC, that are approved by regulation promulgated by the Commissioner for use in determining the minimum standard of valuation for such policies; for policies or contracts issued on or after January 1, 1961, and prior to January 1, 1966, either such tables or, at the option of the company, the Class (3) Disability Table (1926); and for policies issued prior to January 1, 1961, the Class (3) Disability Table (1926). Any such table shall, for active lives, be combined with a mortality table permitted for calculating the reserves for life insurance policies;

f.   For accidental death benefits in or supplementary to policies - for policies issued on or after January 1, 1966, the 1959 Accidental Death Benefits Table or any accidental death benefits table, adopted after 1980 by the NAIC, that is approved by regulation promulgated by the Commissioner for use in determining the minimum standard of valuation for such policies; for policies issued on or after January 1, 1961, and prior to January 1, 1966, either such table or, at the option of the company, the Inter-Company Double Indemnity Mortality Table; and for policies issued prior to January 1, 1961, the Inter-Company Double Indemnity Mortality Table. Either table shall be combined with a mortality table permitted for calculating the reserves for life insurance policies;

g. For group life insurance, life insurance issued on the substandard basis and other special benefits - such tables as may be approved by the Commissioner.

(3) Except as provided in subdivision (4) of this subsection, the minimum standard for the valuation of all individual annuity and pure endowment contracts issued on or after the operative date of this subdivision (3), as defined herein, and for all annuities and pure endowments purchased on or after such operative date under group annuity and pure endowment contracts, shall be the Commissioner's reserve valuation methods defined in subsections (d) and (d-1) and the following tables and interest rates:

a. For individual annuity and pure endowment contracts issued prior to April 19, 1979, excluding any disability and accidental death benefits in such contracts - the 1971 Individual Annuity Mortality Table, or any modification of this table approved by the Commissioner, and six percent (6%) interest for single premium immediate annuity contracts, and four percent (4%) interest for all other individual annuity and pure endowment contracts;

b. For individual single premium immediate annuity contracts issued on or after April 19, 1979, excluding any disability and accidental death benefits in such contracts - the 1971 Individual Annuity Mortality Table or any individual annuity mortality table, adopted after 1980 by the NAIC, that is approved by regulation promulgated by the Commissioner for use in determining the minimum standard of valuation for such contracts, or any modification of these tables approved by the Commissioner, and seven and one-half percent (7 ½%) interest;

c. For individual annuity and pure endowment contracts issued on or after April 19, 1979, other than single premium immediate annuity contracts, excluding any disability and accidental death benefits in such contracts - the 1971 Individual Annuity Mortality Table or any individual annuity mortality table, adopted after 1980 by the NAIC, that is approved by regulation promulgated by the Commissioner for use in determining the minimum standard of valuation for such contracts, or any modification of these tables approved by the Commissioner, and five and one-half percent (5 ½%) interest for single premium deferred annuity and pure endowment contracts and four and one-half percent (4 ½%) interest for all other such individual annuity and pure endowment contracts;

d. For all annuities and pure endowments purchased prior to April 19, 1979, under group annuity and pure endowment contracts, excluding any disability and accidental death benefits purchased under such contracts - the 1971 Group Annuity Mortality Table, or any modification of this table approved by the Commissioner, and six percent (6%) interest;

e. For all annuities and pure endowments purchased on or after April 19, 1979, under group annuity and pure endowment contracts, excluding any disability and accidental death benefits purchased under such contracts - the 1971 Group Annuity Mortality Table or any group annuity mortality table, adopted after 1980 by the NAIC, that is approved by regulation promulgated by the Commissioner for use in determining the minimum standard of valuation for such annuities and pure endowments, or any modification of these tables approved by the Commissioner, and seven and one-half percent (7 ½%) interest.

After July 1, 1975, any company may file with the Commissioner a written notice of its election to comply with the provisions of this subdivision (3) after a specified date before January 1, 1979, which shall be the operative date of this subdivision for such company, provided, a company may elect a different operative date for individual annuity and pure endowment contracts from that elected for group annuity and pure endowment contracts. If a company makes no such election, the operative date of this subdivision for such company shall be January 1, 1979.

(4) a. Applicability of This Subdivision. The interest rates used in determining the minimum standard for the valuation of:

1. All life insurance policies issued in a particular calendar year, on or after the operative date of subdivision (e)(4) of G.S. 58-58-55,

2. All individual annuity and pure endowment contracts issued in a particular calendar year on or after January 1, 1982,

3. All annuities and pure endowments purchased in a particular calendar year on or after January 1, 1982, under group annuity and pure endowment contracts, and

4. The net increase, if any, in a particular calendar year after January 1, 1982, in amounts held under guaranteed interest contracts

shall be the calendar year statutory valuation interest rates as defined in this subdivision.

b. Calendar Year Statutory Valuation Interest Rates.

1. The calendar year statutory valuation interest rates, I shall be determined as follows and the results rounded to the nearer one-quarter of one percent (¼ of 1%):

I. For life insurance,

$I = .03$ plus $W (R1 - .03)$ plus $W/2 : (R2 - .09)$;

II. For single premium immediate annuities and for annuity benefits involving life contingencies arising from other annuities with cash settlement options and from guaranteed interest contracts with cash settlement options,

$I = .03$ plus $W (R - .03)$

where $R1$ is the lesser of R and $.09$,

$R2$ is the greater of R and $.09$,

R is the reference interest rate defined in this subdivision, and W is the weighting factor defined in this subdivision,

III. For other annuities with cash settlement options and guaranteed interest contracts with cash settlement options, valued on an issue year basis, except as stated in II above, the formula for life insurance stated in I above shall apply to annuities and guaranteed interest contracts with guarantee durations in excess of 10 years and the formula for single premium immediate annuities stated in II above shall apply to annuities and guaranteed interest contracts with guarantee duration of 10 years or less,

IV. For other annuities with no cash settlement options and for guaranteed interest contracts with no cash settlement options, the formula for single premium immediate annuities stated in II above shall apply,

V. For other annuities with cash settlement options and guaranteed interest contracts with cash settlement options, valued on a change in fund basis, the formula for single premium immediate annuities stated in II above shall apply.

2.   However, if the calendar year statutory valuation interest rate for any life insurance policies issued in any calendar year determined without reference to this sentence differs from the corresponding actual rate for similar policies issued in the immediately preceding calendar year by less than one-half of one percent (½ of 1%), the calendar year statutory valuation interest rate for such life insurance policies shall be equal to the corresponding actual rate for the immediately preceding calendar year. For purposes of applying the immediately preceding sentence, the calendar year statutory valuation interest rate for life insurance policies issued in a calendar year shall be determined for 1980 (using the reference interest rate defined for 1979) and shall be determined for each subsequent calendar year regardless of when subdivision (e)(4) of G.S. 58-58-55 becomes operative.

c.   Weighting Factors.

1.   The weighting factors referred to in the formulas stated above are given in the following tables:

I.   Weighting Factors for Life Insurance:

Guarantee Duration (Years)	Weighting Factors
10 or less	.50
More than 10, but not more than 20	.45
More than 20	.35

      For life insurance, the guarantee duration is the maximum number of years the life insurance can remain in force on a basis guaranteed in the policy or under options to convert to plans of life insurance with premium rates or nonforfeiture values or both which are guaranteed in the original policy;

II.   Weighting factor for single premium immediate annuities and for annuity benefits involving life contingencies arising from other annuities with cash settlement options and guaranteed interest contracts with cash settlement options:

.80

III. Weighting factors for other annuities and for guaranteed interest contracts, except as stated in II. above, shall be as specified in tables (i), (ii), and (iii) below, according to the rules and definitions in (iv), (v) and (vi) below:

(i) For annuities and guaranteed interest contracts valued on an issue year basis:

Guarantee Duration (Years)	Weighting Factor For Plan Type		
	A	B	C
5 or less:	.80	.60	.50
More than 5, but not more than 10:	.75	.60	.50
More than 10, but not more than 20:	.65	.50	.45
More than 20:	.45	.35	.35

(ii) For annuities and guaranteed interest contracts valued on a change in fund basis, the factors shown in (i) above increased

	Plan Type		
	A	B	C

279

by: .15 .25 .05

(iii) For annuities and guaranteed interest contracts valued on an issue year basis (other than those with no cash settlement options) which do not guarantee interest on considerations received more than one year after issue or purchase and for annuities and guaranteed interest contracts valued on a change in fund basis which do not guarantee interest

Plan Type		
A	B	C

rates on considerations received more than 12 months beyond the valuation date, the factors shown in (i) or derived in (ii) increased by: .05 .05 .05

(iv) For other annuities with cash settlement options and guaranteed interest contracts with cash settlement options, the guarantee duration is the number of years for which the contract guarantees interest rates in excess of the calendar year statutory valuation interest rate for life insurance policies with guarantee duration in excess of 20 years. For other annuities with no cash settlement options and for guaranteed interest contracts with no cash settlement options, the guarantee duration is the number of years from the date of issue or date of purchase to the date annuity benefits are scheduled to commence.

(v) Plan type as used in the above tables is defined as follows:

Plan Type A: At any time policyholder may withdraw funds only (1) with an adjustment to reflect changes in interest rates or asset values since receipt of the funds by the insurance company, or (2) without such adjustment but in installments over five years or more, or (3) as an immediate life annuity, or (4) no withdrawal permitted.

Plan Type B: Before expiration of the interest rate guarantee, policyholder may withdraw funds only (1) with an adjustment to reflect changes in interest rates or asset values since receipt of the funds by the insurance company, or (2) without such adjustment but in installments over five years or more, or (3) no withdrawal permitted. At the end of interest rate guarantee, funds may be withdrawn without such adjustment in a single sum or installments over less than five years.

Plan Type C: Policyholder may withdraw funds before expiration of interest rate guarantee in a single sum or installments over less than five years either (1) without adjustment to reflect changes in interest rates or asset values since receipt of the funds by the insurance company, or (2) subject only to a fixed surrender charge stipulated in the contract as a percentage of the fund.

(vi) A company may elect to value guaranteed interest contracts with cash settlement options and annuities with cash settlement options on either an issue year basis or on a change in fund basis. Guaranteed interest contracts with no cash settlement options and other annuities with no cash settlement options must be valued on an issue year basis. As used in this section, an issue year basis of valuation refers to a valuation basis under which the interest rate used to determine the minimum valuation standard for the entire duration of the annuity or guaranteed interest contract is the calendar year valuation interest rate for the year of issue or year of purchase of the annuity or guaranteed interest contract, and the change in fund basis of valuation refers to a valuation basis under which the interest rate used to determine the minimum valuation standard applicable to each change in the fund held under the annuity or guaranteed interest contract is the calendar year valuation interest rate for the year of the change in the fund.

d. Reference Interest Rate.

1. The reference interest rate referred to in paragraph b of this subdivision shall be defined as follows:

I. For all life insurance, the lesser of the average over a period of 36 months and the average over a period of 12 months, ending on June 30 of the calendar year next preceding the year of issue, of Moody's Corporate Bond Yield Average - Monthly Average Corporates, as published by Moody's Investors Service, Inc.

II. For single premium immediate annuities and for annuity benefits involving life contingencies arising from other annuities with cash settlement options and guaranteed interest contracts with cash settlement options, the average over a period of 12 months, ending on June 30 of the calendar year of issue or year of purchase, of Moody's Corporate Bond Yield Average - Monthly Average Corporates, as published by Moody's Investors Service, Inc.

III. For other annuities with cash settlement options and guaranteed interest contracts with cash settlement options, valued on a year of issue basis, except as stated in II above, with guarantee duration in excess of 10 years, the lesser of the average over a period of 36 months and the average over a period of 12 months, ending on June 30 of the calendar year of issue or purchase, of Moody's Corporate Bond Yield Average - Monthly Average Corporates, as published by Moody's Investors Service, Inc.

IV. For other annuities with cash settlement options and guaranteed interest contracts with cash settlement options, valued on a year of issue basis, except as stated in II above, with guarantee duration of 10 years or less, the average over a period of 12 months, ending on June 30 of the calendar year of issue or purchase, of Moody's Corporate Bond Yield Average - Monthly Average Corporates, as published by Moody's Investors Service, Inc.

V. For other annuities with no cash settlement options and for guaranteed interest contracts with no cash settlement options, the average over a period of 12 months, ending on June 30 of the calendar year of issue or purchase, of Moody's Corporate Bond Yield Average - Monthly Average Corporates, as published by Moody's Investors Service, Inc.

VI. For other annuities with cash settlement options and guaranteed interest contracts with cash settlement options, valued on a change in fund basis, except as stated in II above, the average over a period of 12 months, ending on June 30 of the calendar year of the change in the fund, of Moody's Corporate Bond Yield Average - Monthly Average Corporates, as published by Moody's Investors Service, Inc.

e. Alternative Method for Determining Reference Interest Rates.

1. In the event that Moody's Corporate Bond Yield Average - Monthly Average Corporates is no longer published by Moody's Investors Service, Inc., or in the event that the NAIC determines that Moody's Corporate Bond Yield Average - Monthly Average Corporates as published by Moody's Investors Service, Inc., is no longer appropriate for the determination of the reference interest rate, than an alternative method for determination of the reference interest rate, which is adopted by the NAIC and approved by regulation promulgated by the Commissioner, may be substituted.

(d) Except as otherwise provided in subsections (d-1) and (g), reserves according to the Commissioner's reserve valuation method, for the life insurance and endowment benefits of policies providing for a uniform amount of insurance and requiring the payment of uniform premiums, shall be the excess, if any, of the present value, at the date of valuation, of such future guaranteed benefits provided for by such policies, over the then present value of any future modified net premiums therefor. The modified net premiums for any such policy shall be such uniform percentage of the respective contract premiums for such benefits that the present value, at the date of issue of the policy, of all such modified net premiums shall be equal to the sum of the then present value of such benefits provided for by the policy and the excess of (1) and (2), as follows:

(1) A net level annual premium equal to the present value, at the date of issue, of such benefits provided for after the first policy year, divided by the present value, at the date of issue, of an annuity of one per annum payable on the first and each subsequent anniversary of such policy on which a premium falls due; provided, however, that such net level annual premium shall not exceed the net level annual premium on the 19-year premium whole life plan for insurance of the same amount at an age one year higher than the age at issue of such policy.

(2) A net one year term premium for such benefits provided for in the first policy year.

Provided that for any life insurance policy issued on or after January 1, 1985, for which the contract premium in the first policy year exceeds that of the second year and for which no comparable additional benefits are provided in the first year for such excess and which provides an endowment benefit or a cash surrender value of a combination thereof in an amount greater than such excess premium, the reserve according to the Commissioner's reserve valuation method as of any policy anniversary occurring on or before the assumed ending date defined herein as the first policy anniversary on which the sum of any endowment benefit and any cash surrender value then available is greater than such excess premium shall, except as otherwise provided in subsection (g), be the greater of the reserve as of such policy anniversary calculated as described in the first paragraph of this subsection and the reserve as of such policy anniversary calculated as described in that paragraph, but with (i) the value defined in subparagraph (1) of that paragraph being reduced by fifteen percent (15%) of the amount of such excess first year premium, (ii) all present values of benefits and premiums being determined without reference to premiums or benefits provided for by the policy after the assumed ending date, (iii) the policy being assumed to mature on such date as an endowment, and (iv) the cash surrender value provided on such date being considered as an endowment benefit. In making the above comparison the mortality and interest bases stated in subdivisions (2) and (4) of subsection (c) shall be used.

Reserves according to the Commissioner's reserve valuation method for: (i) life insurance policies providing for a varying amount of insurance or requiring the payment of varying premiums; (ii) group annuity and pure endowment contracts purchased under a retirement plan or plan of deferred compensation, established or maintained by an employer (including a partnership or sole proprietorship) or by an employee organization, or by both, other than a plan providing individual retirement accounts or individual retirement annuities under section 408 of the Internal Revenue Code, as now or hereafter amended; (iii) disability and accidental death benefits in all policies and contracts; and (iv) all other benefits, except life insurance and endowment benefits in life insurance policies and benefits provided by all other annuity and pure endowment contracts, shall be calculated by a method consistent with the principles of this subsection except that any extra premiums charged because of impairments or special hazards shall be disregarded in the determination of modified net premiums.

(d-1)   This subsection shall apply to all annuity and pure endowment contracts other than group annuity and pure endowment contracts purchased under a retirement plan or plan of deferred compensation, established or maintained by an employer (including a partnership or sole proprietorship) or by an employee organization, or by both, other than a plan providing individual retirement accounts or individual retirement annuities under section 408 of the Internal Revenue Code, as now or hereafter amended.

Reserves according to the Commissioner's annuity reserve method for benefits under annuity or pure endowment contracts, excluding any disability and accidental death benefits in such contracts, shall be the greatest of the respective excesses of the present values, at the date of valuation, of the future guaranteed benefits, including guaranteed nonforfeiture benefits, provided for by such contracts at the end of each respective contract year, over the present value, at the date of valuation, of any future valuation considerations derived from future gross considerations, required by the terms of such contract, that become payable prior to the end of such respective contract year. The future guaranteed benefits shall be determined by using the mortality table, if any, and the interest rate, or rates, specified in such contracts for determining guaranteed benefits. The valuation considerations are the portions of the respective gross considerations applied under the terms of such contracts to determine nonforfeiture values.

(e)   In no event shall a company's aggregate reserves for all life insurance policies, excluding disability and accidental death benefits, issued on or after the effective date of this section, be less than the aggregate reserves calculated in accordance with the methods set forth in subsections (d), (d-1), (g) and (h) of this section and the mortality table or tables and rate or rates of interest used in calculating nonforfeiture benefits for such policies. In no event shall the aggregate reserves for all policies, contracts, and benefits be less than the aggregate reserves determined by the qualified actuary to be necessary to render the opinion required by subsection (i) of this section.

(f) Reserves for all policies and contracts issued before the effective date of this section may be calculated, at the option of the company, according to any standards that produce greater aggregate reserves for those policies and contracts than the minimum reserves required by the laws in effect immediately before that date.

Reserves for any category of policies, contracts or benefits as established by the Commissioner, issued on or after the effective date of this section may be calculated, at the option of the company, according to any standards that produce greater aggregate reserves for such category than those calculated according to the minimum standard herein provided, but the rate or rates of interest used for policies and contracts, other than annuity and pure endowment contracts, shall not be higher than the corresponding rate or rates of interest used in calculating any nonforfeiture benefits provided for therein.

Any such company that adopts any standard of valuation producing greater aggregate reserves than those calculated according to the minimum standard herein provided may, with the approval of the Commissioner, adopt any lower standard of valuation, but not lower than the minimum herein provided. Provided, however, that for the purposes of this section, the holding of additional reserves previously determined by a qualified actuary to be necessary to render the opinion required by subsection (c) of this section shall not be deemed to be the adoption of a higher standard of valuation.

(g) If in any contract year the gross premium charged by any life insurance company on any policy or contract is less than the valuation net premium for the policy or contract calculated by the method used in calculating the reserve thereon but using the minimum valuation standards of mortality and rate of interest, the minimum reserve required for such policy or contract shall be the greater of either the reserve calculated according to the mortality table, rate of interest, and method actually used for such policy or contract, or the reserve calculated by the method actually used for such policy or contract but using the minimum valuation standards of mortality and rate of interest and replacing the valuation net premium by the actual gross premium in each contract year for which the valuation net premium exceeds the actual gross premium. The minimum valuation standards of mortality and rate of interest referred to in this subsection are those standards stated in subdivisions (1), (2) and (4) of subsection (c).

Provided that for any life insurance policy issued on or after January 1, 1985, for which the gross premium in the first policy year exceeds that of the second year and for which no comparable additional benefit is provided in the first year for such excess and which provides an endowment benefit or a cash surrender value or a combination thereof in an amount greater than such excess premium, the foregoing provisions of this subsection (g) shall be applied as if the method actually used in calculating the reserve for such policy were the method described in subsection (d), ignoring the second paragraph of subsection (d). The minimum reserve at each policy anniversary of such a policy shall be the greater of the minimum reserve calculated in accordance with subsection (d), including the second paragraph of that subsection, and the minimum reserve calculated in accordance with this subsection (g).

(h) In the case of any plan of life insurance which provides for future premium determination, the amounts of which are to be determined by the insurance company based on then estimates of future experience, or in the case of any plan of life insurance or annuity which is of such a nature that the minimum reserves cannot be determined by the methods described in subsections (d), (d-1), and (g), the reserves which are held under any such plan must:

(1) Be appropriate in relation to the benefits and the pattern of premiums for that plan, and

(2) Be computed by a method which is consistent with the principles of this Standard Valuation Law, as determined by regulations promulgated by the Commissioner.

(i) Every life insurance company doing business in this State shall annually submit the opinion of a qualified actuary as to whether the reserves and related actuarial items held in support of the policies and contracts specified by the Commissioner by rule are computed appropriately, are based on assumptions that satisfy contractual provisions, are consistent with previously reported amounts, and comply with applicable laws of this State. The Commissioner by rule shall define the specifics of this opinion and add any other items deemed to be necessary to its scope. Every life insurance company, except as exempted by or pursuant to rule, shall also annually include in the opinion required by this subsection, an opinion of the same qualified actuary as to whether the reserves and related actuarial items held in support of the policies and contracts specified by the Commissioner by rule, when considered in light of the assets held by the company with respect to the reserves and related actuarial items, including but not limited to the investment earnings on the assets and the considerations anticipated to be received and retained under the policies and contracts, make adequate provision for the company's obligations under the policies and contracts, including but not limited to the benefits under and expenses associated with the policies and contracts. The Commissioner may provide by rule for a transition period for establishing any higher reserves that the qualified actuary may deem to be necessary in order to render the opinion required by this subsection.

(j)   Each opinion required by subsection (i) of this section shall be governed by the following provisions:

(1)   A memorandum, in form and substance acceptable to the Commissioner as specified by rule, shall be prepared to support each actuarial opinion.

(2)   If the insurance company fails to provide a supporting memorandum at the request of the Commissioner within a period specified by rule or the Commissioner determines that the supporting memorandum provided by the insurance company fails to meet the standards prescribed by the rules or is otherwise unacceptable to the Commissioner, the Commissioner may engage a qualified actuary at the expense of the company to review the opinion and the basis for the opinion and prepare such supporting memorandum as is required by the Commissioner.

(3)   The opinion shall be submitted with the annual statement reflecting the valuation of such reserve liabilities for each year ending on or after December 31, 1994.

(4)   The opinion shall apply to all business in force including individual and group health insurance plans, in form and substance acceptable to the Commissioner as specified by rule.

(5)   The opinion shall be based on standards adopted from time to time by the actuarial standards board and on such additional standards as the Commissioner may by rule prescribe.

(6) In the case of an opinion required to be submitted by a foreign or alien company, the Commissioner may accept the opinion filed by that company with the insurance supervisory official of another state if the Commissioner determines that the opinion reasonably meets the requirements applicable to a company domiciled in this State.

(7) For the purposes of this section, "qualified actuary" means a member in good standing of the American Academy of Actuaries who meets the requirement set forth in such rules.

(8) Except in cases of fraud or willful misconduct, the qualified actuary shall not be liable for damages to any person (other than the insurance company and the Commissioner) for any act, error, omission, decision, or conduct with respect to the actuary's opinion.

(9) Disciplinary action by the Commissioner against the company or the qualified actuary shall be defined in rules by the Commissioner.

(10) Any memorandum in support of the opinion, and any other material provided by the company to the Commissioner in connection therewith, shall be kept confidential by the Commissioner and shall not be made public and shall not be subject to subpoena, other than for the purpose of defending an action seeking damages from any person by reason of any action required by this section or by rules adopted under this section; provided, however, that the memorandum or other material may otherwise be released by the Commissioner (i) with the written consent of the company or (ii) to the American Academy of Actuaries upon request stating the memorandum or other material is required for the purpose of professional disciplinary proceedings and setting forth procedures satisfactory to the Commissioner for preserving the confidentiality of the memorandum or other material. Once any portion of the confidential memorandum is cited by the company in its marketing or is cited before any governmental agency other than a state insurance department or is released by the company to the news media, all portions of the confidential memorandum shall be no longer confidential.

(k) The Commissioner shall adopt rules containing the minimum standards applicable to the valuation of health plans. The Commissioner may also adopt rules for the purpose of recognizing new annuity mortality tables for use in determining reserve liabilities for annuities and may adopt rules that govern minimum valuation standards for reserves of life insurance companies. In adopting these rules, the Commissioner may consider model laws and regulations promulgated and amended from time to time by the NAIC.

(l) The Commissioner may adopt rules for life insurers for the following matters:

(1) Reserves for contracts issued by insurers.

(2) Optional smoker-nonsmoker mortality tables permitted for use in determining minimum reserve liabilities and nonforfeiture benefits.

(3) Optional blended gender mortality tables permitted for use in determining nonforfeiture benefits for individual life policies.

(4) Optional tables acceptable for use in determining reserves and minimum cash surrender values and amounts of paid-up nonforfeiture benefits.

(5) Assumptions for policyholder withdrawal rates for use in determining minimum reserve liabilities.

In adopting these rules, the Commissioner may consider model laws and regulations promulgated and amended from time to time by the NAIC. (1945, c. 379; 1959, c. 484, s. 1; 1961, c. 255, ss. 1-3; 1963, c. 791, ss. 1, 2; 1975, c. 603, s. 1; 1979, c. 409, ss. 1-6; 1981, c. 761, ss. 1-5; 1985, c. 666, s. 46; 1991, c. 720, s. 19; 1993, c. 452, ss. 52-56; 1999-219, s. 10; 2001-334, s. 17.1; 2007-127, ss. 17, 18.)

§ 58-58-55. Standard nonforfeiture provisions.

(a) This section shall be known as the Standard Nonforfeiture Law for Life Insurance.

(b) In the case of policies issued on or after the operative date of this section, as defined in subsection (h), no policy of life insurance, except as stated in subsection (g), shall be delivered or issued for delivery in this State unless it shall contain in substance the following provisions, or corresponding provisions which in the opinion of the Commissioner are at least as favorable to the defaulting or surrendering policyholder as are the minimum requirements hereinafter specified and are essentially in compliance with subsection (f1) of this section:

(1)   That, in the event of default in any premium payment after premiums have been paid for at least one full year in the case of ordinary insurance or three full years in the case of industrial insurance, the company will grant, upon proper request not later than 60 days after the due date of the premium in default, a paid-up nonforfeiture benefit on a plan stipulated in the policy, effective as of such due date, of such amount as may be hereinafter specified. In lieu of such stipulated paid-up nonforfeiture benefit, the company may substitute, upon proper request not later than 60 days after the due date of the premium in default, an actuarially equivalent alternative paid-up nonforfeiture benefit which provides a greater amount or longer period of death benefits or, if applicable, a greater amount or earlier payment of endowment benefits.

(2)   That, upon surrender of the policy within 60 days after the due date of any premium payment in default after premiums have been paid for at least three full years in the case of ordinary insurance or five full years in the case of industrial insurance, the company will pay, in lieu of any paid-up nonforfeiture benefit, a cash surrender value of such amount as may be hereinafter specified.

(3)   That a specified paid-up nonforfeiture benefit shall become effective as specified in the policy unless the person entitled to make such election elects another available option not later than 60 days after the due date of the premium in default. Nothing herein shall prevent the use of an automatic premium loan provision.

(4)   That, if the policy shall have become paid up by completion of all premium payments or if it is continued under any paid-up nonforfeiture benefit which became effective on or after the third policy anniversary in the case of ordinary insurance or the fifth policy anniversary in the case of industrial insurance, the company will pay, upon surrender of the policy within 30 days after any policy anniversary, a cash surrender value of such amount as may be hereinafter specified.

(5)   In the case of policies which cause on a basis guaranteed in the policy unscheduled changes in benefits or premiums, or which provide an option for changes in benefits or premiums other than a change to a new policy, a statement of the mortality table, interest rate, and method used in calculating cash surrender values and the paid-up nonforfeiture benefits available under the policy. In the case of all other policies, a statement of the mortality table and

interest rate used in calculating the cash surrender values and the paid-up nonforfeiture benefits available under the policy, together with a table showing the cash surrender value, if any, and paid-up nonforfeiture benefit, if any available under the policy on each policy anniversary either during the first 20 policy years or during the term of the policy, whichever is shorter, such values and benefits to be calculated upon the assumption that there are no dividends or paid-up additions credited to the policy and that there is no indebtedness to the company on the policy.

(6) A statement that the cash surrender values and the paid-up nonforfeiture benefits available under the policy are not less than the minimum values and benefits required by or pursuant to the insurance law of the state in which the policy is delivered; an explanation of the manner in which the cash surrender values and the paid-up nonforfeiture benefits are altered by the existence of any paid-up additions credited to the policy or any indebtedness to the company on the policy; if a detailed statement of the method of computation of the values and benefits shown in the policy is not stated therein, a statement that such method of computation has been filed with the Commissioner in which the policy is delivered; and a statement of the method to be used in calculating the cash surrender value and paid-up nonforfeiture benefit available under the policy on any policy anniversary beyond the last anniversary for which such values and benefits are consecutively shown in the policy.

Any of the foregoing provisions or portions thereof not applicable by reason of the plan of insurance may, to the extent inapplicable, be omitted from the policy.

The company shall reserve the right to defer the payment of any cash surrender value for a period of six months after demand therefor with surrender of the policy.

(c) Any cash surrender value available under the policy in the event of default in a premium payment due on any policy anniversary, whether or not required by subsection (b), shall be an amount not less than the excess, if any, of the present value, on such anniversary, of the future guaranteed benefits which would have been provided for by the policy, including any existing paid-up additions, if there had been no default, over the sum of (i) the then present value of the adjusted premiums as defined in subsection (e), corresponding to premiums which would have fallen due on and after such anniversary, and (ii) the amount of any indebtedness to the company on the policy.

Provided, however, that for any policy issued on or after the operative date of subdivision (4) of subsection (e) as defined therein, which provides supplemental life insurance or annuity benefits at the option of the insured and for an identifiable additional premium by rider or supplemental policy provision, the cash surrender value referred to in the first paragraph of this subsection shall be an amount not less than the sum of the cash surrender value as defined in such paragraph for an otherwise similar policy issued at the same age without such rider or supplemental policy provision and the cash surrender value as defined in such paragraph for a policy which provides only the benefits otherwise provided by such rider or supplemental policy provision.

Provided, further, that for any family policy issued on or after the operative date of subdivision (4) of subsection (e) as defined therein, which defines a primary insured and provides term insurance on the life of the spouse of the primary insured expiring before the spouse's age 71, the cash surrender value referred to in the first paragraph of this subsection shall be an amount not less than the sum of the cash surrender value as defined in such paragraph for an otherwise similar policy issued at the same age without such term insurance on the life of the spouse and cash surrender value as defined in such paragraph for a policy which provides only the benefits otherwise provided by such term insurance on the life of the spouse.

Any cash surrender value available within 30 days after any policy anniversary under any policy paid up by completion of all premium payments or any policy continued under any paid-up nonforfeiture benefit, whether or not required by subsection (b), shall be an amount not less than the present value, on such anniversary, of the future guaranteed benefits provided for by the policy, including any existing paid-up additions, decreased by any indebtedness to the company on the policy.

(d) Any paid-up nonforfeiture benefit available under the policy in the event of default in a premium payment due on any policy anniversary shall be such that its present value as of such anniversary shall be at least equal to the cash surrender value then provided for by the policy or, if none is provided for, at least equal to that cash surrender value which would have been required by this section in the absence of the condition that premiums shall have been paid for at least a specified period.

(e) (1) This subdivision (1) of subsection (e) shall not apply to policies issued on or after the operative date of subdivision (4) of subsection (e) as defined therein. Except as provided in the third paragraph of this subdivision, the adjusted premiums for any policy shall be calculated on an annual basis and shall be such uniform percentage of the respective premiums specified in the policy for each policy year, excluding any extra premiums charged because of impairments or special hazards, that the present value, at the date of issue of the policy, of all such adjusted premiums shall be equal to the sum of (i) the then present value of the future guaranteed benefits provided for by the policy; (ii) two percent (2%) of the amount of insurance, if the insurance be uniform in amount, or of the equivalent uniform amount, as hereinafter defined, if the amount of insurance varies with duration of the policy; (iii) forty percent (40%) of the adjusted premium for the first policy year; (iv) twenty-five percent (25%) of either the adjusted premium for the first policy year or the adjusted premium for a whole life policy of the same uniform or equivalent uniform amount with uniform premiums for the whole of life issued at the same age for the same amount of insurance, whichever is less. Provided, however, that in applying the percentages specified in (iii) and (iv) above, no adjusted premium shall be deemed to exceed four percent (4%) of the amount of insurance or uniform amount equivalent thereto. The date of issue of a policy for the purpose of this subsection shall be the date as of which the rated age of the insured is determined.

In the case of a policy providing an amount of insurance varying with duration of the policy, the equivalent uniform amount thereof for the purpose of this section shall be deemed to be the uniform amount of insurance provided by an otherwise similar policy containing the same endowment benefit or benefits, if any, issued at the same age and for the same term, the amount of which does not vary with duration and the benefits under which have the same present value at the date of issue as the benefits under the policy, provided, however, that in the case of a policy providing a varying amount of insurance issued on the life of a child under age 10, the equivalent uniform amount may be computed as though the amount of insurance provided by the policy prior to the attainment of age 10 were the amount provided by such policy at age 10.

The adjusted premiums for any policy providing term insurance benefits by rider or supplemental policy provision shall be equal to (i) the adjusted premiums for an otherwise similar policy issued at the same age without such term insurance benefits, increased, during the period for which premiums for such term insurance benefits are payable, by (ii) the adjusted premiums for such term insurance, the foregoing items (i) and (ii) being calculated separately and as specified in the first two paragraphs of this subsection except that, for the purposes of (ii), (iii) and (iv) of the first such paragraph, the amount of insurance or equivalent uniform amount of insurance used in the calculation of the adjusted premiums referred to in (ii) of this paragraph shall be equal to the excess of the corresponding amount determined for the entire policy over the amount used in the calculation of the adjusted premiums in (i).

Except as otherwise provided in subdivisions (2) and (3) of this subsection, all adjusted premiums and present values referred to in this section shall for all policies of ordinary insurance be calculated on the basis of the Commissioner's 1941 Standard Ordinary Mortality Table, provided that for any category of ordinary insurance issued on female risks, adjusted premiums and present values may be calculated according to an age not more than three years younger than the actual age of the insured, and such calculations for all policies of industrial insurance shall be made on the basis of the 1941 Standard Industrial Mortality Table. All calculations shall be made on the basis of the rate of interest, not exceeding three and one-half percent (3 1/2%) per annum, specified in the policy for calculating cash surrender values and paid-up nonforfeiture benefits. Provided, however, that in calculating the present value of any paid-up term insurance with accompanying pure endowment, if any, offered as a nonforfeiture benefit, the rates of mortality assumed may not be more than one hundred and thirty percent (130%) of the rates of mortality according to such applicable table. Provided, further, that for insurance issued on a substandard basis, the calculation of any such adjusted premiums and present values may be based on such other table of mortality as may be specified by the company and approved by the Commissioner.

(2) This subdivision (2) of subsection (e) shall not apply to ordinary policies issued on or after the operative date of subdivision (4) of subsection (e) as defined therein. In the case of ordinary policies issued on or after the operative date of this subdivision (2) as defined herein, all adjusted premiums and present values referred to in this section shall be calculated on the basis of the Commissioner's 1958 Standard Ordinary Mortality Table and the rate of interest specified in the policy for calculating cash surrender values and paid-up nonforfeiture benefits, provided that such rate of interest shall not exceed three and one-half percent (3 1/2%) per annum except that a rate of interest not exceeding four percent (4%) per annum may be used for policies issued on or after July 1, 1975, and prior to April 19, 1979, and a rate of interest not exceeding five and one-half percent (5 1/2%) per annum may be used for policies issued on or after April 19, 1979, and, provided that for any category of ordinary insurance issued on female risks, adjusted premiums and present values may be calculated according to an age not more than six years younger than the actual age of the insured; provided, however, that in calculating the

present value of any paid-up term insurance with accompanying pure endowment, if any, offered as a nonforfeiture benefit, the rates of mortality assumed may be not more than those shown in the Commissioner's 1958 Extended Term Insurance Table. Provided, further, that for insurance issued on a substandard basis, the calculation of any such adjusted premiums and present values may be based on such other table of mortality as may be specified by the company and approved by the Commissioner.

After May 12, 1959, any company may file with the Commissioner a written notice of its election to comply with the provisions of this subdivision (2) after a specified date before January 1, 1966. After the filing of such notice, then upon such specified date (which shall be the operative date of this subdivision (2) for such company), this subdivision (2) shall become operative with respect to the ordinary policies thereafter issued by such company. If a company makes no such election, the operative date of this subdivision (2) for such company shall be January 1, 1966.

(3) This subdivision (3) of subsection (e) shall not apply to industrial policies issued on or after the operative date of subdivision (4) of subsection (e) as defined therein. In the case of industrial policies issued on or after the operative date of this subdivision (3) as defined herein, all adjusted premiums and present values referred to in this section shall be calculated on the basis of the Commissioner's 1961 Standard Industrial Mortality Table and the rate of interest specified in the policy for calculating cash surrender values and paid-up nonforfeiture benefits, provided that such rate of interest shall not exceed three and one-half percent (3 1/2%) per annum except that a rate of interest not exceeding four percent (4%) per annum may be used for policies issued on or after July 1, 1975, and prior to April 19, 1979, and a rate of interest not exceeding five and one-half percent (5 1/2%) per annum may be used for policies issued on or after April 19, 1979; provided, however, that in calculating the present value of any paid-up term insurance with accompanying pure endowment, if any, offered as a nonforfeiture benefit, the rates of mortality assumed may be not more than those shown in the Commissioner's 1961 Industrial Extended Term Insurance Table. Provided, further, that for insurance issued on a substandard basis, the calculation of any such adjusted premiums and present values may be based on such other table of mortality as may be specified by the company and approved by the Commissioner.

After June 11, 1963, any company may file with the Commissioner a written notice of its election to comply with the provisions of this subdivision (3) after a specified date before January 1, 1968. After the filing of such notice, then upon such specified date (which shall be the operative date of this subdivision (3) for such company), this subdivision (3) shall become operative with respect to the industrial policies thereafter issued by such company. If a company makes no such election, the operative date of this subdivision (3) for such company shall be January 1, 1968.

(4) a. This subdivision shall apply to all policies issued on or after the operative date of this subdivision (4) of subsection (e) as defined herein. Except as provided in paragraph g of this subdivision, the adjusted premiums for any policy shall be calculated on an annual basis and shall be such uniform percentage of the respective premiums specified in the policy for each policy year, excluding amounts payable as extra premiums to cover impairments or special hazards and also excluding any uniform annual contract charge or policy fee specified in the policy in a statement of the method to be used in calculating the cash surrender values and paid-up nonforfeiture benefits, that the present value, at the date of issue of the policy, of all adjusted premiums shall be equal to the sum of (i) the then present value of the future guaranteed benefits provided for by the policy; (ii) one percent (1%) of either the amount of insurance, if the insurance be uniform in amount, or the average amount of insurance at the beginning of each of the first 10 policy years; and (iii) one hundred twenty-five percent (125%) of the nonforfeiture net level premium as hereinafter defined. Provided, however, that in applying the percentage specified in (iii) above no nonforfeiture net level premium shall be deemed to exceed four percent (4%) of either the amount of insurance, if the insurance be uniform in amount, or the average amount of insurance at the beginning of each of the first 10 policy years. The date of issue of a policy for the purpose of this subdivision shall be the date as of which the rated age of the insured is determined.

b. The nonforfeiture net level premium shall be equal to the present value, at the date of issue of the policy, of the guaranteed benefits provided for by the policy divided by the present value, at the date of issue of the policy, of an annuity of one per annum payable on the date of issue of the policy and on each anniversary of such policy on which a premium falls due.

c. In the case of policies which cause on a basis guaranteed in the policy unscheduled changes in benefits or premiums, or which provide an option for changes in benefits or premiums other than a change to a new policy, the adjusted premiums and present values shall initially be calculated on the assumption that future benefits and premiums do not change from those stipulated at the date of issue of the policy. At the time of any such change in the benefits or premiums the future adjusted premiums, nonforfeiture net level premiums and present values shall be recalculated on the assumption that future benefits and premiums do not change from those stipulated by the policy immediately after the change.

d. Except as otherwise provided in paragraph g of this subdivision, the recalculated future adjusted premiums for any such policy shall be such uniform percentage of the respective future premiums specified in the policy for each policy year, excluding amounts payable as extra premiums to cover impairments and special hazards, and also excluding any uniform annual contract charge or policy fee specified in the policy in a statement of the method to be used in calculating the cash surrender values and paid-up nonforfeiture benefits, that the present value, at the time of change to the newly defined benefits or premiums, of all such future adjusted premiums shall be equal to the excess of (A) the sum of (i) the then present value of the then future guaranteed benefits provided for by the policy and (ii) the additional expense allowance, if any, over (B) the then cash surrender value, if any, or present value of any paid-up nonforfeiture benefit under the policy.

e. The additional expense allowance, at the time of the change to the newly defined benefits or premiums, shall be the sum of (i) one percent (1%) of the excess, if positive, of the average amount of insurance at the beginning of each of the first 10 policy years subsequent to the change over the average amount of insurance prior to the change at the beginning of each of the first 10 policy years subsequent to the time of the most recent previous change, or, if there has been no previous change, the date of issue of the policy; and (ii) one hundred twenty-five percent (125%) of the increase, if positive, in the nonforfeiture net level premium.

f. The recalculated nonforfeiture net level premium shall be equal to the result obtained by dividing (A) by (B) where

(A) Equals the sum of

(i) The nonforfeiture net level premium applicable prior to the change times the present value of an annuity of one per annum payable on each anniversary of the policy on or subsequent to the date of the change on which a premium would have fallen due had the change not occurred, and

(ii) The present value of the increase in future guaranteed benefits provided for by the policy, and

(B) Equals the present value of an annuity of one per annum payable on each anniversary of the policy on or subsequent to the date of change on which a premium falls due.

g. Notwithstanding any other provisions of this subdivision to the contrary, in the case of a policy issued on a substandard basis which provides reduced graded amounts of insurance so that, in each policy year, such policy has the same tabular mortality cost as an otherwise similar policy issued on the standard basis which provides higher uniform amounts of insurance, adjusted premiums and present values for such substandard policy may be calculated as if it were issued to provide such higher uniform amounts of insurance on the standard basis.

h. All adjusted premiums and present values referred to in this section shall for all policies of ordinary insurance be calculated on the basis of (i) the Commissioner's 1980 Standard Ordinary Mortality Table or (ii) at the election of the company for any one or more specified plans of life insurance, the Commissioner's 1980 Standard Ordinary Mortality Table with Ten-Year Select Mortality Factors; shall for all policies of industrial insurance be calculated on the basis of the Commissioner's 1961 Standard Industrial Mortality Table; and shall for all policies issued in a particular calendar year be calculated on the basis of a rate of interest not exceeding the nonforfeiture interest rate as defined in this subdivision for policies issued in that calendar year. Provided, however, that:

1. At the option of the company, calculations for all policies issued in a particular calendar year may be made on the basis of a rate of interest not exceeding the nonforfeiture interest rate, as defined in this subdivision, for policies issued in the immediately preceding calendar year.

2. Under any paid-up nonforfeiture benefit, including any paid-up dividend additions, any cash surrender value available, whether or not required by subsection (b), shall be calculated on the basis of the mortality table and rate of interest used in determining the amount of such paid-up nonforfeiture benefit and paid-up dividend additions, if any.

3. A company may calculate the amount of any guaranteed paid-up nonforfeiture benefit including any paid-up additions under the policy on the basis of an interest rate no lower than that specified in the policy for calculating cash surrender values.

4. In calculating the present value of any paid-up term insurance with accompanying pure endowment, if any, offered as a nonforfeiture benefit, the rates of mortality assumed may be not more than those shown in the Commissioner's 1980 Extended Term Insurance Table for policies of ordinary insurance and not more than the Commissioner's 1961 Industrial Extended Term Insurance Table for policies of industrial insurance.

5. For insurance issued on a substandard basis, the calculation of any such adjusted premiums and present values may be based on appropriate modifications of the aforementioned tables.

6. Any ordinary mortality tables, adopted after 1980 by the NAIC, that are approved by regulation promulgated by the Commissioner for use in determining the minimum nonforfeiture standard may be substituted for the Commissioner's 1980 Standard Ordinary Mortality Table with or without Ten-Year Select Mortality Factors or for the Commissioner's 1980 Extended Term Insurance Table.

7. Any industrial mortality tables, adopted after 1980 by the NAIC, that are approved by regulation promulgated by the Commissioner for use in determining the minimum nonforfeiture standard may be substituted for the Commissioner's 1961 Standard Industrial Mortality Table or the Commissioner's 1961 Industrial Extended Term Insurance Table.

i. The nonforfeiture interest rate per annum for any policy issued in a particular calendar year shall be equal to one hundred and twenty-five percent (125%) of the calendar year statutory valuation interest rate for such policy as defined in the Standard Valuation Law, rounded to the nearer one quarter of one percent (1/4 of 1%).

j. Notwithstanding any other provision in this Chapter to the contrary, any refiling of nonforfeiture values or their methods of computation for any previously approved policy form which involves only a change in the interest rate or mortality table used to compute nonforfeiture values shall not require refiling of any other provisions of that policy form.

k. After the effective date of this subdivision (4) of subsection (e), any company may file with the Commissioner a written notice of its election to comply with the provisions of this subdivision after a specified date before January 1, 1989, which shall be the operative date of this subdivision for such company. If a company makes no such election, the operative date of this subdivision for such company shall be January 1, 1989.

(e1)   In the case of any plan of life insurance which provides for future premium determination, the amounts of which are to be determined by the insurance company based on then estimates of future experience, or in the case of any plan of life insurance which is of such a nature that minimum values cannot be determined by the methods described in subsections (b), (c), (d), or (e) herein, then:

(1)   The Commissioner must be satisfied that the benefits provided under the plan are substantially as favorable to policyholders and insureds as the minimum benefits otherwise required by subsections (b), (c), (d), or (e) herein;

(2)   The Commissioner must be satisfied that the benefits and the pattern of premiums of that plan are not such as to mislead prospective policyholders or insureds;

(3)   The cash surrender values and paid-up nonforfeiture benefits provided by such plan must not be less than the minimum values and benefits required for the plan computed by a method consistent with the principles of this Standard Nonforfeiture Law, as determined by regulations promulgated by the Commissioner;

(4)   Notwithstanding any other provision in the laws of this State, any policy, contract, or certificate providing life insurance under any such plan must be affirmatively approved by the Commissioner before it can be marketed, issued, delivered, or used in this State.

(f)   Any cash surrender value and any paid-up nonforfeiture benefit, available under the policy in the event of default in a premium payment due at any time other than on the policy anniversary, shall be calculated with allowance for the lapse of time and the payment of fractional premiums beyond the last preceding policy anniversary. Any values referred to in subsections (c), (d) and (e) may be calculated upon the assumption that any death benefit is payable at the end of the policy year of death. The net value of any paid-up additions, other than paid-up term additions, shall be not less than the amounts used to provide such additions. Notwithstanding the provisions of Section 3 [subsection (c)], additional benefits payable (i) in the event of death or dismemberment by accident or accidental means, (ii) in the event of total and permanent disability, (iii) as reversionary annuity or deferred reversionary annuity benefits, (iv) as term insurance benefits provided by a rider or supplemental policy provision to which, if issued as a separate policy, this section would not apply, (v) as term insurance on the life of a child or on the lives of children provided in a policy on the life of a parent of the child, if such term insurance expires before the child's age is 26, is uniform in amount after the child's age is one, and has not become paid up by reason of the death of a parent of the child, and (vi) as other policy benefits additional to life insurance and endowment benefits, and premiums for all such additional benefits, shall be disregarded in ascertaining cash surrender values and nonforfeiture benefits required by this section, and no such additional benefits shall be required to be included in any paid-up nonforfeiture benefits.

(f1)   This subsection, in addition to all other applicable subsections of this section, shall apply to all policies issued on or after January 1, 1985. Any cash surrender value available under the policy in the event of default in a premium payment due on any policy anniversary shall be in an amount which does not differ by more than two-tenths of one percent (2/10 of 1%) of either the amount of insurance, if the insurance be uniform in amount, or the average amount of insurance at the beginning of each of the first 10 policy years, from the sum of (1) the greater of zero and the basic cash value hereinafter specified and (2) the present value of any existing paid-up additions less the amount of any indebtedness to the company under the policy.

The basic cash value shall be equal to the present value, on such anniversary, of the future guaranteed benefits which would have been provided for by the policy, excluding any existing paid-up additions and before deduction of any indebtedness to the company, if there had been no default, less the then present value of the nonforfeiture factors, as hereinafter defined, corresponding to premiums which would have fallen due on and after such anniversary. Provided, however, that the effects on the basic cash value of supplemental life insurance or annuity benefits or of family coverage, as described in subsection (c) or (e)(1), whichever is applicable, shall be the same as are the effects specified in subsection (c) or (e)(1), whichever is applicable, on the cash surrender values defined in that subsection.

The nonforfeiture factor for each policy year shall be an amount equal to a percentage of the adjusted premium for the policy year, as defined in subsection (e)(1) or (e)(4), whichever is applicable. Except as is required by the next succeeding sentence of this paragraph, such percentage:

(1) Must be the same percentage for each policy year between the second policy anniversary and the later of (i) the fifth policy anniversary and (ii) the first policy anniversary at which there is available under the policy a cash surrender value in an amount, before including any paid-up additions and before deducting any indebtedness, of at least two-tenths of one percent (2/10 of 1%) of either the amount of insurance, if the insurance be uniform in amount, or the average amount of insurance at the beginning of each of the first 10 policy years; and

(2) Must be such that no percentage after the later of the two policy anniversaries specified in the preceding item (1) may apply to fewer than five consecutive policy years.

Provided, that no basic cash value may be less than the value which would be obtained if the adjusted premiums for the policy, as defined in subsection (e)(1) or (e)(4), whichever is applicable, were substituted for the nonforfeiture factors in the calculation of the basic cash value.

All adjusted premiums and present values referred to in this subsection shall for a particular policy be calculated on the same mortality and interest bases as are used in demonstrating the policy's compliance with the other subsections of this section. The cash surrender values referred to in this subsection shall include any endowment benefits provided for by the policy.

Any cash surrender value available other than in the event of default in a premium payment due on a policy anniversary, and the amount of any paid-up nonforfeiture benefit available under the policy in the event of default in a premium payment shall be determined in manners consistent with the manners specified for determining the analogous minimum amounts in subsections (b), (c), (d), (e)(4), and (f). The amounts of any cash surrender values and of any paid-up nonforfeiture benefits granted in connection with additional benefits such as those listed as items (i) through (vi) in subsection (f) shall conform with the principles of this subsection (f1).

(g) The provisions of this section shall not apply to any of the following:

(1) Industrial sick benefit insurance as defined in Articles 1 through 64 of this Chapter,

(2) Reinsurance,

(3) Group insurance,

(4)   Pure endowment,

(5)   Annuity or reversionary annuity contract,

(6)   Term policy of uniform amount, which provides no guaranteed nonforfeiture or endowment benefits, or renewal thereof, of 20 years or less, for which uniform premiums are payable during the entire term of the policy,

(7)   Term policy of decreasing amount, which provides no guaranteed nonforfeiture or endowment benefits, on which each adjusted premium, calculated as specified in subsection (e), is less than the adjusted premium so calculated, on a term policy of uniform amount, or renewal thereof, which provides no guaranteed nonforfeiture or endowment benefits, issued at the same age and for the same initial amount of insurance and for a term of 20 years or less expiring before age 71, for which uniform premiums are payable during the entire term of the policy,

(8)   Policy, which provides no guaranteed nonforfeiture or endowment benefits, for which no cash surrender value, if any, or present value of any paid-up nonforfeiture benefit, at the beginning of any policy year, calculated as specified in subsections (c), (d) and (e), exceeds two and one-half percent (2 1/2%) of the amount of insurance at the beginning of the same policy year, nor

(9)   Policy which shall be delivered outside this State through an agent or other representative of the company issuing the policy.

For purposes of determining the applicability of this section, the age at expiry for a joint term life insurance policy shall be the age at expiry of the oldest life.

(h)   After March 6, 1945, any company may file with the Commissioner a written notice of its election to comply with the provisions of this section after a specified date before January 1, 1950. After the filing of such notice then upon such specified date (which shall be the operative date for such company) this section shall become operative with respect to the policies thereafter issued by such company. If a company makes no such election, the operative date of this section for such company shall be January 1, 1950.

(i)   For any single premium whole life or endowment insurance policy subject to subdivisions (e)(2) and (e)(3) of this section, a rate of interest not exceeding six and one-half percent (6 1/2%) per annum may be used. (1945, c. 379; 1959, c. 484, s. 2; 1961, c. 255, ss. 4-7; 1963, c. 791, ss. 3, 4; 1975, c.

603, ss. 2, 3; 1979, c. 409, ss. 7-9; 1981, c. 761, ss. 6-14; 1991, c. 720, ss. 19, 31; 1993, c. 452, ss. 57-59.)

§ 58-58-60: Repealed by Session Laws 2003-144, s. 2, effective October 1, 2004.

Vision Books Order Form

Fax Orders:	1-980-299-5965
Phone Orders:	1-704-898-0770
E-mail Orders:	www.visionbooks.org
Mail Orders:	Vision Books, LLC P.O. Box 42406 Charlotte, NC 28215

Shipp To:
Name_____
Address_____
City_____State_____Zip_____
Phone_____Fax_____
Email_____@_____

Bill To: We can bill a third party on your behalf.
Name_____
Address_____
City_____State_____Zip_____
Phone____(_____)_____Fax_____
Email_____@_____

Pamphlet Number ($15.00 Each)	Qty	Total Cost
_____	_____	_____
_____	_____	_____
_____	_____	_____
_____	_____	_____
_____	_____	_____
_____	_____	_____
_____	_____	_____
<u>Full Volume Set 1-92</u>	<u>92 Pamphlets</u>	<u>1,380.00</u>

Free Shipping Shipping & Handling on Full Volume Orders
Add $1.00 Shipping & Handling per pamphlet $_____

Total Cost $_____

Thank you for your support. Management!

DID YOU ENJOY THIS BOOK?

Vision Books, LLC would like to hear from you! If you or someone you know has been fasely imprisoned, we would like to hear your story. If the 'North Carolina Criminal Law and Procedure' has had an effect in your life or if you have suggestions, we would like to hear from you. Send your letters to:

Vision Books, LLC
Attn: Staff Writers
P.O. Box 42406
Charlotte, NC 28215
Email: staff@visionbooks.org

Order Additional Copies:

Fax Orders:	1-980-299-5965
Phone Orders:	1-704-898-0770
E-mail Orders:	www.visionbooks.org
Mail Orders:	Vision Books, LLC P.O. Box 42406 Charlotte, NC 282

www.ingramcontent.com/pod-product-compliance
Lightning Source LLC
Chambersburg PA
CBHW051627170526
45167CB00001B/90